Sufi Deleuze

Sufi Deleuze

Secretions of Islamic Atheism

MICHAEL MUHAMMAD KNIGHT

Fordham University Press
NEW YORK   2023

Copyright © 2023 Fordham University Press

All rights reserved. No part of this publication may be reproduced, stored in a retrieval system, or transmitted in any form or by any means—electronic, mechanical, photocopy, recording, or any other—except for brief quotations in printed reviews, without the prior permission of the publisher.

Fordham University Press has no responsibility for the persistence or accuracy of URLs for external or third-party Internet websites referred to in this publication and does not guarantee that any content on such websites is, or will remain, accurate or appropriate.

Fordham University Press also publishes its books in a variety of electronic formats. Some content that appears in print may not be available in electronic books.

Visit us online at www.fordhampress.com.

Library of Congress Cataloging-in-Publication Data available online at https://catalog.loc.gov.

Printed in the United States of America

25 24 23   5 4 3 2 1

First edition

for Jibreel

Contents

	Introduction: Secrets and Secretions	1
1	Deleuze and Tafsir: The Rhizomatic Qur'an	25
2	People of the Sunna and the Assemblage: Deleuzian Hadith Theory	61
3	Beyond Theology: Sufism as Arrangement and Affect	84
4	The Immanence of Baraka: Bodies and Territory	104
5	Arm Leg Leg Arm Head: Five Percenter Theologies of Immanence	119
	Conclusion: The Seal of Muslim Pseudo	144
	Acknowledgments	155
	Notes	157
	Bibliography	171
	Index	181

Sufi Deleuze

Introduction: Secrets and Secretions

> *Immanence can be said to be the burning issue of all philosophy because it takes on all the dangers that philosophy must confront, all the condemnations, persecutions, and repudiations that it undergoes. This at least persuades us that the problem of immanence is not abstract or merely theoretical. It is not immediately clear why immanence is so dangerous, but it is. It engulfs sages and gods.*
> —GILLES DELEUZE AND FELIX GUATTARI, *What Is Philosophy?*

> *He who understood the mystery of Reality*
> *became vaster than the vast heaven;*
> *Mullah says that Muhammad ascended to the heavens,*
> *Sarmad says that the heavens descended to Muhammad.*
> —SARMAD, QUOTED IN RAKSHAT PURI AND KULDIP AKHTAR, "Sarmad, the Naked Faqir"

It was on the fifth day of the Jamia Millia Islamia's Deleuze and Guattari camp/conference in New Delhi that I deterritorialized my flows in a taxi and spent the rest of the afternoon visiting shrines for the tombs of Sufi masters and other holy people. The most popular *dargah* complex housed the tomb of Nizamuddin Awliya (1238–1325), Sufi master in the Chistiyya order. A surrounding market had expanded as an outward emanation from the dargah, which positioned Nizamuddin's tomb at the deepest center of a labyrinthine network of vendors, insulating the quiet shrine space against the noise and vibrations of Delhi traffic. Neighboring Nizamuddin's dargah was the shrine of his student, Amir Khusrow (1253–1325), who pioneered the Sufi musical tradition of *qawwali*. I offered prayers at the *dargahs*—prayers in an Islamic sense as not merely private conversations within the heart but also performances with my body, a series of prescribed motions and positions and vocalizations. To move my body in accordance with prayer scripts while still wearing my conference badge with Deleuze and Guattari's faces had me thinking about Deleuzian *namaz*, Deleuzian *salat*, *du'a*, *dhikr*. In Deleuzian terms, the question wouldn't be whether the named object of the prayer was "real"—for Deleuze, it wasn't—but what the body-at-prayer could *do*, what productive linkages and enhancements of powers it could achieve with other bodies in this world, on this ground. At least as much as religion can be defined as a "belief system," it's also a body system. To think of my prayers at the dargahs primarily as acts of "faith," in which a condition of the soul preceded the movements of the body, rather than as the body producing an interior sense of Islam through relations to spaces and other bodies, would leave out the parts that Deleuze might have found most productive.

Less than one hundred yards from Nizamuddin stood the dargah for one of the most significant Sufi masters in North American Islam, Hazrat Inayat Khan (1882–1927), who had belonged to Nizamuddin's lineage of the Chistiyya and went on to found a new Sufi order with himself as the initiatic master. Outside Inayat Khan's shrine complex, I found the familiar symbol for his order, a star and crescent inside a winged heart. I purchased some musty old copies of the order's famous orange-covered book series at the front office and then walked up to the tomb, remembering that one of my mentors, the Islamic heresiologist and "Anarcho-Sufi" Hakim Bey, had come to this place more than fifty years earlier. It was the orange-covered books that had brought him here. Facing the master's tomb like Hakim Bey must have in the 1960s, I mouthed a silent al-Fatiha. I was once Bey's official biographer and occasionally his personal driver, carting him to hang out with Inayat Khan's grandson at the Inayati order's North American center. I was also an initiate in his own "Moorish Orthodox" order with the name Mikail El, but we had our split, and my Hakim Bey biography just became a reflection on father-son breaks and failed master-disciple connections. We hadn't spoken in years, but like Bey said when someone asked if he was still a Sufi, "I never quit anything"; as I keep collecting and reassembling, I might have forgotten him at the bottom of the toybox, but he's still in there. Our history filled the space between Inayat Khan's body and mine.

I did not know what Deleuze would have done with the shrine or this moment, or if he'd know what he *could* do with a Hazrat Inayat Khan dargah machine. My head remained plugged into earlier lectures and panels: it was technically day two of the conference but followed a Deleuze and Guattari camp in which I attended sixteen lectures in three days, crushing myself under what was basically a semester of grad school compressed into a weekend. The three-day camp was an immersion experience in which I intensified my speaking and thinking and dreaming in Deleuzian, and now I couldn't help but process Sufi dargahs with Deleuzian tools. My Sufism and my Deleuze were both fragments of fragments, broken off and now coming together. The next day, I'd go back to the

Deleuze and Guattari conference with Hazrat Inayat Khan's *The Divinity of the Human Soul* in my bag.

The dargahs are sites for heavy concentrations of *baraka*, which conveys multiple ideas. The term clumsily appears in English translation as "blessings," which fails to capture everything that happens at the shrines and doesn't feel very Deleuzian: the pursuit of blessings suggests a celestial hierarchy distributing golden chips from above. If you've been blessed, we have to ask: Blessed by *what*? Who sent the blessings *down* upon you, and from *where*? Because God is supposed to be the real source of baraka, its heaven-to-earth flow inevitably signals a divine transcendence; baraka enters into this world as a flow from *outside the world*, necessarily a higher plane superior to the world. The flow of baraka maps an ontological hierarchy. But in Islamic studies, scholarship has problematized the rendering of baraka as mere "blessings" and called for a rethinking of baraka as something else, a force or energy that circulates between special places, materials, scripts, and actions on a shared plane, flowing in routes that won't always trace back to the golden chip distributor. Baraka is not a feeling of "bliss" or "beatitude." It's a force. *The* Force. When Muhammad spits into a fatigued camel's mouth and gives it the energy to run, the prophetic saliva achieves a baraka transmission. The camel body in turn transmits baraka to other bodies when men slaughter it and distribute its baraka-infused meat among their community. The Prophet did not limit baraka as strictly a flow from his own body: the *hadith* corpus, the literary body reporting his words and actions, describes baraka as locatable in specific plants, animals, days, months, and words. Baraka exists in a circulation between bodies that alters their conditions and powers, and the flow takes place right here on our plane. With or without an origin that transcends the world and establishes vertical hierarchies between planes of being, baraka also exists as a materially accessible flow in the world, moving horizontally across this plane.

Baraka without a judge? To imagine baraka as movement between bodies on the plane of immanence, rather than a funneling down of credits from the plane of transcendence, could provoke a mystical atheism that affirms the vibrations of life, reverses the vertical chain of being in which our low world depends upon a higher world for value and meaning, and decenters the holder of the golden chips. Such a radical move comes with possible social, legal, and political consequences. Historically, non-Muslims have also come to the dargahs in pursuit of baraka, whether or not "baraka" was their word for the forces that flowed from the tombs. If Hindu visitors connect to Islamic dargah machines and plug their bodies into its baraka flows without fulfilling a Muslim checklist of proper faith confessions and divinely prescribed actions—a surprisingly common occurrence in the precolonial world, before modern reifications of religion and competing Islamic and Hindu nationalisms—something changes in the relation between baraka and, to say it in Deleuze's words, "the system of the judgments of God."[1] This site of encounter allows for a promiscuity of linkages—not even a temporary liminal space between separate monoliths but, as Dominique Sila-Khan argues in her concept of the threshold, potentially "a permanent opening into a world of multiple values."[2] When the Muslim shrine can benefit non-Muslim bodies, enabling baraka's distribution to the worshipers of "idols," baraka's immanence in the world becomes a potential escape from the system, a Deleuzian line of flight into unstable futures.

For some revivalist forces, this is a prime threat posed by the Islamic shrine. If dargahs hold power as loci of immanent baraka, Islam lacks a stable center both on the physical map (since shrine culture enables an infinite proliferation of possible centers) and in terms of universal authority over the tradition (since custodianship of Islam becomes more intensely molecularized and local). The cityscapes of Delhi, Lahore, Harar, Touba, Qom, Fez, Damascus, and Cairo, covered in baraka-transmitting sites, scatter baraka and power throughout the world. This could help to explain why the Saudi state, in a project to preserve its hyper-striated holy city of Mecca as the only appropriate site of pilgrimage and maintain its own truthmaking regime as the ultimate center of "orthodox" Islamic gravity, has promoted the destruction of Islamic shrines within and beyond its borders. Around the world, Sunni revivalist projects have bulldozed and bombed shrines and flattened the landscape, producing the antithesis of what Deleuze usually means by "smooth space." Of course, there's more than one way to neutralize the dargah's power: In Pakistan, the state did not resort to bulldozing shrines, but rather changed the narratives surrounding them, reconstructing entombed holy people from their previous characterizations as saints and mystics into shari'a-compliant clerical scholars, 'ulama. Both state and non-state actors that oppose the dargah recode baraka not as an energy flow between bodies, but rather the golden chips that you earn for obedience to a divinely arranged rational order, a positive judgment of God accessible exclusively through following prescriptions from trained experts.

As modern Sunni revivalisms shut down immanent baraka flows and enforce clerical textualisms in their place, the surviving dargah opens a potential route out of the territory. This was the esoteric fruit that I found in shrines located adjacent to grand, imposing masjids. Not all of the saints are human: just outside of Delhi, people frequented the ruins of a fourteenth-century palace complex, Firoz Shah Kotla, as a dargah for various "jinn-saints" who could transmit baraka or intervene in their lives.[3] Encounters with jinns can open lines of flight and lead to the creation of new things: Mir Babar Ali Anis (1803–74), for example, wrote a lamentation for the tragic martyrdom of the Prophet's grandson Husayn—nearly twelve centuries earlier—based on what he heard from Zafar Jinn, a jinn who had been at Karbala and witnessed it firsthand.[4] These lines of flight from "canonical" Islam, however, were opened by the canon itself, which tells people that jinns are real and can involve themselves in the world of humans. Textualists might frown upon the practices around Firoz Shah Kotla, but it's a body of authorized texts that makes Firoz Shah Kotla possible, naming ruins as popular dwelling-places for jinns.

Around the shrine of Muhammad Sa'id Sarmad (d. 1659), located across the street from Delhi's giant Jama Masjid, one finds a small occult marketplace of talismans, amulets, magical instruments, letter/number charts, and astrological booklets, technologies, and archives counter to what some might call Islamic "orthodoxy" and the schematics of its trained experts. But if you can directly access baraka at the bodies of advanced mystics (who themselves might have been outside the bounds of a jurist-defined orthodoxy) and attract beneficent energies or ward off malevolent forces through the artifacts at a dargah's market, perhaps you don't really need the trained experts. I purchased a set of four brass nails covered in engraved Qur'an verses, supplications to 'Ali, and rows of

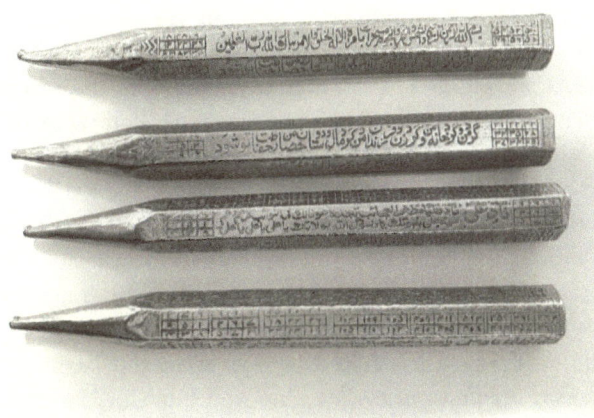

FIGURE 1. Baraka nails. Author's collection.

magical number squares. The idea was that you place one of these nails in each corner of a room, aiming them into the center. The nails act as baraka missiles. You won't find that prescription in hadith canon or any classical work of Islamic jurisprudence, but it's Islam as formulated and understood on the street, which I'd argue is more truly "mainstream" than scholars who speak with the shelves of pretty books behind them. Maybe the trained experts don't own Islam like they think they do.

In addition to the baraka nails, I picked up a biography of Sarmad (actually one of two saints buried inside) in both English and Hindi editions. Speaking to the tension between responsible Islamic jurisprudence and the mystical line of flight, Sarmad's shrine in the shadow of Delhi's enormous Friday *masjid* was built upon the site of his execution by the state. The biography calls him Sarmad Shaheed, Sarmad the Martyr. In terms of confessional identity and modes of knowledge, Sarmad manifested Deleuze's Body without Organs (BwO), experimenting with the strata, attaching and freeing himself, resisting any particular system's acts of control while opening himself to radical connections. He was born into a rabbinical Jewish family in Kashan, memorized biblical literatures, became Muslim, studied under the neo-Platonist philosopher and Ithna 'Ashari Shi'i theologian Mulla Sadra, ventured to South Asia as a merchant, and lost his mind in ecstatic love for a Hindu boy named Abhay Chand. Listening to Abhay Chand recite *ghazal* poetry, Sarmad would go into mystical intoxication. Abhay Chand's parents insisted on separating them, provoking Sarmad to sit naked at Abhay Chand's door until they were finally reunited. Sarmad then gave up clothes altogether and wandered the streets naked. He stopped cutting his hair and fingernails and wrote poetry that indulged in paradox and contradiction, simultaneously claiming and mocking every religion. He worshiped Hindu gods in one verse and denounced them in another; he denied Muhammad's heavenly ascension but also personally identified with the Prophet. In Delhi he befriended Mughal crown prince Dara Shikoh, who had forged his own linkages between Vedanta philosophy and *wujudi* Sufism, locating spaces for Mahadeva, Vishnu, and Brahman in the Qur'an as angels and recognizing the Vedas as divine revelations. Sarmad predicted that Dara Shikoh would rule, but Dara Shikoh's more arborescently Sunni brother Aurangzeb won the family power struggle. Aurangzeb ordered Dara Shikoh's execution and then turned his attention to the naked dervish. He commanded Sarmad to recite the *shahadah*, the Islamic testimony to monotheism (*la ilaha illa Allah*, "no god but God") and Muhammad's prophethood. Sarmad only offered the first words, the "negative part": *la ilaha*, "no god." In the biography sold at the shrine, Sarmad explains,

"I am still not able to see Allah; when I see him, I shall go ahead."[5] His blood now legal, the saint was beheaded as an apostate. A legend holds that Sarmad was executed in Aurangzeb's palace and that his head rolled on its own to the Jama Masjid, reciting poetry along the way. One narrative depicts the severed head as proclaiming, "I am taking my case to the court of the Prophet Muhammad."[6]

The enshrinement of an executed queer Hindu Jewish Sufi Muslim freethinking saint of immanence next to the second-largest masjid in the world as a locus of baraka might lead us to questions. Masjids and shrines have complex and unstable relations. At the shrine of Sufi saint Miyan Mir (1550–1635) in Lahore, I heard the story that Dara Shikoh had originally collected red bricks for the shrine, but Aurangzeb stole them to build Badshahi Masjid, his giant display of imperial power and commitment to "orthodox" Sunni Islam. For a Deleuzian rethinking of Sufism, is there a more on-the-nose metaphor than appropriated bricks? It would be easy to generalize these relations as pointing to a timeless conflict between "legal" and "spiritual" dimensions of Islam, but mystics and their tombs are not always at odds with state power. In some historical settings, the mystic's body provides exactly the kind of site that an imperial orthodoxy needs. The Ottoman Empire honored the master Ibn al-'Arabi's tomb in Damascus with a masjid/shrine complex: the masjid upstairs, the shrine downstairs. Masjids and shrines often occupy the same territory. Though dead bodies have always served as sites of contest for competing Islamic territorialities, much of the strife between masjids and shrines is uniquely modern. All the Islamic shrines that had been bulldozed and bombed in recent decades could have been destroyed prior to the invention of bulldozers and bombs, and Sarmad has been enshrined next to the Friday masjid longer than the United States of America has existed as a sovereign nation. The global antagonism toward shrines does not emanate as a straight flow from an antimodern "traditional Islam," but rather speaks from a hypermodern Sunni revivalism and the disappearance of Sunni mystical kingship models—Mughal and Ottoman and Timurid monarchs claiming the caliphate and even semi-messianic status with Sufi vocabularies and evidence from astrological tables[7]—in favor of modern nation-states with rational authorization and a reliable citation of scriptures. Relocating Sarmad's place in Islam, the biography sold at his shrine seems to adjust its narrative dials for contemporary sensibilities. While acknowledging Sarmad's habit of nakedness and infatuation with a Hindu boy, the book leaves out some of his theological promiscuity, emphasizing his legitimacy as an eccentric but mostly normative Muslim. When he gets weird, it's only because the supreme lovers of God sometimes get weird in ways that conventional believers won't understand, but he's still sincere and safely within the bounds of the territory. Sarmad's engagement of other traditions is erased; Sarmad appears as a more firmly committed Muslim than Dara Shikoh, who becomes implicated as "lacking firmness in faith and softness about religious practice" for his attachment to Hindu traditions.[8] While giving the report of Sarmad's refusal to say the shahadah, the book asserts that after Sarmad's martyrdom, the full testimony of faith was heard from his body three times. And when postmortem Sarmad sought justice for himself in the court of the Prophet, his own teacher rebuked him, reminding Sarmad that he had reached his desired destination and had been patient all his life up to this point. Even the tyrannical, fanatical Aurangzeb is portrayed as holding some respect for Sarmad's advanced gnosis.[9] Both the executed heretic and intolerant emperor undergo de-/reterritorializations in the projects of those who can use them.

Thinking about Sarmad with his long fingernails and Deleuze with his long fingernails, I was not only a reader of concepts, but a body in which things happened. As Judith Butler writes in *Gender Trouble*, "Despite the dislocation of the subject that the text performs, there is a person here."[10] Deleuze did not believe in a fixed, stable self but wrote and spoke with a self-referential voice anyway. So a person, even if a fluid multiplicity of multiplicities plugging in and out of other multiplicities, moved between Deleuze camp and Sufi shrines and then went back to a room to sort the artifacts. Skimming lecture notes in taxis and doing namaz next to dead bodies loaded with power, the fluid multiplicity felt like an assemblage converter for something new, a Deleuzian Sufism, and asked what that would mean. Deleuze wasn't writing mystical poems for a Beloved beyond the clouds. If Sufism were defined in the most simplistically broad terms (and just about *any* definition of Sufism, whether broad or focused, might be doomed from the start) as the pursuit of experiential knowledge of a transcendent god, the fluid multiplicity wondered how such a tradition could combine powers with a philosopher of pure immanence, for whom atheism was a natural given. And then, despite its fragmentation and instability, the fluid multiplicity wrote with first-person pronouns, even possessives. My Sufism, my Deleuze.

Islam and Deleuzian Theology

As it has manifested thus far in a growing number of projects, the scholarly "Deleuze and religion" question fixates on a tension between Deleuze's ontology of immanence—in which Being's origins, purpose, power, and value depend not on something outside or beyond, because there is no outside/beyond, but remain immanent in itself—and theologies of transcendence, in which a god who creates the world necessarily stands not only outside and beyond it, but *above* it. With belief in transcendence comes a possibility of transcendent values: timeless, unchanging, and pure "judgments of God" free from the polluting and corrupting touch of the world. The world of human thoughts, feelings, and values, hopelessly fluid and flimsy, must therefore surrender itself to regulation from above. Supplementing the transcendence of supernaturalist theism and God's revealed instructions, Islamic tradition privileges a historical transcendence in the moment of Islam's origins with the Prophet and his community, represented as an untouchable golden age seemingly standing outside of time. By this model, chronological distance from the pure past leads inevitably to a chain of successive degradation, inferior copies of copies, meaning that the present generation of Muslims must recognize itself as the worst in history. At the end of the world, the Prophet promises, Islam will have degraded to such a point that there will be no observable differences between Muslims and other communities. We see a similar phenomenon in Mahayana Buddhism with the "end of the Dharma" doctrine, first developed by a Chinese contemporary of Muhammad (the Pure Land patriarch Daocho, 562–645 CE), which held that as human beings became further removed from the Buddha with the passage of time, Buddhism declined. No longer able to do the work themselves, Buddhists would then become increasingly reliant on the transcendent compassion of Buddha Amitabha in his hundred thousand billion buddha-fields.[11]

A neo-traditionalist argument, buzzing with complaints about "postmodernism" and "secular" academia, would charge that without timeless truths imported from a plane of transcendence, there can be no truths at all. The Prophet and those closest to him (which would mean different things between Sunni and Shi'i historical narratives) cannot be judged but become the system of judgment: without the transcendent values and norms that they project across time and space, we are unable to formulate meaning for ourselves and are thus doomed to rootless, unstable relativism. Multiple bodies of Islamic knowledge makers, authorized by their constructed links to the sacred past, claim a kind of trickle-down transcendence in their own right as the Prophet's heirs. During a public performance of slavery apologetics in 2017, Jonathan A. C. Brown relied on this transcendence to deflect criticism: "The Prophet of God, *salla Allahu alayhi wa salam*, had slaves. He had slaves. There's no denying that. Are you more morally mature than the Prophet of God? No, you're not."[12] Muslim condemnations of slavery, however, also refer to timeless values established by the original Muslim community, arguing that a close read of the Prophet's personal example—with awareness of his own historical setting and its limits—demands abolition as the truest expression of his ethics. For Deleuze, as Daniel W. Smith has argued, transcendence (which does not have to be theological in nature but can also find expression in "secular" forms) "is what prevents ethics."[13] In an acentered and univocal existence without transcendence subjugating life and imposing universal norms, Deleuze envisions philosophy on the plane of immanence as perpetual experimentation and creation of the new, which multiplies the possibilities for life. Whether or not this requires atheism depends on what exactly you need god machines to do.

While the tension between immanence and transcendence has remained crucial to a developing corpus of Deleuzian theology, this conversation has regularly privileged Western Christian thinkers and canons, neglecting non-Christian traditions and failing to consider Islamic archives. Even projects that attempt to push back against Deleuzian theology's Christocentrism take part in its perpetuation. Daniel Colucciello Barber's *Deleuze and the Naming of God* (2014) makes an important intervention in Deleuzian theology, but explicitly leaves out non-Christians: "When I talk in this book about religion, I talk about Christianity."[14] Even when discussing Malcolm X, Barber does not engage Malcolm as actually working with a theology (whether that of Elijah Muhammad or Malcolm's later Sunni reconversion) that could speak to the problem of divine transcendence. Barber rationalizes a particular Euro-American-Christocentrism with claims on "the historical force that Christianity exerts on our present moment . . . it is precisely because of the hegemony of Christianity in relation to the act of naming God that I am focusing on Christian theology."[15] Christianity, he argues, "remains the primary analogate among religions."[16] Given the "sort of historical pressure that Christianity still exerts on the contemporary imagination," Barber comfortably speaks only to/of Christianity, which still does not mean Christianity as a global multiplicity defined by the extraordinary heterogeneity of its molecular expressions—not the infinite local expressions of folk Catholicism, Latter-Day Saints, John Song, African Pentecostalism, or my snake-handling evangelist grandfather in West Virginia—but chiefly elite thinkers, usually white men, in Western intellectual genealogies.[17]

What is this planet on which Barber lives, the frustrated Islamic studies scholar must ask, where *Muslims do not meaningfully exist*, and *only* Christianity leaves a mark on *the* contemporary imagination? Whose present moment does not contribute to what Barber considers *our* present moment? Who is the "our" to which Barber's present moment belongs?

Barber ironically suggests that his exclusion of non-Christian resources somehow challenges Christian hegemony "in alliance with a dechristianization of the discourse of religion," serving a possible de-Christianized future.[18] While recognizing and appreciating Barber's awareness of Euro-Christian global hegemony and its impact on "religion" as a concept, I am not convinced that yet another monograph in which religion means *theology*, and theology means *Christian* theology, and Christian theology means the work of *Western European* and *American* Christian theologians and post-Christian philosophers—while insisting that non-Christians can/should take part in this conversation too—meaningfully opens the portal.

Revelation comes *down* to the world; the Arabic word used most regularly in reference to the Qur'an's revelation, *nazul*, precisely signifies "descent." According to canonical hadiths, God descends nightly from the highest heaven to the lowest and calls out to those asking for his forgiveness. In Muhammad's supreme authorizing experience, his night journey, he goes *up*. For a "Deleuze and Islamic theology" project, the problem of transcendence would remain critical, and there's enough resonance and overlap between traditions that a Deleuzo-Islamic theology could benefit from developments in Christian (or Christocentric) engagements of Deleuze such as Barber's insightful work. But the focused "Deleuze and Islam" conversation remains to be had. To think about a Deleuzo-Islamic theology could lead in a number of directions: We could try to wrestle Deleuze into compromise with Islamic theology and soften the consequences of his atheism, following a line of flight in which Deleuze ironically circles us back into the structures of orthodoxy. We could search Islam for ontologies of immanence and potential interlocutors for Deleuze among thinkers that he never would have considered (as Daniel Tutt has done with Mulla Sadra)[19] or put Deleuze to work toward new approaches to Islamic theologies. Again, whether you can assemble a fruitful Deleuzo-Islamic theism or place for Deleuzian immanence in Islam depends on the limits of your Deleuzianism and your Islam. Alan Badiou asserts that despite his resistance to Platonist transcendence, Deleuze still upholds an emanationist ontology;[20] while contested, this claim provides one opening. The emanationism espoused by Ibn Sina/Avicenna and refuted by al-Ghazali failed to win the orthodoxy contest but remains an *Islamic* emanationism. As Laura Marks argues, "The presence of Ibn Sina's thought in Deleuze is relatively easy to discover, for he was the magister, influencing almost every strain of Islamic and Western medieval thought."[21] Many readers of Deleuze (and Deleuze himself), while appreciating Avicenna's importance for Western intellectual tradition, would fail to catch Avicenna's Muslim context and full range of references, such as his use of Sufi terms,[22] and therefore miss him as an "Islamic philosopher" (or, in Deleuze's case, miss the idea of "Islamic philosophy" as a thing that already exists, rather than a hypothetical possibility). But if Deleuze has no Duns Scotus or (whether directly or indirectly) Spinoza without Avicenna's impact, Deleuze is already Islamic.[23] We could extend Deleuze's claimed tradition of the univocity of being (to which Deleuze views himself as an heir and perhaps the truest fulfillment, a "Seal of Univocity?") to include Islamic figures such as the Andalusian theosopher Ibn al-'Arabi, whose thought provoked anxieties over monism and pantheism similar to the legacies of Duns Scotus and Spinoza, and get Deleuzo-wujudism.[24] Connecting the right pieces, we might end up with a Deleuzo-Farabi assemblage, Deleuzo-Mulla Sadra, Deleuzo-Ikhwan as-Safa, or Deleuzo-Suhrawardi Illuminationism. But the project should ask for more than simply showing Deleuze's genealogy to be entangled with Muslim thinkers, finding Muslims who said Spinoza-ish things, or bringing Islamic references into the Deleuze-and-theology conversation.

If Suhrawardi saw himself as a reviver of Plato's teachings, instructed by a dream vision in which Aristotle came to Suhrawardi and confessed Plato's superiority, his Ishraqi version of emanation just sends us running in circles on the question of transcendence or playing a shell game in which the neo-Platonism bean gets moved from Christian to Islamic containers. Islamic neo-Platonism does not produce the Nietzschean "inversion of Platonism" that Deleuze pursued.[25] Islamic neo-Platonism addresses God's need to be *more* transcendent, not exactly a Deleuzian problem. And Deleuze's valorization of "pure immanence" doesn't open itself to apophatic or "negative" theologies in the same way as the thought of Jacques Derrida, whose work has been appropriated in service of negative theology and even productively placed in conversation with classical Sufi masters such as Ibn al-'Arabi.[26] If an apophatic theology ultimately preserves and intensifies a supreme being's removal from life, only rendering that being *more* unknowable, ineffable, and transcendent, are we really doing something "Deleuzian"? God the rational creator, judge, and arborescent order-maker can be switched out with God as a cosmic Mr. Potato Head of rootless organless multiplicity and chaos, but as Petra Carlsson Redell has pointed out in her critique of Christo-Deleuzian theologies, dressing up the transcendent singular sky-lord as a new rhizomatic god of immanence doesn't solve the Deleuzian theology problem.[27] So long as God remains an object for theology to represent, Redell argues, it makes no difference "how 'eternally changing,' 'fluid,' 'schizoid' or 'tehomic' God might be perceived or described to be."[28]

I don't know if "Can a Deleuzian believe in God or not?" is the most interesting question that one can ask. Before smuggling theism into Deleuze or trying to produce a theism that might satisfy Deleuze's priorities—collaborating with Deleuze to create a new hybrid Deleuzian-theism-baby, to recall his famous metaphor of entering authors from behind and impregnating them, that's both monstrous to him and unmistakably his[29]—I want to first preserve Deleuze's atheism without immediately excavating it for a hidden secret of *tawhid*. Deleuze, resisting the priestly disease of "interpretosis,"[30] isn't entirely open to a textual esotericism that seeks to penetrate his words and turn his atheism into a disguise for the unseen god, but a Deleuzo-Islamic theology could lead in another direction—extracting an atheism from within Islam, an alternate motivating system in which you read the Qur'an like you're the Deleuzian lobster-god collecting and sorting with your pincers.

Obviously, many Muslims and non-Muslims alike would find the suggestion of an "Islamic atheism" (and Deleuze's image of God-as-lobster) to be beyond absurd. *Islam* literally signifies "surrender" and "submission," and the capitalized Islam, in its popular plain-sense meaning, refers to a tradition of surrender/submission to the singular and supremely *other* God of Abraham (who could be represented in degrees of anthropomorphism, but not as a crustacean). There's a sizeable corpus of non-Muslims writing about Islam, many of them relatively sympathetic, who perceive an uncompromising monotheism to be Islam's ultimate essence. Many Muslim bodies of literature would assert the same (as Kecia Ali's work on biographies of the Prophet demonstrates, apologetic and polemical works can end up collaborating toward a shared outline of essential bullet points).[31] In the popular "five pillars" model for thinking about Islam, the first pillar is the shahadah, the testimony to God's unity and Muhammad's prophethood. This is believed to be the gate through which one passes to enter the tradition. When I was sixteen years old, I reinvented myself as a Muslim with no ceremony or ritual other than walking into a masjid and repeating the testimony in Arabic and English before witnesses. How could one formulate an "Islamic" denial of God's unity? And to deny the first half of the shahadah inevitably means repudiating the second, since erasing God would mean denying Muhammad's claims about himself.

I find my launch pad here at the claim from Deleuze and Guattari in *What Is Philosophy?* that there is "always an atheism to be extracted from religion."[32] We usually don't think of atheism as internal to a religion, developing through the logics and codes of the thing that it denies, waiting to reveal itself from within; nor would it be obvious to everyone that atheism might take a particular form in relation to the specific religion from which it was extracted. Deleuze and Guattari write that Jewish thought contained an atheism that found its fulfillment with "the atheist Spinoza."[33] If the atheism that emerges from within Christianity is somehow specifically Christian, I want to know the specific atheism that might secrete from Islam, an "Islamic" atheism. Exploring the dargahs of Delhi as baraka zones without concentrating on a particular god as baraka's source (even when I recited the god's names), I thought that perhaps I was taking part in an Islamic atheism. But I was also captivated by Deleuze and Guattari's casual assertion that Christianity "secretes" atheism more than any other religion;[34] why would Christianity excel over other religions in its capacity for this secretion? How would Deleuze go about measuring religions' atheistic secretions to compare them?

To read Islam through a Deleuzian lens or follow a Deleuzian departure into Islamic thought could mean that I'm doing comparative theology, especially given the nascent tradition of Christian, post-Christian, or Christian-adjacent "Deleuzian theology." A project of Deleuzo-Islamic theology would necessarily engage Deleuze's reception and appropriation by theologians working with Christian materials, the present state of Deleuzian theology as a new Christian or post-Christian tradition. But a Deleuzian theology project, regardless of the particular tradition in which the theology takes place, cannot be reducible to a matter of thinkers and texts speaking to other thinkers and texts, safely outside history—a kind of academic transcendence. Nor can it impose the hegemony and coherence upon a tradition that comparative theology tends to demand. To place a tradition's theology into conversation with a thinker from outside, asking whether the two can find some resonance or harmony or contribute to each other, starts with a troubled assumption that the tradition is fundamentally united and whole, that it indeed possesses a singular theology that would enable us to present the thinker and tradition as two individuals speaking to one another. The meeting of Deleuze and Islam, in this case, would mean investigating sacred sources such as the Qur'an and hadith and performing acts of interpretation to recover possible meanings from them or privileging specific giants of Islamic thought, premodern elite luminaries (men) such as al-Ghazali or Avicenna, and treating them as spokesmen for a supposedly unified theological system. If you want to meet Deleuze with an Islamic monism, you can have an Islamic monism; those resources are readily available. If you want to put Deleuze to work for a theology, however, this dialogue-between-elite-men approach misses a prime Deleuzian concern: the assemblage as relation of powers. Islamic theology, like Christian theology, only comes to us in a recognizable shape through centuries of conflict and struggle.

From what ingredients was Islamic theology assembled, under what circumstances, and by what forces? What creative possibilities and minor voices were obscured in the process? How did the crystallization of an "Islamic theology" regulate and suppress its internal heterogeneity, potential for change, and capacity for connections to an outside? In what ways did this crystallization fail to complete its work, still allowing for the creation of new connections and multiplicities? Historical Islam reveals an abundance of ways that diverse thinkers and communities reproduce God and the Prophet as concepts; the lived reality of Islam is messier than the notion of a singular "Islamic theology" could accommodate. Deleuze's most fruitful contribution to an Islamic theology could be the way that he affirms multiplicity: at the start of *A Thousand Plateaus*, Deleuze and Guattari remind us that "since each of us was several, there was already quite a crowd."[35] Which Deleuze (or Deleuzo-Guattari) are we putting to work? If we take this seriously, we're left with little hope for a theological exchange between Deleuze, being not one but several Deleuzes, and fifteen centuries of accumulated global Islamic tradition, at least not without violent acts of territorialization on our part. The Deleuzian assemblage won't let you forget that. I can't imagine a Deleuzian encounter with Islam that only receives content from the "official" pulpit at Jama Masjid while neglecting the martyred naked Sufi's shrine and occult marketplace across the street. If the Islam that Deleuze meets is multiple, the encounter never ends: each side of the exchange is forever new. And to the extent that Deleuze's project seeks to invert Platonism, we cannot extract one artifact from the Islamic multiplicity and grant it the privilege of representing "true" Islam as the best possible execution of a pure and perfect blueprint while also envisioning a chain of degradation in which the lesser "heterodox" options offer only increasingly corrupted copies as they are further distanced from the pure. Deleuzo-Islam affirms bad copies.

While I usually avoid bringing terms such as "orthodoxy," "heterodoxy," "heresy," and "syncretism" into Islamic studies contexts (because first, these concepts are derived from Christian histories and have limited application outside the history of European Christianity; second, in the academic study of religion, these terms tend to rely on uncritical and ahistorical essentialisms), I argue that Deleuzian Islamic theology, as much as it can say things about divine attributes and immanence and representation, must confront orthodoxy as a social construction that privileges some voices and erases others. This is the difference between thinking about immanence as an abstracted theological problem and thinking about theology itself as something immanent *inside* the world. If strata represent the "judgments of God" that Deleuze resists, orthodoxy—which very straightforwardly and literally claims to represent the judgments of God—manifests a process of stratification in God's name. Orthodoxy constitutes the fabrication of a tradition's legitimate center (and in contrast, its illegitimate margins). Orthodoxy demands the management of unmanageable chaos, the governing and limiting of multiplicity, and the policing of imagined boundaries. Of the terms in Islamic vocabulary that could serve as rough translations for heresy, *bida'* and *zandaqa*, the former refers to "innovation," signifying a departure from the original pure template of Islam as embodied by the Prophet; the latter derives from a suspicion that some Muslims secretly adhered to Manicheanism while publicly claiming Islam; zandaqa eventually became a catch-all for any transgression against established Muslim norms.[36] If orthodoxy's prime terrors appear as imposing change upon a timeless ideal and improperly mixing the pure with outside dirt, Deleuzo-Islam must pursue an inversion of orthodoxy. The Islamic orthodoxy-making technologies of transmission chains, initiatic lineages, textual canons, scholarly consensus (*'ijma*), and scriptural canon all reproduce Deleuze's most despised image: the centralizing, hierarchically ordered tree. Informed by assemblage theory, a Deleuzo-Islamic theology must instead rethink Islam as a dynamic, variegating rhizome defined by connections to its outside with multiple points of entry and exit. Islam-as-rhizome affirms positive relations to heterodoxy, which is to say a conception of Islamic theology as forever heterogeneous, always in flux, never in its finished form or accessible in its original state, but always a plastic proto-Islam in development. Insofar as it seeks escape from orthodoxy's strata, Deleuzian theology manifests as a praxis of heresiology, a study of the tradition's dangerous lines of flight through which it mutates into a new creation: where they can be found, what opens them, the outsides to which they lead, and what causes them to become closed or blocked.

Even while inconsistently patrolling the border and celebrating pathways of creative experimentation, Deleuzian Islam could still mark its outer limits. Deleuzian theology, before we ever ask about God, means that we take seriously Deleuzian denials of the quest for origins and purity and think about what it means for Islam on the ground, here in this world of flesh-and-blood bodies, when Deleuze and Guattari declare, "We should stop believing in trees"[37]—that is, the organs by which Islam becomes organ-ized. A Deleuzian BwO rhizome-Islam does not have to revel in absolute chaos and perpetual deconstruction all the time, but it still exhibits a release from the need for Islam to remain forever clear and unchanged, strictly arranged by genealogies of knowledge and permission throughout and beyond time. Every assemblage contains energies that potentially scatter its components as well as those that hold the components together. Ask the Deleuzian question "What can Islam do?" and witness the forces that either expand or contract the range of possible answers.

Entering into Deleuze's work along with the corpus of supplementary literatures and a whole field of "Deleuze studies" surrounding it, I found encouragement in the "methodological breather" taken by Alexander G. Weheliye in *Habeas Viscus: Racializing Assemblages, Biopolitics, and Black Feminist Theories of the Human* (2014). Weheliye warns that making use of Deleuze and Guattari could lead a project into "the quagmire of orthodox Deleuzianism," which reads Deleuze "exclusively within the western European philosophical tradition."[38] The notion of "orthodox Deleuzianism" struck me as a paradox, given that some of my most fulfilling moments with Deleuze came from using him as a tool—or rather, a weapon—upon theological orthodoxy. But concentric circles of priests have formed around Deleuze, radiating meaning from the center to the outside. Newcomers to the Deleuzian territory can achieve preliminary initiation through his more accessible interpreters, who have produced numerous user's guides to his major works and "Deleuze dictionaries" that navigate readers through his unique (and sometimes unstable) vocabulary, concepts, and references. This all looks like the start of a territory; and like territories, its proper boundaries and limits have been contested, and authorized gatekeepers patrol the checkpoints. As the field of literatures using Deleuze expands beyond the territory's furthest reaches and control, we also see Deleuzian revivalists making Salafi calls for a return to the text and what Deleuze "actually" says while issuing *takfir* on thinkers who have deviated from the original sources.[39]

Turning away from "doctrinaire Deleuzians" and a "strict Deleuzianism" that enforce "a proper form of being Deleuzian," Weheliye finds fruitful encounters with Deleuze through scholars who use Deleuze for projects of critical race studies, queer theory, and other milieus "beyond the snowy masculinist precincts of European philosophy."[40] As in my appropriations of a figure such as Ibn al-'Arabi, I don't need Deleuze to produce a unified system that fails to function if any of the parts are broken or missing. This project represents another experiment in a world outside the territory of Deleuze—or, for that matter, orthodox Deleuzianism.

It should be made clear that I do not look to Deleuze's work with the expectation that he might say something directly useful *about* Islam and/or Muslims. Deleuze was not particularly well-read in Islamic studies, and his rare engagements of Islam share the weaknesses found in his treatments of just about everything outside Europe.[41] Like his nomadology, Deleuze's references to Islam and Muslims speak to the limits of his personal Orientalism and the intellectual genealogies that inform him.[42] I make the charge (with some mixed feelings, because I don't want to feed efforts to reinscribe Deleuze as an alt-right icon)[43] that Deleuze was an anti-Muslim racist. When discussing the French hijab ban, Deleuze resorts to the standard Islamophobic trope of "creeping shari'a," asking, "Is this issue merely the first phase of a larger strategy?" and outlining a scenario in which Muslim minority groups manage to make increasingly aggressive demands on French society. In Deleuze's creeping-shari'a doomsday scenario, the allowance of hijab in public schools can lead to a "second phase" that consists of "the right to Islamic prayer in the class room," and then a "third phase" that includes raising objections to Voltaire as "an offense to Muslim dignity." For evidence that his anti-Islamic bigotry doesn't mean that he's a racist, Deleuze then declares that Arabs don't need religion for their identity, because secular Arabs exist.[44] Recalling Weheliye's insights, I find comfort in the growing assemblage of Deleuze studies, which expands Deleuze's reach beyond his personal limits and makes use of his concepts without necessarily upholding his own transcendence as a universal and all-encompassing authority. Gathering and sorting particles from Deleuze to make my Deleuzo-Islamic arrangement, I extract the parts that are useful and leave other parts behind.

If Deleuze only views Islam from an Orientalist airplane window, pronouncing racist judgments from 30,000 feet above the world, I want to zoom in his lens, bring him back to earth, and show him the schizzes of local Islam that split up the monolith. In Lahore's Sultan Pura section, I visited the shrine of Ghoray Shah (d. 1594), a fourteenth-century saint directly descended from the Prophet. He was a child saint whose palsy caused him to shake. The boy loved horses—hence the honorific "Ghoray (Horse) Shah"—and devotees reportedly offered him toy horses in exchange for the fulfillment of their prayers. After his father scolded him over the miracles-for-toys program, Ghoray Shah died of grief at five years old. Through the centuries since, devotees have been leaving horse figures at his tomb. I've heard it suggested that the practice, along with the legend of Ghoray Shah, could have supplanted rites from an older, pre-Islamic regime: perhaps in some forgotten time for a now-forgotten god, visitors to the site offered *real* horses in sacrifice, and the post-Islamic regime did not erase the site but recoded it with new stories and meanings. But in the Islam of modern globalizing Sunni revivalisms and transnational networks, for which "local" comes to mean "inauthentic," even the toy horses have slowly disappeared as modern universalisms molarize Islam's molecular packs, capturing local flows within their judgments and textualist inhibitions. For a Deleuzian conversation with Islam, I don't want Deleuze reading Suhrawardi's particular emanationism; I want Deleuze as a tool for looking at the specific milieus in which Greek philosophical tradition and Zoroastrian angelologies become recognizably Islamic resources, the Qarmatiyya deterritorialized the Black Stone from the Ka'ba in an attack based on astrological readings, Elijah Muhammad understood the Black Stone as a representation of his own self, Muslim astrologers affirmed Muhammad as Lord of the Jupiter-Saturn Conjunction, Persian Sufis produced a tradition of *kufriyyat* ("infidelity") poetry celebrating idolatry as the veil over a secret Islamic gnosis, and the Satpanthis conceptualized 'Ali as Vishnu and Fatima as Lakshmi, recoding the Prophet's household as avatars of Hindu gods. Islamic tradition is overcoded with arborescent genealogical functions but also lives and grows as a rhizome, and Deleuze and Guattari tell us that the "rhizome is an anti-genealogy."[45] Genealogical charts and evolutionary trees don't account for the virus that transmits a genetic blueprint from one host to another, giving us the cat with baboon DNA.[46] A straightforward genealogy of Islam doesn't show the channels through which occult traditions could smuggle Hermes Trimegistus across borders to become the antediluvian esotericist Enoch and then find a place in the Qur'an as the prophet Idris.[47] I don't want Deleuze reading Avicenna; I want Deleuze at Ghoray Shah's dargah, holding a clay horse in his hands and building on Supreme Mathematics.

Islam at large is the full egg, the earth, the Body without Organs, littered with escape routes from forces that stratified the territory, gridded the land to direct (limit) our movement, and restricted the acceptable range of difference with their systems of divine judgment. The project is not to accept the organism's illusion of regulated flows and reliable hegemony at face value, nor to destroy the organs, but to look for points at which the *organization* can turn from its cultivated arborescence to its internal rhizomatic tendencies, opening portals into new experimentation.

Experimentation, not annihilation. I am not deconstructing into oblivion. You can't just "blow apart the strata without precautions," Deleuze and Guattari warn.[48] Reckless and absolute deterritorialization can lead to capture by a black hole that lands you back on the strata, the codings of divine judgment—as in the "Wahhabi" bulldozing of the Ottoman world piece by piece, a deterritorialization from the old imperial order to more intensely redraw the territory. Between the shocks and traumas of our deterritorializations, we recover and reassemble. In *A Thousand Plateaus*, Deleuze and Guattari dial down the revolution of *Anti-Oedipus* and give repeated cautions of the Body without Organs gone wrong, bodies that had only dumped their organs and destroyed themselves. "You don't reach the BwO by wildly destratifying," they write, and "You don't do it with a sledgehammer, you use a very fine file."[49] Some of my tools here, such as an attritioned student of Malcolm X in 1960s Harlem who left the masjid and named himself Allah, might be sledgehammers, but I remember that Deleuze and Guattari tell us, "You have to keep enough of the organism for it to reform each dawn."[50] In hadith canon, Muhammad promises that the earth will consume all of the human corpse except for the coccyx (*'ajba al-dhanab*, literally "strange tail"), from which the human was created and from which it would be reconstituted on the day of resurrection.[51] The line of flight offered by Islamic atheism can always circle back into the territory. I suggest that as absolute a disintegration as an "Islamic atheism" might appear, it could ironically preserve the 'ajba al-dhanab for a future return.

The Arrangement

Following this introduction, chapters 1 and 2 concern the sacred sources, the Qur'an and hadith corpus. In Chapter 1, I first introduce the Qur'an with an eye for Deleuze's taxonomy of root-books, fascicular root-books, and rhizome-books in *A Thousand Plateaus*, in part to challenge Deleuze's passing reference to the Qur'an as a supremely authoritarian root-book that forbids interpretation. To think about Deleuze as a tool for engaging the Qur'an, I must ironically move past what Deleuze himself says *about* the Qur'an; with limited exposure to Islamic studies, Deleuze lacks the resources to think of the Qur'an as something other than a "Muslim Bible." I trace the genealogies of colonial knowledge that inform Deleuze's rare mentions of the Qur'an and then turn to the Qur'an as it lives in the world, leading to an alternative conception of the Qur'an as a Deleuzian rhizome-book. I then take us beyond the "Muslim Bible" framework and reintroduce the Qur'an through the multiplicity of ways that it functions in Muslim lives as things other than a scripture to be read and interpreted, including ritual, aesthetic, sensory, magical, and occult technologies. While decentering interpretation as the privileged mode for engaging the Qur'an, this chapter also explores ways in which Muslims derive meaning from the Qur'an's content, including the Qur'an's internal structure. I introduce key themes in Qur'an interpretation and commentary (*tafsir*) and then offer a Deleuzian framework for exploring the Qur'an without resorting to searches for its "true" meaning. In the process, this chapter pushes back against the genealogies of colonial knowledge production that narrow the Qur'an's possibilities within the limits of the "Muslim Bible" model, in part reading Deleuze against Deleuze.

Chapter 2 explores the hadith corpus, the thousands of narrations reporting Muhammad's sayings and actions, through the lens of Deleuzian assemblage theory to examine its rhizomatic and arborescent tendencies. The hadith corpus, unlike the Qur'an, is not a singular "book" with fixed content, but a mass of oral traditions, disseminated by thousands of reporters across multiple generations, codified within countless volumes of varying canonical privilege, and subject to rigorous evaluation by master critics. Like any assemblage, this corpus exhibits strata that stabilize and contain its flows, but also deterritorialize lines of flight. The *isnad*, the chain of transmission history that accompanies each hadith, might appear unavoidably arborescent: tracking different versions of a hadith through its isnads produces textual history as an authorizing tree and centralizes orthodoxy-making power in the hands of a coterie of clerical scholars. The isnad names centers and margins. However, consideration of isnads also reveals the internal multiplicities that characterize the hadith corpus: the presence of competing networks that eventually become collectively territorialized as a singular "Sunni tradition" with the rise of textual canon. Isnads expose significant heterogeneities that have been obscured in the Sunni hadith corpus, such as local schools of thought (illustrated, for one example, by the theological and legal differences between hadiths from Basra as opposed to Kufa). For both the mechanics of its production and openings in its content, the aural tradition of hadith still exhibits lines of flight that resist sectarian stratification and orthodoxy-policing. This chapter disassembles the hadith corpus to look at the process by which it became assembled, revealing the creative and rhizomatic power that it still contains.

Chapter 3 considers foundations for a Deleuzian Sufism, starting not with doctrines and concepts but with Sufism as lived assemblages defined by relations between bodies. Sufi intellectual tradition offers a wealth of resources for imagining theologies of immanence, exhibited in the charges of monism and pantheism leveled against Sufi thinkers such as Ibn al-'Arabi (1165–1240), alternately praised and reviled as *shaykh al-akbar*, the "greatest shaykh," or *shaykh al-akfar*, the "most heretical shaykh," and whose theology of *wahdat al-wujud* (the unity of being) would seem to invite immediate dialogue with Deleuze's favorite theologians, Spinoza and Duns Scotus. In this chapter, however, I prioritize the embodied theologies found in the *khanaqah*, the Sufi lodge, locating a Deleuzian Sufism in the connections through which Sufi bodies enhance each other and collaborate in the making of Sufism as not only scriptural exegesis or a theorizing of mystical experience, but an assemblage with material content.

Chapter 4 examines the question of baraka as it relates to transcendence and immanence, with focus on Jannat al-Baqi, a cemetery in Medina that hosts the graves of numerous heroes from early Islam (such as Muhammad's grandchildren, his wife A'isha, the caliph 'Uthman, and many others). With the emergence of the modern Saudi state in 1925, the various mausolea that had been constructed (and reconstructed, following earlier destruction by Sunni revivalists) throughout Jannat al-Baqi were demolished in accordance with the state's "Wahhabi" platform and its transcendence-favoring model of baraka. Tension between divergent models of baraka continues to manifest in contemporary disputes over the Islamic legitimacy of shrine culture. In numerous modern contexts, various neo-traditionalist forces such as the Saudi state and ISIS have bulldozed and bombed long-standing Muslim shrines in part as a rejection of baraka's immanence, thereby privileging their own brands of textualist revivalism. The question of whether baraka flows entirely from beyond the world or can be seen as a flow between bodies in the world—and of course, the question of who decides—holds profound consequences for what counts as legitimate Islam in a given setting.

Chapter 5 explores an Islamic theology of pure immanence, the construction of divinity found with Five Percenter tradition. In 1960s Harlem, a former Muslim and student of Malcolm X who had renamed himself Allah began teaching young Black men to reject the notion of an invisible, transcendent "mystery god" in the sky. He argued that instead of worshiping what they could not see, they must recognize themselves as "true and living" gods of the universe—not "incarnations" or "manifestations" of a greater supreme being, but *gods* themselves. Allah interpreted his own name with a backronym of "Arm Leg Leg Arm Head," illustrating the divinity of the human form, and taught Islam as "I Self Lord Am Master," an affirmation of Islam as his own nature rather than surrender to transcendent forces.

As Allah's young gods carried his theology throughout New York, Allah eventually became the venerated figurehead of a new religious movement known as the Five Percenters. While teenagers in police custody told officers that their name signified the "five percent of Muslims who smoke and drink," the "five percent" actually referred to a belief in "poor righteous teachers" who would liberate the consciousness of the masses (the 85 percent) from the control of religious leaders (the 10 percent). Allah ultimately told his young followers that they were not only gods, but also that each of them was entitled to *his* divine name, thereby decentralizing the movement and ensuring that no charismatic leader or hierarchical institution would take over after his death. Decades later, Five Percenter tradition survives not only in New York but also nationally and even internationally, perhaps best known for the deep roster of hip hop artists (such as the Wu-Tang Clan, Rakim, Nas, and Jay Z, among many others) who claim affiliation or otherwise refer to the tradition in their lyrics. While Five Percenters spread their theology across the world, however, prison systems throughout the United States declared the Five Percenters a "security threat group" and denied them constitutionally protected rights of conscience, practice, and assembly as a religious community. As incarcerated Five Percenters in multiple states sued for their constitutional freedom of conscience, prison systems opposed their claims to religion in part through an argument that Five Percenters were not properly "religious" and thus had no claim to the protected rights of religions if they did not believe in a higher power greater than themselves. State prison systems moved with the full power of their machinery to crush the theology of an immanent Black divine, enforcing a theology of God as transcendent beyond Blackness.

While some voices in any assemblage are louder than others, Five Percenter theology remains theoretically acentered and multiple. Some Five Percenters will articulate their godhood in pantheistic tones that sound Spinozist or wujudi; others remain entirely materialist and offer Marxist critiques of religion. In its broadest characterization, I would present Five Percenter doctrine as a rejection of supernaturalist theologies that position divinity as a transcendent Other outside the self. Could the Five Percenter concept of God find categorization as "Islamic"? Five Percenters themselves answer that question in diverse ways. Most Five Percenters reject self-identification as Muslims, since a Muslim *submits* to Allah and a Five Percenter *is* Allah; but many Five Percenters, even those who identify as non-Muslims, still make claims on Islam (sometimes in terms of a "way of life" rather than a "religion") and articulate their personal divinity through reference to the Qur'an, hadith traditions, various strands within Shi'ism, Sufi figures such as al-Hallaj, Ibn al-'Arabi, and Bullhe Shah, and participation in Muslim communities, whether Sufi orders or Sunni and Shi'i masjids. Islam as Allah accessed it was primarily the Nation of Islam led by Elijah Muhammad; while the Nation certainly did care about modes of Islamic authority such as Qur'an interpretation, there is no evidence that Allah had personally presented his concepts as an exegesis of the Qur'an and hadith canon or otherwise engaged "classical" Islamic archives. However, I argue that tracing the "roots" of Five Percenter tradition defies arborescent "family tree" models but works most productively with a "rootless" rhizomatic model in which the origins are multiple and continually reconstructed. With a reading of the numerous (and often contradictory) resources from throughout Islamic tradition that become tools in the Five Percenters' theology of immanent Black godhood and the routes through which Five Percenter discourses and more "classical" or "traditional" Islamic concepts and practices flow into each other, this chapter envisions the possibilities for an "Islamic atheism" to be secreted from the tradition.

In Islamic interpretive traditions, "seal" (*khatm*) can signify a conclusion but also a confirmation. My concluding discussion, "The Seal of Muslim Pseudo," reassembles the themes and arguments of the book and imagines Deleuzo-Islam as a tradition characterized by theological immanence and ongoing destratification through a positive relationship to change and mixture, an Islam that remains unfinished and continually informed by its encounters.

1 / Deleuze and Tafsir: The Rhizomatic Qur'an

> ... *the Koran goes the furthest in this direction.*
> —DELEUZE AND GUATTARI, *A Thousand Plateaus*

What direction? Where does the Qur'an go, and why does it go the furthest? And when Deleuze and Guattari tracked the Qur'an's course, what tools did they have at their disposal? In this decontextualized fragment from *A Thousand Plateaus*, after all, they do claim to know something about the Qur'an; they assert an analytical mastery over the artifact, name its orientation, and lay down their own strata upon it as "judgments of God." Before examining what Deleuze and Guattari claim to know about the Qur'an, I want to consider how they know what they think they know.

Their claim to knowledge of the Qur'an does not necessarily concern what the Qur'an *says* or *means*, because Deleuze and Guattari promise to never ask this question of any book.[1] They remain suspicious of attempts to retrieve meanings from a text's interior that interpreters imagine were hiding there all along. The text has no interior: when the insect crawling across a page comes to a crease, it might think that it has penetrated into the page's depths, but only encounters the foldings that have been performed upon a flat surface. Deleuze and Guattari even create a diagnosis for compulsive hermeneutics: "interpretosis."[2] When they proclaim with confidence that the Qur'an goes further than other books in a particular direction, they're not acting as *mufassirs* of the text and asserting that the Qur'an prescribes this direction in its own words. They don't support their claim with a citation of any specific verse; they aren't even claiming to have read the Qur'an at all.

But still, they claim *something*. Without taking a position on what the Qur'an says or what it means when it says things, Deleuze and Guattari still speak as authoritative experts regarding the Qur'an's life in the world. Unconcerned with what the book tells them about itself, they ask different questions: What other machines can plug into a particular book-machine and make it work? What can a book *do*? They want to know how a book either represents the world or connects to it and how the machine works (or does not).

The machines that can plug into the Qur'an-machine include Deleuze and his concepts, but Deleuze himself is not the one to make those connections. The excerpt from *A Thousand Plateaus* cited earlier amounts to one of only two references to the Qur'an in the pair of immense volumes that comprise *Capitalism and Schizophrenia* and the only explicit mention of the Qur'an by name. This lack of engagement, however, provides an opportunity, because even if Deleuze did not produce a "Deleuzian" treatment of the Qur'an, his concepts can be creatively appropriated for projects beyond his expertise or interest. A Deleuzian tafsir of the Qur'an, in which a Deleuze system is retrieved from his words to understand and comment upon a Qur'an system, would be less compelling to me than the idea of entering Deleuze into an assemblage with the Qur'an, experimenting with Deleuze's conceptual tools to see what they open in the revelation. There are no fixed, stable systems here, only fluxes between bodies that might make something new.

While I'm not looking for Deleuze to say useful things about the Qur'an, I nonetheless have to return to this quote from *A Thousand Plateaus* in which Deleuze and Guattari identify the direction in which the Qur'an supposedly goes furthest. Deleuze and Guattari tell us, "There is no difference between what a book talks about and how it is made."[3] Their passing commentary on the Qur'an—again, a commentary that they can make without citing any verse or demonstrating that they've read the book—reveals much about how *their* books were made, the outside through/on which their books exist, and the machines into which they are plugged. The conversation starts with Orientalism.

The Colonial Genealogy of One Half-Sentence in *A Thousand Plateaus*

Back to the direction in which the Qur'an goes furthest. Let's recover some of the context for Deleuze's and Guattari's diagnosis:

> It is now the book, the most deterritorialized of things, that fixes territories and genealogies. The latter are what the book says, and the former the place at which the book is said. The function of interpreta-

tion has totally changed. Or it disappears entirely in favor of a pure and literal recitation forbidding the slightest change, addition, or commentary (the famous "stultify yourself" of the Christian belongs to this passional line; the Koran goes the furthest in this direction).[4]

The direction in which the Qur'an exceeds all other books, according to Deleuze and Guattari, is textualist authoritarianism, manifested with the "root-book" of stable territories and genealogies that allows for no movement in its possibilities: no change, no multiplicity of expression, no dynamic or creative work with the text, no engaged communities of ongoing interpretation, only "pure and literal recitation." Deleuze and Guattari have a distaste for arborescent genealogies, but we can draw a family tree for these feelings about the Qur'an, tracing their assessment to an Orientalist master narrative concerning Islam's essential nature and possible futures. Tomoko Masuzawa observes this narrative's formation in *The Invention of World Religions*, describing a process by which Islam came to be popularly imagined as "the epitome of stifling rigidity, intolerance, and fanaticism." This representation, Masuzawa explains, became "a familiar theme, mechanically repeated by one treatise after another, in flagrant disregard of the diversity and obvious malleability evidenced in the vast domain of the actual Islamic world."[5]

A casual survey of Orientalists writing about the Qur'an reveals the map that Deleuze and Guattari would trace. Sir William Muir (1819–1905) pairs the Qur'an and Muhammad's sword together as "the most stubborn enemies of Civilisation, Liberty, and the Truth which the world has yet known."[6] Writing in 1880–81, Robertson Smith derides the Qur'an as singularly "the bulwark of all prejudices and social backwardness in the East" and insists that if the "Mohammedan people" are to make any progress, it would require that "a freer attitude be taken up towards the Koran."[7] Three decades later, Martin Hartmann makes a similar demand that in order to join modern civilization, Muslims must apply contemporary methods of biblical criticism to their Qur'an.[8] John Arnott MacCulloch, in *Religion, Its Origin and Forms* (1904), characterizes Islam in his "Mohammedanism" chapter as distinct for its "frankest literalism" and adds, repeating a previous scholar's diagnosis of Islam as "lifeless," that "Islam has shown itself unable to develop" due to the "absolute authority of the Quran."[9] In 1944, Giorgio Levi Della Vida confidently asserts, "The *Leitmotiv* of the religious history of Islam is the desperate attempt to get rid of the rigid literalism of the Koran."[10] Central to this narrative of scripturalist backwardness is an assumption that the Qur'an's author, described by one nineteenth-century scholar in very Deleuzo-Guattarian phrasing as a "typical Oriental despot," imposes a uniquely demanding totalism over its readers, even within the passional regime's genre of sacred scripture. The Qur'an's readers in turn are presumed to accept this arrangement or struggle helplessly against it.[11] The Orientalists' diagnosis of Muslims' subjugation under the Qur'an typically goes hand in hand with an articulation of Islamic monotheism with qualifiers such as "absolute," "uncompromising," "rigid," and "pure," as when a reverend writing in 1888 gives Islam credit for at least teaching a "pure, rigid, austere monotheism."[12] "The Koran insistently inculcates monotheism in its most absolute and uncompromising form," Lucy M. Garnett tells us in 1911.[13] These adjectives travel consistently between works of major and minor authors alike.

These assessments of Islam's "absolute" monotheism must be understood in light of a shapeshifting European anti-Semitism that could move across the centuries between theological hatred (i.e., Jews as Christkillers) and modern racial pseudo-science (Jews as genetic pollutants) and conspiracy theory (Jews orchestrating world events to their advantage from behind the scenes). Judaism was scapegoated during the Enlightenment as illustrating the wrong kind of religion, characterized by immutable laws, superstitious ritualism, antirational faith in miracles and other bizarre stories, and the unquestioned authority of scripture, all foils to the ultimate triumph of reason.[14] The vicious anti-Semitism found in Enlightenment philosophers such as Immanuel Kant (1724–1804), who advocated a "pure moral religion" that entailed a "euthanasia of Judaism,"[15] would intersect with rising Aryanist ideology, in which the imagined monolith of Aryan peoples was mirrored by their antithesis, the imagined monolith of Semitic peoples.

While Western writers either condemned Christianity for its Jewish origins (in the interests of liberation from religion or an alternative pagan revivalism) or sought to deracialize Jesus from his Jewishness, Islam became an intensification of everything deemed objectionable in Judaism. Ernest Renan (1823–92), who worked to distance Jesus and Christianity from their Jewish milieu, would assert that Islam, not Christianity, was the true successor to Judaism, since Christianity exhibited an Aryan essence and left Semitic religion behind. Renan both deterritorialized Jesus from his Jewish origins (asserting that Jesus, having grown up in Galilee, had not been a product of the "Semitizing" desert) and racialized Sufism away from Islam, arguing that Sufism's creativity and sophisticated systematization of mystical experience signaled that it was entirely a product of Iranian (that is, Aryan) flows, owing nothing to Arab (that is, Semitic) Islam. Renan made his case in part by contrasting Semitic and Aryan theologies, the former being strictly monotheistic, the other more pantheistic; in contrast to the Semitic god, an unfathomable master above the world who occasionally sent revelations to human prophets, the Aryan god actually entered the world and became human, meaning that Aryan religion did not share in the Semitic dependence on a divinely revealed book.[16] Renan's diagnosis resonates in part with Kant, who perceived Islam as shallow rote ritualism but gave Persians (Aryans) credit for their poetry and refined taste, offering the explanation that they were "not such strict followers of Islam" as Sunnis and maintained a "tolerably mild interpretation of the Koran."[17]

An Aryanist writer in 1932 describes the Qur'an as teaching "the strict monotheism of the Semitic peoples as opposed to the actual polytheism of the Farther East, and as opposed to the practical polytheism of the West" and argues that "the polytheism of the Nicene creed is dying out" in favor of the "uncompromising monotheism of Sinai" shared by Muslims and Jews.[18] Other authors of the period describe Judaism as "the stubborn advocate of an absolute monotheism," Muhammad as the "apostle of a rigid monotheism,"[19] the Qur'an as borrowing from the Jews' "absolute monotheism" and "pure monotheism,"[20] and Iranian Shi'ism as "the revolt of the Aryan against Semitic monotheism" (in contrast to Ibn 'Abd al-Wahhab, reformer of Islam in the Arabian Peninsula, whose monotheism is termed properly "absolute" and "strictest").[21] German theologian Otto Pfleiderer writes in 1904 that "Islamism shares the monotheistic, rigidly theocratic and legalistic character of Judaism, without its national limitation. . . . Islamism is the Jewish idea of theocracy carried out on a larger scale by the youthful national vigor of the Arabians, well calculated to discipline raw barbaric peoples, but a brake on the progress of free human civilization."[22] H. G. Wells also praises Islam's "uncompromising monotheism, void of any Jewish exclusiveness, which is sustained by the Koran."[23]

This uncompromising and unphilosophical monotheism serves a racially disabled population that requires, as James T. Bixby, writing in 1895, explains, a "simple creed . . . one which needs no elaborate metaphysical explanations, but is comprehensible by the most ignorant, even at the first recital."[24] Bixby praises Islam for "inciting martial ardor" and "putting faith before a new people in a form, most simple and easily graspable, for meeting half-way the weaknesses of Oriental peoples," while noting Islam's inadequacy: "But for the quieter and more solid victories of peace and the needs of higher civilizations, for promoting social liberty and personal development, it is not well-fitted."[25] Bixby wants to at least give Islam credit for speaking to less-evolved peoples at their own level: "While, then, I do not regard Islam as a religion adapted to foster the highest civilization and to be a final faith for *humanity of the best type* [italics mine], nevertheless, to meet the wants of barbaric and semi-civilized nations, it has admirable qualifications."[26] The stiffness of the Qur'an's monotheism thus appears to have been inherent to its human author's ancestral stock, linking Islam to Judaism not in the language of contemporary interfaith dialogue as branches of an "Abrahamic" monotheistic tradition in which Christianity also shares, but rather as a racialized expression of the limited Semitic intellect and its hostility to sophisticated theological abstractions. In a 1912 volume on Iranian religion, a scholar describes Semitic peoples as adhering to a common "rigid monotheism—a monotheism less philosophic than religious,"[27] while the 1897 monograph *The Aryan Race: Its Origins and Its Achievements* tells us, "There is nothing to indicate the least native tendency of the Semitic mind toward philosophy."[28]

As the same tropes of "absolute" and "uncompromising" monotheism and scripturalism circulate among Orientalist scholarship and popular literature on Islam, these works contribute to a shared narrative of Islam as a Semitic nation-building enterprise, expressed with pretensions toward universalism and bound in an intensified version of the Bible. According to this narrative, absolutist Semitic monotheism finds its purest expressions not in theology, philosophy, mysticism, or art, but *law*, reducing religion to a set of divinely ordered permissions and prohibitions. Narratives of Semitic religions as enforcing an authoritarian, under-theorized monotheism at the price of their civilizational progress underwent shifts across the twentieth century. While becoming less explicitly racialized with the post–World War II decline of overt Aryanism, they would continue to inform the dominant Western imaginary of Islam throughout the entirety of Deleuze and Guattari's lives. In his classic *Mohammedanism* (1949), H. A. R. Gibb repeats the standard accounts of Islamic monotheism as "uncompromising," "simple, rigid, and austere" and a "pure Abrahamic" revival while upholding the Qur'an as Islam's unquestioned center; offering "the final and most perfect solutions for all questions of belief and conduct," he argues, the Qur'an's doctrines and prescriptions "have remained in all ages the core and inspiration of the Muslim religious life."[29] The same imaginary emanates from W. Montgomery Watt, Deleuze and Guattari's prime scholarly citation on Islam, when he issues the declaration (which would become a popular truism of Muslims' apologetic "Intro to Islam" pamphlets) that Islam is best understood not as a mere "religion," but rather a complete "way of life" that "permeates the whole fabric of society."[30] Watt himself analyzed Islam through a lens of racial essentialism, as when he observes, "Fear of the near appearance of the Divine has deep roots in Semitic consciousness," to make sense of

Muhammad's first experiences of prophethood.³¹ Whether or not Deleuze and Guattari actually believed in races or racial essences, white supremacy's archive remained the hill on which they stood to speak with confidence about Jews, Muslims, and books.

The connections between Deleuze and this sea of Aryanist discourses become most explicit in the plateaus "1227: Treatise on Nomadology" and "7000 B.C.: Apparatus of Capture." In these plateaus, Deleuze and Guattari ground their analysis of states and war machines in the work of philologist and comparative mythologist Georges Dumezil (1898–1986), whose "complex relationship to the Aryanist research of the Third Reich" and precise connection to fascism have been debated and whose work regardless became meaningful for advocates of European pagan revivalism as well as those who wanted to romanticize specific social hierarchies as "natural" for the Aryan race.³² In their universalizing theories, Deleuze and Guattari rely on Dumezil specifically for his dualist distribution of power, expressed in mythology between legislator gods and magician gods. Having developed his theory from observing Indo-Iranian-Germanic (that is, Aryan) continuities and envisioning a distinct "Indo-European" (again, Aryan) mythological framework, Dumezil (and Deleuze and Guattari following him) identifies the same legislator and magician gods under different names across Indo-European societies: Mitra is thus Tyr; Varuna is Odin.³³ Deleuze hails Dumezil as "exemplary" and asserts that "no one has better analyzed the generic and specific differences between religions, and also the differences in parts and functions between the gods of a particular, single religion."³⁴ In the second half of the twentieth century, French Orientalist (and Deleuze and Guattari's later reference point for the possibility of "an Islamic philosophy,"³⁵ as well as a chief source on Iran for Foucault)³⁶ Henri Corbin continued to swim in the Indo-European theory as his work imagined metaphysical resonances between Germany and Iran, even articulating what Steven M. Wasserstrom calls an "unreconstructed Aryan triumphalism" throughout his work.³⁷ Corbin's scholarship served the interests of the Pahlavi regime, which sought to decenter Islam as but one element within a perennialist narrative of Iranian (Aryan) spirituality reaching back to the time of Cyrus.³⁸ Hamid Algar charges that Corbin shares resonance with earlier race theorists such as Arthur de Gobineau in his vision of Islam's internal divide as a conflict between Aryans (Iranians) and Semites (Arabs) and that Corbin had merely "transferred the dichotomy from the biological to the spiritual plane."³⁹ In his discussion of Corbin's Sufi master Frithjof Schuon (1907–98), who repeated and elaborated upon common tropes of nineteenth-century Aryanism ("the Aryan tends to be a philosopher whereas the Semite is above all a moralist"),[40] Gregory A. Lipton forcefully demonstrates that the twentieth-century academic study of Sufism (and by extension, Islam at large) in Western universities remained deeply entangled in ideologies of European ethno-racial-religious superiority over Jewish and Muslim Semitism.[41]

Again, none of this is to say that Deleuze and Guattari consciously adhere to Aryanism or any theory of white supremacy; the point is that this discourse shaped their historical moment so profoundly that they could not have avoided exposure. That's the story of their stray remark about the Qur'an. Deleuze and Guattari first use Judaism to illustrate their theory and then casually mention the Qur'an as the prime specimen of such a book that exceeds Jewish scripture and goes furthest of all. While "587 B.C.–A.D. 70: On Several Regimes of Signs" has been read as a "radical extension of Protestant Christianity,"[42] it can also be considered a less radical extension of Aryanism.

Islam, perceived as exceeding all other monotheisms in its refusal to cede territory, must therefore possess the book that exceeds all other literature in doing the things that Deleuze and Guattari personally find troubling about monotheism and its tree-book literature ("We're tired of trees.... They've made us suffer too much").[43] Throughout the nineteenth and twentieth centuries, this expectation of the Qur'an was disseminated and routinized so successfully in Western scholarship and popular media that it graduated from colonial ideology into common sense, allowing Deleuze and Guattari to reproduce it without bothering to cite a source. There is no source; the world is their source. In the knowledge regime inherited by two intellectuals of a twentieth-century colonial power that had subjugated most of Muslim Africa, this vision of the Qur'an was close enough to a natural and obvious given that they neither owed a specific author credit for articulating it first nor felt a burden to prove their claim, whether using the Qur'an's text or secondary scholarship.

Prior to their tracing of the Qur'an's supposed trajectory, Deleuze and Guattari make *Capitalism and Schizophrenia*'s first reference to the Qur'an in *Anti-Oedipus*, in their universal history "Savages, Barbarians, Civilized Men." This section charts the shift from a "primitive" people's "territorial machine" to the next stage, a "despotic machine" (which itself will become decoded under the next stage, the "civilized capitalist machine"). The despotic machine is characterized by a rising despot who rebels against the old tribal systems and alliances to create a new social order with himself positioned as the embodied will of a god. In the despotic machine, graphism initially aligns with the voice but then takes it over, imprisoning the voice by setting it into writing.[44] Describing the despotic text's subjugation of the voice, they turn to the Qur'an's circulation in Africa:

> Andras Zempleni shows how, in certain regions of Senegal, Islam superimposes a plane of subordination on the old plane of connotation of animist values: "The divine or prophetic word, written or recited, is the foundation of this universe; the transparence of the animist prayer yields to the opacity of the rigid Arab verse; speech (*fe ver be*) rigidities into formulas whose power is ensured by the truth of the Revelation and not by a symbolic or incantatory efficacy. ... The Moslem holy man's learning refers to a hierarchy of names, verses, numbers, and corresponding beings—and if necessary, the verse will be placed in a bottle filled with pure water, *the verse water shall be drunk*, one's body will be rubbed with it, and one's hands will be washed with it." Writing—the first deterritorialized flow, drinkable on this account: it flows from the signifier.[45]

Deleuze, Guattari, and Zempleni are wrong to think of this "drinkable" Qur'an as necessarily a negotiation between Senegal's "old plane" of "animism" and rigid Islamic textualism. Rudolph Ware in particular has powerfully critiqued the "African fetish" and "syncretism" models with which Orientalist scholarship has treated Islam in West Africa. "Drinking the Qur'an certainly represents no animist innovation," Ware writes; "the practice is probably as old as Islam itself."[46] Traditions of ingesting the Qur'an and/or liquids infused with its energies can be found among the Salaf, the earliest Muslim generations, whose practices hold a canon-making authority[47] and remain globally popular Islamic practices, found not only in these "certain regions of Senegal" but also in Pakistan, Indonesia, Egypt, Morocco, Yemen, Turkey, Iran, India, and conceivably anywhere that you find Muslims.[48]

Practices of ritualized text veneration and the use of material copies of texts as magical technologies, as well as the question of power relations between local indigenous traditions and a globalizing textualist religion, can also be found in Buddhist tradition.[49] The European study of religion, however, had grown increasingly sympathetic to Buddhism from the nineteenth century onward as Aryanists reconstructed the Buddha into one of their own, even comparing Buddha and Hitler as exemplars of a mutual "Indo-Germanic" essence.[50] Since Buddhism was favorably racialized as Aryan, Aryanists could not imagine it as a religion of scripture veneration, which was the hallmark of negatively racialized Semitic religion; Buddhism could not illustrate Deleuze and Guattari's despotic semiotics with the same punch as Judaism and Islam. Instead, Deleuze and Guattari mention Buddha's tree as an example of the tree that becomes a rhizome.[51]

While acknowledgment in *Anti-Oedipus* of the Qur'an's lived complexity as a book that can become deterritorialized and form productive connections in non-book modes (in this case, as a drinkable talisman that supposedly expresses Islam's "plane of subordination on the old plane of animist values") could be read in friction with *A Thousand Plateaus*'s presentation of the Qur'an as immovable stone tablet demanding only recitation, Deleuze and Guattari do not explicitly mention the Qur'an by name here. We technically don't know that they connect this drinking of "rigid Arab verse . . . ensured by the truth of the Revelation" to the Qur'an. Given their frenetic citational spree through global history, archaeology, anthropology, psychoanalysis, and other disciplines, the shallowness of their reading in Islam, and their capacity for mistakes such as mislocating the Pacific island of New Guinea in Africa, it's a legitimate question. But even if we give their citation of Zempleni the benefit of the doubt, Deleuze and Guattari still enforce Orientalist visions of the Qur'an's relationship to other traditions—namely, as a weaponized call to subordination and domination on behalf of a prophetic warlord's despotic machine. Islam finds its characterization here in the supposed "opacity of the rigid Arab verse," the absolute dominance of its scripture and "plane of subordination" that it imposes, and the textualist *hierarchy* that privileges the knowledge of the "Moslem holy man," rendering the Qur'an an essential illustration of their larger narrative about signification in the despotic machine.

Deleuze and Guattari make their second reference to the Qur'an, in which they tell us that the Qur'an goes further than other books in its resistance to interpretation or modification of any kind, in *A Thousand Plateaus*. Again, the Qur'an is referenced in close proximity to despots and their regimes. Deleuze and Guattari's referent for understanding Islam and the Qur'an remains Judaism and the Bible (as filtered through Western Christian intellectual histories). In the plateau "587 B.C.–A.D. 70: On Several Regimes of Signs" (dated for the two destructions of the Temple that forced the Jews to wander in exile), Deleuze and Guattari draw a contrast between the "paranoid, signifying, despotic regime" and the "passional or subjective, postsignifying, authoritarian regime."[52] Here, the despotic regime locates its despot-god at the center of concentric circles in which the despot-god's words undergo constant interpretation by authorized mediators; the first of this regime's definitive principles holds that "the sign refers to another sign, ad infinitum."[53] The latter "passional" and "postsignifying" regime emerges after a set of signs breaks away from the "irradiating circular network" to "work on its own account."[54] For a paradigmatic example of this break, Deleuze and Guattari refer to the Hebrew exodus from Egypt: the Jewish nation "detaches from the Egyptian imperial network of which it was a part and sets off down a line of flight into the desert."[55] The line of flight, however, repeats the world from which it offered escape. Against the pharaonic despot-god, the Jews respond with "the most authoritarian of subjectivities" and "the most passional and least interpretive of delusions"[56] while preserving their nostalgia for the despotic regime left behind; this nostalgia informs the establishment of a new kingdom with its own king and "a temple that would finally be solid."[57] At this "mixed semiotic," the Jews enter into the passional regime.[58]

As opposed to the despotic regime, in which meaning was centered upon the face of the despot-god and his interpretation by priestly experts, the passional regime presents a "sacred written Book" that obscures the face in favor of stone tablets that have internalized the world to become "the unique book, the total work, all possible combinations inside the book, the tree-book, the cosmos-book."[59] The expanding circles through which the despot-god's words undergo interpretation and mediation are gone as the sacred written Book becomes all things and all-powerful. Even when the tree-book's content is not expressly theological (Wagner, Mallarme, Joyce, Marx, and Freud become "Bibles" in their own rights),[60] Deleuze and Guattari see this "book worship" as drawn from the heritage of monotheism, reflecting a "monotheistic need for a single fount of wisdom."[61] The tree-book's delusion finds expression in "monotheism and the Book. The strangest cult."[62] And it is here that Deleuze and Guattari trace an old map to determine the Qur'an's orientation, telling us that as the Qur'an represents the most severe of territorializing books, it prohibits all creative agency from the reader and demands only literal recitation.

Deleuze and Guattari position *A Thousand Plateaus* within a unique taxonomy of books that consists of three categories: the root-book, fascicular root-book, and rhizome-book. As their names suggest, these categories speak to *A Thousand Plateaus*'s theme of assemblages as chiefly characterized either by their arborescent tendencies, meaning their hierarchical orders and capacities for resisting change, or their rhizomatic tendencies, meaning their fluid arrangements and openness to change. Deleuze and Guattari present *A Thousand Plateaus* as their model of a rhizome-book, a book that no longer seeks to represent or reproduce the world with a unitary truth but instead forms infinite connections with its outside, thereby remaining capable of endless transformations. The open, unstable, experimental rhizome-book appears as an antidote to the root-book and also the fascicular root-book ("to which our modernity pays willing allegiance"), characterized by the root-book's loss of its principal root and grafting of an "immediate, indefinite multiplicity of secondary roots."[63] The supreme root-book is the Bible, but there's more than one Bible in the world (i.e., Wagner, Mallarme, Joyce, Marx, and Freud), and the truest specimen of the tree-making "Bible" genre, more Bible than the Bible itself, is the Qur'an. Muhammad in the Deleuzo-Guattarian imaginary thus becomes an exaggerated Moses, the most extreme case of prophetic despotism.

Deleuze and Guattari point out that every assemblage contains forces that push it both toward and away from the tree; even the most intensely arborescent cosmos-book should offer a secret escape to the Body without Organs. Rethinking the Qur'an as a rhizome also provides a line of flight from the rampant Orientalism of *Capitalism and Schizophrenia*—which, if we follow the Deleuzo-Guattarian tension of the assemblage, would contain arborescent cosmos-book tendencies of its own.

Qur'an Machines

Rethinking the Qur'an's arborescence, we should first detach the Qur'an from Deleuze's apparent assumption that the Qur'an can be regarded as Islam's Bible, doing what bibles do but exceeding all other bibles in its absolutism. While it could seem intuitive and obvious to think of the Qur'an as the "Muslim Bible," the Bible itself is not a timelessly stable artifact: its powers and functions have changed amidst historical events (such as the Reformation), technological advancements (i.e., modern printing and industrialization making books cheap and widely accessible), epistemological shifts (such as standardized education producing higher mass literacy), and the rise of secularism and the modern individual, for whom religion undergoes reconstruction as a private and personal journey. All these forces combine to produce a modern Christianity in which the Bible is taken for granted as *the* central site at which one learns Christian truths. In this modern Christianity, it becomes reasonable for the first time in history to assume that an average committed Christian personally possesses his or her own copy of the Bible, which she studies with faith in her personal walk with the Word. Whatever Deleuze thinks the Bible does, neither the Bible nor the Qur'an could not have done that in the same way across all historical contexts. If the Qur'an looks like the Bible now, we need to recognize that both the Bible and Qur'an have been transformed.

Some scholars of Islam have suggested that rather than think of the Qur'an as the "Muslim Bible," a better comparison (while still clumsy and troubled) would name the Qur'an as the "Muslim Christ." This repositioning of the Qur'an could disrupt its standing in the Deleuzo-Guattarian framework, since their account of Christianity's break from Judaism relies in part on an opposition between Christians embracing holy paintings (the face of Christ) and Judaic iconoclasm anchored to scripture. Janell Watson, building on the insights of Eva Kuryluk, calls this the triumph of a "visual son" over his "linguistic father."[64] Without substantive readings in Islamic art history, I don't know if Deleuze and Guattari could reprocess the Qur'an in such terms. Contrary to popular Western mythology that envisions Islam as the most forceful iconoclasm (with especially vehement rejections of prophetic faciality), Muslims also boast a rich tradition of visual art, including paintings that depict the Qur'an's narratives and scenes from the Prophet's life, even with images of Muhammad bearing a fully exposed face. The Ayatollah Khomeini, for example, particularly favored a popular poster of Muhammad as a young man. Moreover, Deleuze and Guattari's opposition between divine faciality and internalized sacred text—Moses is denied a vision of God's face, they remind us, but instead receives immutable stone tablets[65]—doesn't apply to the life of Muhammad, who receives both a divinely revealed scripture and even, in a widely circulated but controversial tradition, sees God in the sensuous "best form" (a beardless young man with curly hair, a crown, sandals of gold, and a green or red robe, reclining on a cushion) with his *physical* eyes.[66]

Between the root-book and rhizome-book stands the fascicular root-book. As an alternative possibility to the rejection of interpretation, Deleuze and Guattari write that in the fascicular root-book, "interpretation survives but becomes internal to the book itself, which loses its circulatory function for outside elements," or "interpretation may reject all intermediaries or specialists and become direct, since the book is written both in itself and in the heart."[67] But despite the multiplicity of its roots, the fascicular root-book remains a kind of root-book, not yet a rhizome, a "strange mystification: a book all the more total for being fragmented."[68]

If Deleuze and Guattari failed to achieve a more historically sophisticated grasp of the Qur'an, it could be worth remembering that they were born around the same time as the modern Saudi state (Deleuze in 1925, Guattari in 1930). The generations preceding them were marked by the decline and disintegration of the Sufism-infused Ottoman Empire and the emergence of the so-called Wahhabi movement in the Hijaz alongside other Sunni revivalisms throughout the world, as well as a diversity of efforts by Muslim intellectuals to recalibrate the textual tradition. Deleuze and Guattari lived their lives and wrote their books across the same decades a fledgling regime rooted in "Wahhabism" assumed control over Mecca and Medina and increasingly presented itself as Islam's natural center and supreme global authority. The Saudi state became a leading producer of the Qur'an both materially (printing and distributing millions of copies of the Qur'an every year, both in Arabic and translation into countless languages) and discursively (disseminating translations through its own scholarly matrix, supplemented with commentaries by its preferred experts). Roughly contemporary to the rise of the Saudi state, the colonial Indian context saw a "Qur'an-only" movement develop as Muslim reformers engaged in pamphlet wars with Hindu reformers, who likewise adopted a modern Vedas-only vision of Hinduism, while Muslims and Hindus alike contended with Christian missionaries. These Muslim reformers, living under a Protestant colonial regime, offered *sola scriptura* arguments that an authentic and pure understanding of Islam required no source but the Qur'an. Reproduced in the twentieth century, the Qur'an would speak to the modern construction of "religions" as units of analysis that could be best accessed and understood as monovalent textual systems, meaning that every "religion" had to make a coherent case for itself with a monological statement of unchanging doctrine.

To call for a Qur'an-only Islam today affirms a method of *tafsir al-qur'an bi-l-qur'an*, treating the Qur'an as its own commentary: the Qur'an can be interpreted, but a reading finds its integrity through sealing off the Qur'an against pollution from outside. The Qur'an thus becomes a fascicular root-book, meaning, in Deleuze and Guattari's words:

> Interpretation survives but becomes internal to the book itself, which loses its circulatory function for outside elements: for example, the different types of coded interpretation are fixed according to axes internal to the book; interpretation is organized according to correspondences between two books, such as the Old and New Testaments, and may even induce a third book suffused by the same element of interiority.[69]

Qur'an-only Muslims deterritorialize the Qur'an from centuries of supplementary textual tradition and then reterritorialize the Qur'an as the center of Muslim life. The move is not reducible to an antimodern return to the glory of primordial Islam and sealing of the Qur'an against the outside, but can also ironically force the opposite, an opening to new modes of engagement. In gender-progressive and feminist Muslim thought, privileging the Qur'an with a sola scriptura argument means narrowing the field of battle and depriving the patriarchy of so much ammunition that it had collected while lording over an intellectual tradition for centuries. The Qur'an is a relatively small book, remains far more accessible via translation than any other Islamic text (such as the mammoth encyclopedic hadith collections), does not require the extensive supplementary literature of hadith science or jurisprudence, and, contrary to popular Western expectations, has never been the dominant source for Islamic law or ritual practice, offering very little content in those areas. Naming the Qur'an as Islam's essential (or only) center becomes an escape from the despot between regimes, a cutting away from accumulated strata to create something new.

Surprising those readers who assume that every religion's center naturally and universally rests in its holy book, Qur'an-only (or Qur'an-centered) discourse also reinvents Islam within the bounds set by modern secularism. Modern Qur'an-only discourse turns the revelation into a root-book in part through an attempt to sever and limit connections to resources beyond its pages, cutting away archives of Islamic law, bodily disciplines, ritual praxis, hadith-based exegesis, mysticism, traditions that some would term "cultural" practices or "folk religion," and whichever method of reading produces the wrong result. The "Qur'an-only Qur'an," more concretely bounded and (in theory) isolated from everything outside the book than had ever been conceivable, attempts to detonate historical Islamic tradition to rely exclusively on itself as a coherent thesis, capturing all possibilities for interpretation within its own covers. The readers have changed, and the modes of reading have changed. The premodern method of atomistic verse-by-verse commentary faces challenge with an intensified modern interest in thematic analysis, which means that each *sura* increasingly undergoes interpretation as a self-contained rhetorical artifact. Even the entire Qur'an can be read as a united whole for whatever an exegete identifies as its important themes, enabling projects of retrieving "the Qur'an's view of gender," "the Qur'an's view of violence," "the Qur'an's view of religious pluralism," etc.

Meanwhile, a growing body of hermeneutics, focused especially on the Qur'an's gendered consequences, turns the Qur'an into a fascicular root-book by cutting away the hope of an original root—namely, the promise of recovering and reconstructing "what the Qur'an really says." Recognizing the subjectivity of human interpretation as inevitable; affirming multiplicity becomes its own answer to the question. If we've surrendered the chance for "real meaning," either to secular literary theory or faith in the infinite possibilities of divine revelation, human commentary is all we have or need. We can prove the Qur'an's status as a queerness-affirming scripture if a commentator has announced it as such. We do not ask "what the Qur'an really says," because this is no longer seen as accessible, but instead ask what the Qur'an's interpreters say. Examining 4:34, the infamous "wife-beating verse," Ayesha Chaudhry looks beyond the Qur'an to the tafsir tradition and reminds us that what we find the Qur'an telling us depends not on the bare words, but rather on the worldviews ("idealized cosmologies") that readers bring to them so people adhering to patriarchal idealized cosmologies find the Qur'an advocating spousal violence and people with egalitarian idealized cosmologies find the Qur'an resisting it. If you believe that the Qur'an is from God and that God shares your sense of justice, then the Qur'an expresses your sense of justice—or at least, if none of us can speak for the Qur'an's author, your human subjectivity is no less a worthy mirror of the Qur'an than other readings. For many of us, a challenge emerges when we don't find the Qur'an repeating our justice back to us, and some would locate the problem in our own hearts rather than the text. When the chance of representing a transcendent authorial intention disappears, interpretation's boundless multiplicity holds the unity of the book together.

In modern reconstructions of Islam, the Qur'an becomes an image of the world in unprecedented departures from its life throughout the previous dozen-plus centuries. So what was the Qur'an before it became a root-book in the modern world? Against the hierarchical, stabilizing, orthodoxy-policing structure of the tree and its roots, Deleuze and Guattari offer the rootless and unstable rhizome, which they present in *A Thousand Plateaus* as the book that they've written. *A Thousand Plateaus* defines the rhizome—and by extension, the rhizome-book of *A Thousand Plateaus* itself—by six principles: (1) its nature of connection, (2) heterogeneity, (3) multiplicity, (4) asignifying rupture, (5) cartography, and (6) decalcomania.[70] These are the principles by which the rhizome-book opposes the root-book and fascicular root-book, remaining creatively open and unpredictable rather than sealing itself off as a self-contained block forever resistant to change. Many Muslims, considering the rhizome on these terms, might agree with Deleuze and Guattari in positioning the Qur'an as the rhizome-book's most excessive antithesis. But Muslim traditions—Islam as understood and lived in the world, rather than only the prescriptions from a specific body of scholarly elite men—also reveal a rhizomatic Qur'an.

Starting with the principle of connection, the rhizome's capacity for proliferating linkages with other multiplicities through which it transforms them and is transformed by them, perpetually creating anew through encounters and exchanges, I ask what the Qur'an can do. What kinds of connections can it achieve? What machines plug into it? What happens if we allow the most pessimistic scenario, temporarily granting

Deleuze and Guattari their ahistorical assertion that the Qur'an denies interpretation and requires only "pure and literal recitation"? If this were indeed the case, the intuitive first guess would be that the Qur'an obviously shuts down chances for creative encounters with the outside. But something changes if "pure and literal recitation" means that the Qur'an cannot undergo translation and movement through the world remains bound to its original Arabic. Does this further constrict the text or open it to new connections? I should reassert here that perhaps a third of what we call "the Muslim world" understands Arabic. If the Qur'an only circulated as "pure and literal recitation," it would be incomprehensible to the vast majority of its believing audience. In this sense, either interpretation has been denied or the power of meaning-making has scattered beyond the domain of reading. Is the Qur'an still a "root-book" if it's no longer discourse? Is it still a book, or have we missed its non-book powers?

I can't know if Deleuze and Guattari ever read the Qur'an, but I wonder if they have ever *heard* it. The name *al-Qur'an* literally means "The Recitation" (or "The Reading," with "reading" as understood within an aural tradition prior to a fully elaborated script or the development of a book culture). The Qur'an sometimes refers to itself as a *kitab* ("writing"/"book") but usually self-defines as the Qur'an in distinction from the *Kitab*, the Bible. It can be reasonably asserted that *recitation*, rather than *reading*, remains the primary mode by which many Muslims form connections with the Qur'an on a daily basis. This is to say that a Muslim who routinely recites short passages of the Qur'an in prayer (with or without comprehension of the Arabic) or listens to trained reciters that beautify the revelation with their voices is not necessarily going to examine the Qur'an as a *book* that offers *content* with the same kind of routine.

Tajwid, the discipline of reciting the Qur'an with tones, performs a kind of calligraphy with the Qur'an's vocalization. Listening to a trained reciter, I have been brought to tears by words that I could not understand. Without interrogating the content, I could open myself to transformation by the Qur'an as a machine for making affects. Tajwid changes the air in the room and my own breath. Whether this recitation is "pure and literal," however, depends on your own criteria. Though widely established as "mainstream Islamic tradition" today, recitation of the Qur'an with melody was a controversial practice in the early centuries of Islam. Of the four Sunni schools that survive today, two (the Malikis and Hanbalis) were characterized by their opposition, one (the Hanafis) contained a multiplicity of positions, and one (the Shafi'is) regarded the practice as permitted. At stake in the legal question, Christopher Melchert argues, was Islam's deterritorialization from Judaism and Christianity, along with tension concerning the permissibility of music and the question of when ornamenting the Qur'an with your voice transgressed a limit and became song.[71]

Is the Qur'an still a book when it makes *sounds* but not *words*? When delivered in that "pure and literal recitation" to non-Arabic speakers, the Qur'an's verses known for softening hearts and its verses that deal with mundane issues such as inheritance laws sound the same. They are beautified by the same classical sciences of tajwid, which do not make distinctions in the melodies due to content. If you do not register words when you hear the Qur'an, the message means less than the technology of affect working upon your body with sound. In my life as a Muslim, I have known numerous masjid aunties and uncles who could not understand the Arabic text, but would nonetheless "read"—that is, vocalize the sounds represented by the letters—every day, completing the Qur'an several times in a year. Some devoted special training to the discipline of tajwid. While they could spot the names of God and other frequent words or phrases, they see and hear the Qur'an as an embodied act of worship, not literary study.

Calligraphic reproductions of particular verses become so complex and abstracted that one no longer "reads" them for meaning. Knowing that the verses on a masjid's wall represent the Qur'an can produce an effect with or without closely examining the words to realize their message; the calligraphy is there for affect and baraka, to transform its viewers and the space. Unfortunately, Islamic calligraphy often receives treatments as a kind of *negation*, as though this tradition exists only because Muslims were supposedly forbidden from making other kinds of sacred art and had to settle for lesser media.

The words can take on new energies and produce new affects when rendered in new forms. The words can even break apart into letters that retain their Qur'an-ness and its powers. The dot under the first letter of the first word in the Qur'an, according to some traditions, represents 'Ali; more precisely, 'Ali is alleged to have proclaimed that he *is* the dot under the letter, which he also named as the innermost heart of the Qur'an. Ibn al-'Arabi would disassemble a word such as *kun*, the divine "Be" with which God created the universe, and interpret its letters: the *kaf* (k) and *nun* (n) representing the *zahir*, and the short vowel *waw* between them signifying the *batin*, calling attention to God's union of manifest and non-manifest in the act of creation.[72] As building-blocks of divine speech that preceded material reality, letters are no longer just letters, but building-blocks in the construction of the universe. The Hurufiyya, literally the "Lettrists," expounded on the metaphysical secrets of letters and gave rise to another movement, the Nuqtaviyya, the "Dot-ists," who derived meanings from the dots appearing above or under letters.[73] Ibn al-'Arabi, who regarded the letters as occupying a world like our own and even a hierarchical order parallel to human arrangements of prophets and *awliya*, ascended into the heavens and had sexual intercourse with the Arabic alphabet.[74]

The power of the letters, deterritorialized from the Qur'an and reterritorialized in amulet form, can transfer to any page. Verses related to medicine or curing (*tibb*) can be extracted from the Qur'an for talismanic functions, but even the letter that starts the word can carry its power in repetition:

ط ط ط ط
ط ط ط ط
ط ط ط ط
ط ط ط ط

Al-Shibli wrote the letter ق, linked to divine names such as al-Qadir (the Powerful), al-Qahhar (the Conqueror), al-Qawi (the Mighty), and al-Qayyum (the Everlasting), not to mention the heart (*al-qalb*), into a man's palm at the center of seven concentric circles, and instructed him to lick it, which expelled the jinn that had possessed him.[75] I can turn this book into an anti-jinn talisman right here:

If your body has been overtaken by jinns, lick the next page. For entertainment purposes only.

"There is no requirement," Brent Adkins writes, "that portions of one book be connected with other portions of the same book, or even other books. To create a rhizome be promiscuous; connect a portion of *A Thousand Plateaus* with a plant, with a feeling, with a song, with a mathematical formula."[76] Does the Qur'an enable promiscuous rhizomatic connections? The Qur'an can sever human-jinn assemblages, as in the previous talisman or the recitation of the final two suras as a defense against sorcery, but the Qur'an also *forms* them in the culture of jinn-enticing talismans, amulets, and the street-Islam beyond canonical texts. As Anna Bigelow observes, a well-circulated legend holds that reciting the 72nd sura (popularly known as Surat al-Jinn) a certain number of times would result in a jinn falling under your control.[77]

My Qur'an is connected to, among other things, chai in Styrofoam cups. I became Muslim in the month of Ramadan. As a detail of my earliest masjid experiences, the Styrofoam cups in which we drank chai at the masjid before starting *tarawih* (the special Ramadan prayers in which the entirety of the Qur'an is recited) became programmed into me as a

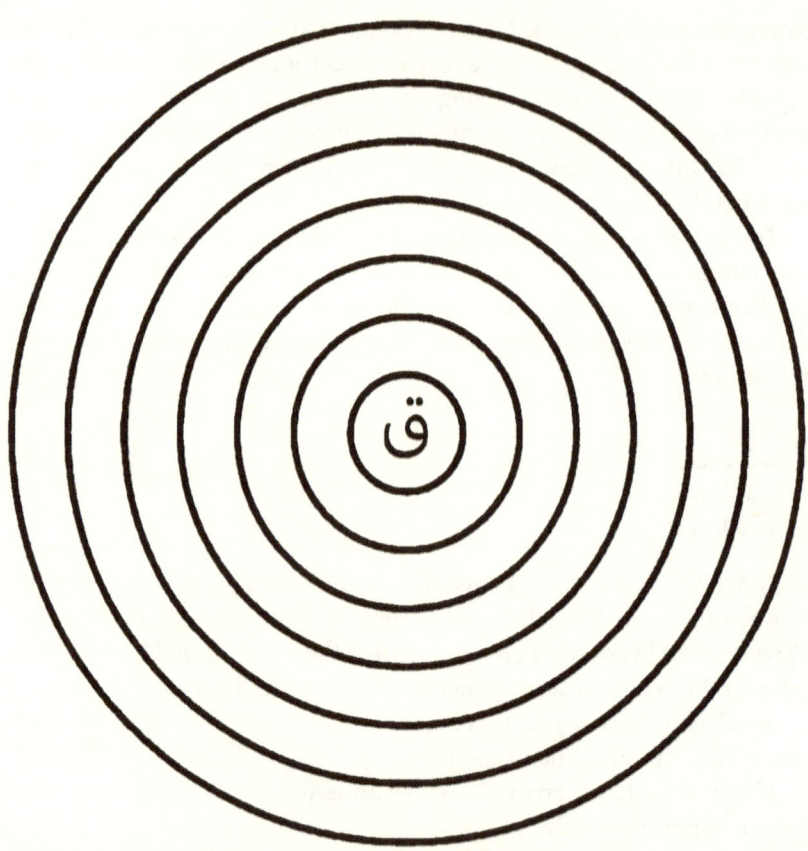

FIGURE 2. Anti-jinn talisman. Author's collection.

sensory trigger for Islamic thoughts and feelings. The Qur'an's recitation in tarawih, while "pure and literal" enough, was not exactly an encounter with messages from a book: as a teenager new to the masjid, I had read parts of the Qur'an in translation, but did not yet have training in Arabic and could not have comprehended what I heard. But I stood for those Arabic recitations with a *sense* of the Qur'an. Something still feels "Qur'anic" if I drink chai in a Styrofoam cup; my condition changes with that precise linkage of Qur'an-machine to Styrofoam-chai-machine. I also connect to the Qur'an through places and smells: on a high shelf sits a boxed Qur'an, the box and the Qur'an itself both ornamented with cloth from the interior *kiswa*, the green curtain hanging inside the Ka'ba (as opposed to the Ka'ba's more famous exterior black kiswa). Perhaps as a trace of the fabric's prior life on the perfumed inner wall of the Ka'ba, the Qur'an preserves a fragrance that flows out whenever I open the box. I don't read, recite, or interpret this Qur'an, but I smell it.

I remember the sensation that came with memorizing a short sura early in my conversion, which felt as though I were absorbing the Qur'an into my body, piece by piece, as well as the awe of meeting a *hafiz*, someone who had memorized the *entire* Qur'an by heart. One afternoon in my teen years, I chose not to rest on a couch when I saw that my hafiz friend was napping on the floor. My declining the couch for the floor was not a religious "requirement" in the narrowest sense but expressed a personal sense of the *adab* (etiquette) that I owed to the revelation. In these corporeal experiences of the Qur'an, the body preserves Muhammad's reception of divine flows as an *event*, a penetration of energies into our world. The hafiz becomes, in Ware's phrasing, a "walking Qur'an."[78] In Deleuzian terms, we might consider such encounters as processes of *becoming-Qur'an*. This does not mean that anyone actually transforms into the Qur'an, but rather that a Muslim body and the Qur'an form a rhizome with each other, sometimes through a connective node like another body that has memorized the Qur'an and recites it with beautiful training, or perhaps chai in a Styrofoam cup that triggers the right neural pathways. The Muslim body works with the Qur'an like the Deleuzo-Guattarian pair of the wasp and orchid. The orchid's qualities attract the wasp, the wasp attempts to mate with the orchid, and thereby the wasp participates in the orchid's cross-pollination. Like the orchid, the Qur'an offers an image or tracing: a mode of humanity, a technology in its material and aural experience of making particular humans. Our bodies become deterritorialized as pieces of the Qur'an's "reproductive apparatus," but also reterritorialize the Qur'an by "transporting its pollen."[79]

> It could be said that the orchid imitates the wasp, reproducing its image in a signifying fashion (mimesis, mimicry, lure, etc.). But this is true only on the level of the strata—a parallelism between two strata such that a plant organization on one imitates an animal organization on the other. At the same time, something else entirely is going on: not imitation at all but a capture of code, surplus value of code, an increase in valence, a veritable becoming, a becoming-wasp of the orchid and a becoming-orchid of the wasp. Each of these becomings brings about the deterritorialization of one term and the reterritorialization of the other; the two becomings interlink and form relays in a circulation of intensities pushing the territorialization even further. There is neither imitation nor resemblance, only an exploding of two

heterogeneous series on the line of flight composed by a common rhizome that can no longer be attributed to or subjugated by anything signifying.[80]

We connect with the Qur'an even when we are not interested in what it says; the Qur'an changes us, and when the "pure and literal recitation" no longer consists of words, we change the Qur'an in perhaps a more substantive way than if we actually edited and revised its script. The Qur'an can become tangible and hold a talismanic material presence in the world, as in the miniature Qur'an that hangs from a rearview mirror—the entire revelation reproduced in an unreadable book smaller than my thumb.

What monster babies were made when Ibn al-'Arabi copulated with the alphabet? I don't know if he penetrated or was penetrated; but in another account, the Qur'an entered his body as a material force and changed him from inside. Ibn al-'Arabi became driven to write poetry after an angel came to him with a piece of white light in its hands. This light, the angel explained, was the sura of the Qur'an popularly named *Ash-Shu'ara*, "The Poets." Ibn al-'Arabi accepted the light from the angel and ingested it. Inside his torso, the light materialized as a growing hair that moved up through his chest and neck, emerging from his mouth as "an animal with a head, tongue, eyes, and lips." The animal embodiment of the sura expanded until its head spanned the eastern and western horizons, but then returned to its original size and reentered Ibn al-'Arabi's body. From that moment on, with the sura inside him, Ibn al-'Arabi could produce poetry "from no reflection and no intellectual process whatsoever."[81] His poetry was an extension of the Qur'an through his body, having developed from a deterritorialized fragment of the Qur'an reterritorializing his chest. The sura's materialization as an animal body denies interpretation, but perhaps not in the same way as a root-book: how does one achieve "pure and literal recitation" of the sura as light, hair, and animal? To think of a Deleuzian approach to the Qur'an as entirely a question of Deleuzian approaches to *books* and *reading* reveals its poverty when the Qur'an acts as non-literature in so many ways.

When we treat the Qur'an as a book, we have also made promiscuous connections. Numerous points in the Qur'an provide secret doors through which you can tunnel out, find yourself in other books, and then reterritorialize those books within the Qur'an's schema, as in Dara Shikoh's reading of "a glorious recitation (*qur'an*), in a book protected . . . a revelation from the lord of the worlds" (56:77–80) as a reference to the Upanishads, which recoded his study under Hindu sages as a pursuit of Islamic knowledge.[82]

Muslim traditions recognize the limits and dangers of translation, which is always subjective interpretation and impossible without inflicting some change upon the words. Translation requires choices. Pious Qur'an translators who strive for the most "pure and literal" translation often remain hesitant to call their works "translations," opting instead for "interpretations." Translation, whether between languages or historical contexts, inevitably attaches the book to new machines. When translators of the Qur'an reproduce the text in biblical registers (with the King James gravitas of "Thou" and "Thy," culturally loaded terms like "faith" and "God," and Anglicized prophet names, turning Musa into Moses and rewriting him as a new character who occupies another fictional universe with all its unique baggage), they might indeed turn the Qur'an into the Muslim Bible. When early Muslims first preached in lands that did not have a preexisting vocabulary for monotheism, what could they call Allah? In China, "Allah" was rendered as "Buddha." Concepts such as prophets and angels were also rewritten in Confucian and Taoist terms. What did these words mean for the Muslims who used them? Translation is inevitably change. Whether "pure and literal" or not, the translated Qur'an cannot help but merge with new forces and change what it can do. At every verse, outside forces flow into the Qur'an and connect themselves to it, even smuggling themselves into the text. This would be unthinkable for Deleuze and Guattari, who insist that the Qur'an resists change more than any other book; but translations of the Qur'an are famous for the "parentheses" game, in which the translator's own explanation of a verse appears within the verse in parentheses, achieving the appearance of organically belonging to the verse. The Arabic remains unchanged, but translation opens a new tunnel between inside and outside. The most notorious culprit of this practice, the Hilali-Khan translation of the Qur'an, enjoys prolific production and dissemination as the translation officially sponsored by the Saudi state—ostensibly the place where Orientalists such as Deleuze and Guattari might expect to find the Qur'an's supposed needs for "pure and literal recitation forbidding the slightest change, addition, or commentary" to be most strictly policed. In a glaring example of the editorial sovereignty that these "fundamentalists" exercise over the text, the Hilali-Khan translation interferes with the opening sura, al-Fatiha, filling in the Qur'an's blanks with its own commentary. In its conclusion, the sura asks for God's guidance on the straight path—those who have received God's favor, not those who have earned God's wrath or gone astray. The Hilali-Khan translation of the final verse reads, "Those on whom You have bestowed Your Grace, not (the way) of those who earned Your Anger (such as the Jews), nor of those who went astray (such as the Christians)."[83] The naming of specific communities does not occur anywhere in the Arabic, which becomes plainly visible to readers of Arabic, since the Hilali-Khan translation provides both the original and translation side by side; in this sense, the book claims to represent an unchanging "pure and literal" reproduction. But because this is a translation and is presumably meant for readers who cannot access the Arabic, the page's juxtaposition of English and Arabic texts gives a false impression that one side perfectly reproduces the other. The added detail about Jews and Christians adheres to a particular interpretive history associated with the Hanbali school that enjoys state support in Saudi Arabia and that tradition's prescription for engaging the Qur'an: if you want further explanation of the Qur'an than the Qur'an itself provides, you look to the canonical hadith corpus. According to Hilali and Khan, this method does not express one interpretive "choice" among many but simply fulfills "what Islam says," which they do not regard as a multiplicity. But it does evidence connections between the Qur'an and its outside; Hilali and Khan plug their Qur'an-machine into a hadith-machine (at first glance, the machine closest to what Deleuze and Guattari think is the only mode of encounter the Qur'an allows), which simultaneously expands and constricts the Qur'an's power to do things. It also illustrates the inadequacies of imagining the Qur'an as the "Muslim Bible," which fails to recognize the array of unique machines, such as this particular version of a hadith-machine, to which the Qur'an can connect.

Engaging the principle of connection in his guide to *A Thousand Plateaus*, Brent Adkins asks, "What might we be able to do with a book ... if we did not suppose that it must be read in the order it was written?"[84] The rhizomatic book, in its proliferation of connections, releases the root-book's demand for arborescent linearity. Offering *A Thousand Plateaus* as their rhizome-book, Deleuze and Guattari encourage the reading of their plataeaus in any order. In contrast to the linear narrative of the Bible, the Qur'an does not follow an arborescent organization of books and chapters. Rather, it appears more like the "series" in Deleuze's *Logic of Sense* or the "plateaus" of Deleuze and Guattari's *Thousand Plateaus* in that each of the Qur'an's suras (literally "forms" or "images") can stand alone without relation to where it appears in the book and that there's no indication that the suras were meant to be read as successive "chapters" in a proper order to construct their unifying thesis. At first glance, the Qur'an has no organizing principle whatsoever, other than size: the suras generally decrease in length as you proceed through the book. The same apparent disorder can persist even within the suras themselves, particularly larger ones, coming and going between topics without always clearly establishing their relation. Numerous non-Muslims through the years have told me that they tried to read the Qur'an but found it painfully repetitive and disjointed; their mistake was assuming that the book starts on the first page, ends on the last page, presents its narratives and arguments with either a thematic or chronological arrangement, and was designed to carry the reader through a satisfying A-to-B journey from the first page to the last. That was my mistake at fifteen, feeling saintly just for plodding through the entirety of the massive second sura, al-Baqara. The Orientalists on whom Deleuze and Guattari would have relied for their window into the Qur'an also treated it like a book that should have an organic beginning and end and expressed frustration with its clear defiance of linearity. Thomas Carlyle (1795–1881) describes the Qur'an as "a wearisome confused jumble, crude, incondite; endless iterations, long-windedness, entanglement; most crude, incondite—insupportable stupidity, in short."[85] The Qur'an was revealed over the course of twenty-three years, but its arrangement in book form holds no relation to chronology; the verses widely believed to represent the earliest revelations appear in the 96th sura, and the verse taken as the closure of the Qur'an is found at 5:3, which deals with dietary regulations and abruptly declares, "On this day I have completed your *din*." The Qur'an does not promise a singular narrative that holds it together as a book. It is not arranged around a consistent story or theme that dominates the others; as a seemingly haphazard arrangement of God's discourse to Muhammad, it offers nothing like a gospel-styled biography of the Prophet and (to the frustration of scholars) very little helpful material in terms of concrete references to his lived experience or historical context. The shorter suras might remain clear and concise and hold to a consistent theme, but the largest suras can display an ostensible thematic patchiness that mirrors the entirety of the Qur'an. In its structure, the Qur'an does not look like it was designed to impose arborescent orders.

If someone insists on engaging the Qur'an only through "pure and literal recitation," forbidding even the most painfully accurate translation and rejecting most or all attempts at human interpretation—and yes, *some* Muslim scholars claimed this as their mode of reading—Deleuze and Guattari still know that reading without interpretation is impossible, right? The Qur'an does not provide explicit instructions for how to interpret or avoid interpretation. The Qur'an acknowledges that verses can be clear or unclear (3:7), but the matter of whether humans can possibly understand unclear verses (and if so, *which* humans?) remains ambiguous, given two equally "literal" recitations of 3:7 that lead to opposite conclusions: either those "firm in knowledge" comprehend the meanings of the unclear and affirm it, or they simply affirm the unclear without needing to comprehend. As with a sign that commands, "DO NOT READ THIS SIGN," one can only decide that the Qur'an forbids interpretation after first subjecting it to interpretation.[86] Deciding upon Hanbali *bi-la kayf* as the only appropriate mode of reading constitutes an intervention outside the Qur'an, a connection with human subjectivities, cultural specificities, and intellectual genealogies outside the words.

Connection is followed by the principle of heterogeneity, which means that the rhizome pursues connections with everything. Historically, despite Orientalist narratives of the Qur'an flattening the terrain wherever it landed and crushing diversity under Semitic monotheist hegemony, heterogeneous connections moved the Qur'an through the world. Some of these connections happened so early in the life of the Qur'an that they changed Islam forever without any chance of turning back. Barely a century after Muhammad's death, the rise of the 'Abbasid caliphate and its imperial translation project would plug the Qur'an into Greek, Persian, and Indian philosophical and scientific archives. Muslim intellectuals, even when preserving the "pure and literal" words of the Qur'an, changed the eyes with which they installed themselves into the Qur'an and processed its meanings. Verses in the Qur'an that seemingly portray an anthropomorphic god who sits in a chair like a man would become overruled by verses that emphasize God's absolute otherness and transcendence. Similarly, if the Qur'an envisioned a flat earth below a domed sky with cords attached to it like a tent—resonant with cosmologies in the region—as scholarship has argued, interpretive tradition rather quickly moved away from this model in favor of extracting a "geocentric, spherical, Aristotelian-Ptolemaic world picture" from the same text.[87] The definitive arguments in classical Muslim theology could read as disputes over various outside machines that might appropriately plug into the Qur'an, whether the Greek philosophical tradition or a growing network of hadith partisans who conceptualized the Qur'an's meanings as accessible only to the extent that Muhammad articulated them to his Companions. The Qur'an did not name or enforce its own terms but remained a smooth space subjected to competing efforts at striation.

At various points of the rhizomatic Qur'an, different connections become possible, as specific verses enable linkages to diverse literatures and resources and the Qur'an expands its powers by hooking up to other books—as in Dara Shikoh finding a pipeline from the Qur'an into the Upanishads. The Brooklyn-based Nubian Islamic Hebrews created an intertextuality between the Qur'an and the book of Revelation by identifying Revelation as Christ's *Injil* referenced in the Qur'an and the Qur'an as the Seventh Seal mentioned in Revelation.[88] Hermeticism becomes Islamic in the Qur'an's mention of the obscure prophet Idris, raised to a "high station" (19:56–57). The Qur'an does not offer any further information regarding Idris, nor does it explain the meaning of his "high station." But in its refusal to nail down Idris's meanings, the Qur'an opens its body for entry from outside. When readers of the Qur'an identified Idris as Enoch, who himself was identified with Hermes, a vast esoteric and occult archive entered the Qur'an's universe. According to the Iraqi Shi'i esotericists of the Ikhwan as-Safa' ("Brothers of Purity"), Idris's "high station" meant that Idris spent thirty years in deep study at the celestial sphere of Saturn, after which he returned to this world and taught astrology to humankind.[89] While many Muslims would take it for granted that astrology is unequivocally prohibited because the Prophet appears to say as much in hadith canon, others can find astrology implicitly recognized in the Qur'an as a divine revelation. I own a brass plate from Iran that displays the twelve Zodiac signs as well as a verse of the Qur'an, likely chosen for its mentions of things for which one might resort to occult technology: "women and sons, heaped sums of gold and silver, branded horses and cattle, and tilled land" (3:14).

In the ninth century CE, a community of Hellenic philosophers and occultists in Harran, attracting caliphal suspicion for its practices of astrology (and possible astrolatry) and unclear theological alignment, made use of Idris to reterritorialize itself as adhering to a non-Muslim—but nonetheless Qur'anically supported—tradition; this move placed them in the same legal category of *ahl al-kitab* as Christians and Jews and

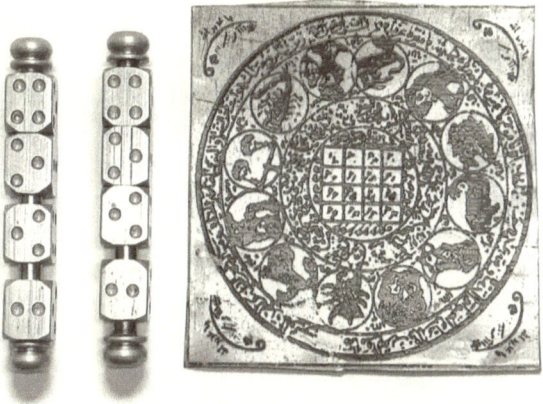

FIGURE 3. Brass Zodiac plate and geomancy dice. Author's collection.

entitled them to the same protections.[90] Both Muslims and non-Muslims employed the opening of flows by 19:56–57 to redraw their boundaries.

The Qur'an can join forces with dreams to make new worlds. One of the most important Sufi commentaries on the Qur'an, Ibn al-'Arabi's *Fusus al-Hikam*, came to him during a dream encounter with the Prophet. Dreams are routes of connection not only for Sufis, but anti-Sufis as well, since Sunni hadith canon presents Muhammad confirming that when he appears in a dream, it is really him. In a moment of "Wahhabi mysticism," Muhsin Khan, co-producer of the Hilali-Khan translation, was inspired to render the Qur'an in English after experiencing a dream in which he drank the Prophet's sweat.[91]

The third principle of the rhizome is multiplicity. "Unlike trees or their roots," Deleuze and Guattari explain, "the rhizome connects any point to any other point."[92] We think of the Qur'an as a singular whole, but it functions only as multiplicity in which some parts are used more often than others, some parts can be used *against* others, and different parts can combine (or reach beyond the book's covers to make connections outside it) in seemingly infinite ways. No obvious center of gravity reigns supreme over the text.

Many readers point to al-Fatiha, the Qur'an's opening sura, as a logical center or point of entry. Indeed, if someone were to mistake the Qur'an for a book to be read in linear fashion from its first page to its last, al-Fatiha (whose popular title literally translates as "the opening") would start that journey. Not knowing anything about the book's layout when I picked up the Qur'an for the first time, I naturally started at the first page. Al-Fatiha is also typically the first sura that a child learns by heart. For its significance to Muslim praxis, al-Fatiha easily stands as the most recited piece of literature in human history. A Muslim who faithfully maintains the practice of praying five times every day in the manner prescribed by Sunni jurisprudential traditions recites al-Fatiha anywhere from seventeen to thirty-three times every day—this range depending on whether s/he performs only the required prayers or adds the encouraged supplementary prayers of the Prophet, and *not* including the numerous other contexts in which someone might recite al-Fatiha, such as tarawih prayers in Ramadan or uses of the sura in healing or protective practices. We could easily argue for al-Fatiha as the Qur'an's center. But if the Qur'an is supposed to operate as an authoritarian set of commands that provides the foundation for every aspect of individual human behavior and the achievement of a well-ordered society, al-Fatiha falls short: a prayer for guidance and mercy, its mere seven verses offer no legal codes, ritual prescriptions, dietary restrictions, moral judgments, or any explicit drawing of boundaries that could imagine a unique and privileged community, a distinct religion with its own territory and capitalized proper name. Al-Fatiha does affirm God's sovereignty over our fates and refers to a "straight path" but offers no concrete information by which we could locate the straight path or identify the community that follows it: if al-Fatiha's seven verses constituted the entirety of the Qur'an, we'd have no idea what distinguished Muslims from Christians or Jews (or even Meccan polytheists, who also called upon God, but as one force among many).

Nor is al-Fatiha the only possible center within the Qur'an. Muslims often read the 36th sura, Ya Sin, for the dying and dead, and numerous traditions of the Prophet attest to its special qualities: Muhammad names Ya Sin the "heart of the Qur'an" and tells his Companions that reciting Ya Sin will bring comfort, peace, and security; in one tradition, he even promises that the reward for Ya Sin's recitation equals that of reciting the *entire* Qur'an ten times. The 55th sura, ar-Rahman, is often imagined in a pair with Ya Sin and was reportedly termed the Qur'an's "adornment" by the Prophet. The 112th sura, popularly titled al-Ahad or al-Ikhlas, consists of only four verses, but some prophetic traditions assert that to recite the sura a mere three times equals recitation of the entire Qur'an in merit.

The rhizome's fourth principle, "asignifying rupture," reflects its resistance against "oversignifying breaks separating structures or cutting across a single structure." The Qur'an is not a box that contains meanings to shield them from an outside. This is the problem of the *ahl al-Qur'an*, the "people of the Qur'an" or "Qur'anists" who claim that their understanding of Islam comes entirely from pure and rational meanings found within the Qur'an's interior. Qur'anists think that they can enter the Qur'an and then seal up the hole behind them, allowing no bacteria from the outside world to follow them in and contaminate the words, forgetting that every reader is already a whole microbiome loaded with protists and fungi and viruses.

The rhizome can be "broken, shattered at a given spot," only to "start up again on one of its old ones, or on new lines."[93] The Qur'an travels across mediums, becoming prayers and MP3s and calligraphic tile art, with no definitive ordering for how these redistributions take place. Which verses do you cut away to plant the Qur'an in a new place, from which you grow the entire Qur'an again? Some choices are popular and intuitive: the verse of God's footstool, Ayat al-Kursi, becomes deterritorialized from the book as necklaces and wall hangings. Wedding invitations are likely to cut and replant the excerpt, "We created you from a single soul, male and female," doubly so if it's an intercultural marriage, since the verse goes on to say, "And we made you into nations and tribes so that you may know one another" (49:13). Sometimes the relationship between content and medium is obvious, but often less so. When verses are reproduced as calligraphic art or a recorded recitation for those who cannot read or comprehend the Arabic for content, the medium obliterates the content apart from what the viewer/listener already *feels* about the Qur'an as an essence. Muslim occultists arrange Arabic letters in patterns and make magic squares with immense powers of healing, protection, or attack. The letters have been deterritorialized from words, verses, and suras, but remain the Qur'an, the entirety of the Qur'an.

The Qur'an deterritorializes itself in the world and reterritorializes the world but is also subject to the world's territoriality. The Qur'an as a rhizome is both the Qur'an as a body of text between two covers and the infinite modes by which the Qur'an can connect with circulating intensities of the world. When the effects of the Qur'an change through these encounters, it's not a matter of "influence," "imitation," "borrowing," or "syncretism," because there is no possibility of a Qur'an existing before the encounter; the Qur'an *is* the Qur'an's rhizome with the world. This rhizomatic Qur'an includes lines of flight, but as *A Thousand Plateaus* warns, "There is still a danger that you will reencounter organizations that restratify everything, formations that restore power to a signifier, attributions that reconstitute a subject—anything you like, from Oedipal resurgences to fascist concretions."[94] The Qur'an-only discourse aims to deterritorialize the Qur'an from the grips of supplementary texts and norm-making institutions that have laid their regulatory strata over the Qur'an. But this deterritorialization can also turn to reterritorialization under a regime of "What the Qur'an *really* says" as ordered by the priorities of a particular group and its own normative assumptions and methodologies, creating a new territory of orthodoxy and blocking off the lines of flight by which one might escape it.

The fifth principle of the rhizome, cartography, stands at first glance in opposition to the sixth, decalcomania. The distinction between them is not always obvious, and Deleuze and Guattari caution against firm and absolute oppositions even when they appear to be setting them up. Mapping is the unpredictable production of the new, while decals reproduce images identically for perfect transferal to other surfaces. When you make maps, you create; when making decals, you trace. The results are consistent and reliable. The rhizome is "a map, not a tracing."[95] But Deleuze and Guattari resist a binary in which mapping is always good, tracing is always bad, and the two must remain locked in irreconcilable opposition. The difference between them lies in the map's orientation "toward an experimentation in contact with the real," compared to tracing's reliability as it turns maps into images and rhizomes into roots.⁹⁶ The Qur'an obviously undergoes tracing when Muslim interpretive traditions valorize the stability of the consonantal skeleton, the Qur'an as preserved by caliphal projects that sought to prevent variability. In theory, the letters of the Qur'an do not change, but are transferred onto new surfaces: quotations and citations, decorative calligraphy, artful recitation, and so on, with the letters' power resting on the perfect repetition of the copy. Even translation of the Qur'an into new languages, while executed with awareness of translation as a speculative and fallible human effort (always a map and never a perfect tracing), envisions "pure" reproduction of the original meanings as its unattainable ideal. But as Deleuze and Guattari tell us that "a new rhizome may form in the heart of a tree,"⁹⁷ the Qur'an could appear to demand decals but inspire mapping. The letters on the page are not technically altered or modified, but can be connected, supplemented, disconnected, and ripped. Our world offers no space blank enough for the Qur'an decal to be transferred without undergoing change; in some corners, this can even lead to the implication that Muhammad's personal subjectivity, the filter through which the Qur'an entered this world, necessarily impacted the Qur'an's appearance in human speech.⁹⁸ The Qur'an produces meanings through more than its words; the words interact with affects and environments and bodies. The tracings are always contextually specific.

Classical Muslim thought abounds with theorizations of the Qur'an as possessing a plainly manifest, external dimension of meaning (its zahir), along with a hidden, interior dimension (the batin). For traditions traced to Ja'far as-Sadiq, the Prophet's direct descendant and sixth Shi'i Imam, the Qur'an actually expresses four levels of meaning, each with its intended audience: the *'ibara* (clear or literal), addressed to the unsophisticated masses who would do best with contemplating a virtually corporeal man-god who sits in a chair; the *ishara* (allegories), meant for the clerical scholars and elite intellectuals; the *lata'if* (subtleties), to be comprehended by the friends of God, the 'awliya or "saints"; and finally the *haqa'iq* (realities), known only to the prophets.⁹⁹ You start at a place that's like reading about sugar; then you look at sugar; then you taste sugar; then you *are* sugar. Another tradition presents as-Sadiq explaining that in addition to the outer meaning, every verse of the Qur'an could hold up to seven layers of inner meanings (*butun*).¹⁰⁰ When the Qur'an mentions seven heavens tiered one above the other (67:3), according to as-Sadiq, that's the book telling you about itself. The Prophet is even reported to have said that he could have loaded seventy camels with just the meanings of al-Fatiha alone.¹⁰¹ The Qur'an's enriched capacity for meanings does not have a singular and necessary political destiny. It can give people tools or take them away; it can provide an opening to liberation or enforce a hierarchical order. The idea of the words containing a secret layer (or layers) of batin meanings concealed below or inside the plain-sense zahir meanings can become a deterritorializing line of flight, but also reterritorialization under a power who draws authority from the batin: These fears informed al-Ghazali's framework for allowing but still regulating allegorical interpretation. As a theologian invested in the Qur'an as a divinely revealed instruction to humanity from outside the world, Al-Ghazali sought a balance between adherence to God's words in their plain-sense limits and the possibility that sometimes God's words fail to make sense on the surface, forcing the reader to find new meanings. This concern also had an immediate political consequence in al-Ghazali's lifetime. Al-Ghazali's project as state propagandist required him to defend a Sunni edifice, which had authorized itself on the basis of rigorous but fallible scholars who inherited a body of transmitted knowledge traceable to the Prophet, against an Isma'ili Shi'i edifice, which could boast an infallible Imam whose knowledge came from the transcendent unseen and who therefore faced no limits in his power to represent the Qur'an's meanings. Sunnis derided Isma'ilis with the pejorative *batiniyya*, charging that Isma'ilis denied God's clear commands in favor of their Imam's claims to superior "secret" knowledge. For al-Ghazali, the Isma'ili claim to hidden meanings transgressed the bounds of acceptable speculation and amounted to *takdhib*, calling the Prophet a liar.[102] Reterritorializing the batin against a mystical master who could claim privileged insider access to the Qur'an, al-Ghazali stratified the batin under the zahir by establishing hermeneutical constraints: One could only resort to seeking the batin of a verse when the zahir was incomprehensible. If the Qur'an tells you not to eat pork, for example, the verse's "literal" meaning conveys a clear instruction with practical "real world" consequences: you could not dodge the divine command by deciding that the pig was only a metaphor for something else. When the Qur'an describes God in anthropomorphic terms, however, we know that God does not "really" have a body or body parts, so such verses cannot be taken literally and must therefore point to an interior meaning. Limiting the conditions by which a verse could say more than its literal meaning allowed, al-Ghazali preserved the Qur'an's openness to theological work while still blocking an esoteric line of flight at its choke point for Isma'ili propaganda.

Ibn al-'Arabi believed that the Qur'an was like a microcosm of the universe in its capacity for expressing God's infinite attributes, and thus overflowed with endless possible meanings: for Ibn al-'Arabi, every interpretation of the Qur'an reflected God's intention. Ibn al-'Arabi was not a religious anarchist or antinomian in relation to the law, nor did the fact that God intended all interpretations require that all interpretations were equal. Ibn al-'Arabi upheld hierarchies of religious difference both in terms of Muslims' relations to non-Muslims and as internal Muslim diversity.[103] As Deleuze and Guattari write, every rhizome contains lines of deterritorialization and lines of segmentarity, and, "You may make a rupture, draw a line of flight, yet there is still a danger that you will reencounter organizations that restratify everything."[104] The rhizomatic Qur'an plugs into both exotericisms and esotericisms, though it is not always a given that one enables movement that the other restrains. At first glance, it would appear that the batin is always the key to deterritorialization and the zahir always reterritorializes; but in a batini regime, a zahiri cutting edge of scripturalist fundamentalism would offer deterritorializing escapes from the master's strata.

Mystical unveilings are not the only paths to the batin. Demystified modern scholars, engaging the Qur'an as a fascicular root-book, find their own lines of flight through projects of reinterpretation that still prioritize a kind of secular batin. To authorize their arguments, modern Muslim intellectuals prioritize the Qur'an—again, often in ways that would have been unprecedented in the premodern world—and work to identify their positions with the interior of the text, as though they have cleared away the sediment of interpretive tradition and rescued the "true" meanings buried deep underneath. The tools vary depending on the scriptural archaeologist: for Sunni revivalists, the proper tools consist of the canonical hadith collections, though these texts in turn require the mediating work of trusted scholars. Interpreters of the Qur'an could bring feminist theory or literary criticism to the text, or the inspired teachings of their mystical masters, or their knowledge of biblical literature or other traditions; some reformist Muslims would bring notions of "historical context" as a key to understanding difficult verses or moving beyond the verses' limitations while remaining faithful to what they regard as the verses' deepest truths. Qur'an-only Muslims believe that with their pure reason, they can place themselves in direct, unmediated encounter with the words and read them exactly for what they mean. Without claiming anything to be truly "universal" for all Muslims everywhere, I can say that for lots and lots of Muslims, there remains a potential for rigorous study of the Qur'an to retrieve deeper meanings and even a promise that these previously undiscovered meanings will solve problems.

Deleuze is not interested in treating books as containers for explorable interiorities. He offers a diagnosis of "interpretosis" for the "disease" of psychoanalysts and priests attempting to decipher signs and recover a hidden reality interior to the text, whether the text in question is a patient's dream or a sacred scripture. Interpretosis of the Qur'an treats the creator of the universe as a patient whose innermost desires can become knowable through diagnostical mastery over his words. A Deleuzian read of the Qur'an cancels the session and pulls God up from the doctor's couch, because the Qur'an has no inner authorial "mind" that rules over the exterior form. If we remain forever stuck on the Qur'an's external surface, we should instead identify the assemblages that the Qur'an forms with the world and the new worlds that these assemblages make possible. An arborescent root-book Qur'an would be imagined as the unified and self-contained repository of all meaning, its value determined by relation to a plane of being higher than our own, but the rhizomatic Qur'an pursues infinite connections to its outside and explodes in multiplicities of meaning without the benefit of a hidden interiority. The inside is not "deeper" than the outside but was created by it on the same plane. The zahir makes and folds the batin. The rhizomatic Qur'an's possibilities include an Islamic atheism when we connect to the Qur'an as divine for its effects in life rather than its placement above life in a vertical hierarchy, engaging the Qur'an not for its origins or what it claims to be or represent but what it does: the ways that it connects to us and our machines, transmitting intensities to our bodies and enhancing our powers. This atheist Qur'an of immanence requires no archaeological dig into its words, no plunging into esoteric depths, no recovery of the hidden, no deeper inside, no higher up.

Conclusions

Deleuze and Guattari saw the publication of *Anti-Oedipus* in 1972 and *A Thousand Plateaus* in 1980. In 1978, between the two volumes, Edward Said produced *Orientalism*. This means that when drawing from an overwhelmingly Western archive to discuss animal-raising nomads or hunter nomads, "Oriental despots," Chinese hexagrams, the "Jewish specificity immediately affirmed in a semiotic system,"[105] Hyksos, Mongols, differences between the sex lives of Crow and Hopi men, New Guinea (which Deleuze and Guattari think is in Africa),[106] "leopard-man societies, etc., in Black Africa,"[107] or the Qur'an, the two volumes of *Capitalism and Schizophrenia* can only speak as participants in, and inescapably products of, a pre-*Orientalism* world, unable to anticipate or respond to Said's annihilation of the anthropologies and histories that nourish their pages (which is not to promise that Deleuze and Guattari rehabilitate their Orientalism in later works). Despite their resistance to trees, Deleuze and Guattari preserve the arborescent transcendence of Europe over the world, writing from a logic that endowed Western historians and colonial ethnographers with the privilege to hierarchically restructure humanity under their own categories and guiding prejudices—to act in this case as the "judgments of God" that stratify the Qur'an and limit its capacity for movement and change. The first obstruction to rethinking the Qur'an as a Deleuzian rhizome-book is Deleuze.

To use Deleuze as a tool for working upon the Qur'an requires a more severe detachment of Deleuze from Orientalism than Deleuze achieved in his own work. It means cutting Deleuze into fragments and discarding some pieces but finding creative new uses for others, making new assemblages, a Deleuze-Qur'an assemblage even if Deleuze despised bibles and thought that the Qur'an was the worst specimen of bible. To this end, I have argued here for relocating the Qur'an in Deleuze's taxonomy of books as a rhizome-book, which opens the Qur'an to a greater multiplicity of experience and meaning-making potentials or rather illuminates the multiplicities already retrievable in historical Islam. These multiplicities can become obscured in the totalizing of the Qur'an as a thesis disseminated in a top-down flow from the highest sphere to our sublunar realm for us to obey as an image of the world, the model of the monotheistic root-book. The Qur'an invites an endless incoherence of heterogeneous and unstable linkages through which meaning is made *in* the world's infinite qur'anic rhizospheres, not handed down from beyond the clouds or the transcendence of a supposedly united and self-contained "classical tradition." Whether the monotheistic root-book requires its opposite to be an *atheistic* rhizome-book is not decided here, but one could question whether the promiscuously connecting qur'anic abstract machine delivers the unity demanded by a *one god, one book* template.

The Qur'an tells us that it exists upon *al-lawh al-mahfuz*, the "preserved tablet" (85:21–22), the precise meaning of which remains open. It is unclear whether this tablet is also the "mother of the book" mentioned elsewhere (43:3–4). Hadith literature supplements the bare description with bonus details: God created the tablet from white pearl with ruby surface, and the tablet contains knowledge of all things in the universe, inscribed in light, with a pen of light. God sent the Qur'an on a descent through the heavens until reaching the Prophet in the sublunar realm, but there are also Sufi traditions identifying the preserved tablet as the believer's heart.[108] Deleuze and Guattari would note such a view of the book in the passional regime, in which the book "may reject all intermediaries or specialists and become direct, since the book is written both in itself and in the heart." For Deleuze and Guattari, this constitutes "the Reformation conception of the book," but again, their biblical understandings of where books can go and what they can do would fail to account for the Qur'an's non-book life in the world.[109]

Inscribed upon the heart, the Qur'an recalls the classical question of the soul's immateriality: if the soul is not material, how would it relate to physical space—how can an immaterial essence be located *inside* a material body? If the Qur'an—the ultimate *real* Qur'an, not the material reproduction of the Qur'an on paper between two covers—exists in its truest form as an inscription on the heart, something changes in our experience of the revelation. The Qur'an is no longer the book to be read and interpreted, nor the supernatural thesis that cannot undergo translation; nor does it lord over us from an incalculably distant outside. The Qur'an receives a new vibrancy and vitality and a capacity for variation: is it really the same Qur'an every time? The Qur'an appears upon infinite hearts with infinite variegation and takes on a kind of agency for producing unique effects within a specific body. The linkage of the Qur'an and the heart, a new Qur'an-heart, drives human bodies as an actant in the material universe, speaking to/from it; the Qur'an can do what it does even without being what it says it is.

In 1996, looking over the edge of apostasy from Islam and experimenting with the fears consuming my body, I desecrated a Qur'an. That same night, I was visited by the Prophet, 'Ali, Hasan, and Husayn in a dream. Without saying a word, they surrounded and held me, and I knew that I was okay, that my attempted apostasy from Islam was somehow Islamic in spirit and contained *within* Islam, if such a thing was thinkable. "Flight" turned out to be a creative, productive thing, a reopening of the territory that made it something new. My escape was not a permanent break from the territory, but only a break in the fence. Years later, a shaman plugged my Qur'an-machine into a *Banisteriopsis caapi* DMT machine and sent me flying off the strata to a vision of Fatima az-Zahra, the Lady of Light. Fatima told me to leave the Qur'an alone; but the next morning, I went back to the masjid and recited the Qur'an with that heretical secret driving my externally normative prayer. I did not *interpret* the Qur'an, but I *used* it. And I hid in my father's bunker on a mountain in West Virginia and performed Burroughs-inspired cut-up experiments with the Qur'an, but also kept a Qur'an untouched. Even when I activated a nuclear deconstruction, something of the Qur'an always remained, enabled me to reconstruct when needed. The Qur'an and my body preserved their connection, a line of flight but also an apparatus of capture. The scapegoat remains an agent of the center, embodying the atheist secretion as an ironic orthodoxy machine.

2 / People of the Sunna and the Assemblage: Deleuzian Hadith Theory

> *The process that creates sedimentary rock proceeds by the sorting out of pebbles of different size and composition, an operation performed by the rivers that transport and deposit the pebbles in homogenous layers at the bottom of the ocean. Then, these loose accumulations are cemented together and transformed into layers of sedimentary rock. These rocks, in turn, may accumulate on top of one another and then be folded by the clash of tectonic plates to produce a larger emergent entity: a folded mountain range like the Himalayas or the Rocky Mountains.*
>
> —MANUEL DELANDA, *Assemblage Theory*

If the most obvious problem in Deleuze's diagnosis of the Qur'an as absolutist root-book denying all interpretation or modification is that Deleuze remains unaware of the various forces that interact with the Qur'an, how would Deleuze's map of Islam change if he knew about hadiths? Deleuze himself does not ask the questions that a Deleuzian might ask of hadiths—how are these machines made, what other machines interact with them to combine powers and become new machines, and what can these machines *do*? But Deleuze's model of the assemblage can become a tool for productive disassembly. To see how the machines have been built and how they work, we first take them apart. Deleuzian hadith analysis illuminates the unstable, rhizomatic tendencies in the sources' construction of Muhammad, undermining the stability and wholeness of that construction and allowing for extractions of Islamic atheism.

The hadiths often undergo representation as a mountainous, singular whole that can be referenced with a capitalized proper name, simply "the Hadith." This deceptive image of unity betrays the hadiths' emergence from a process of interactions between heterogeneous objects and flows, pebbles and rivers: thousands of discrete textual artifacts that were taught and transmitted by thousands of scholars spanning multiple generations, locations, and ideologies, catalogued in numerous sizeable archives with varying degrees of canonical power. Each stage in the formation of the hadith corpus manifests a gathering of multiplicities and their consolidation within larger new orders.

The river's work of collecting, sorting, and arranging occurs at the level of each hadith, which itself operates as a series of relations between multiplicities: not only Muhammad and the Companion who serves as an eyewitness reporter of his words and behavior, but also the successive generations of reporters who transmitted these accounts as oral traditions, ultimately passing the report to those scholars who compiled the textual canon. A hadith establishes its credentials by providing its isnad, the genealogical chain that names all the transmitters through whom it had passed. The isnad is no less critical a component of the hadith than the *matn*, the hadith's discursive content; premodern master critics asserted that a hadith's reliability was to be determined not through personally subjective analysis of the text, but rather by measuring the integrity of its transmitters and the nature of linkages between them.[1] Even when discussing an absurd or obviously forged hadith, such as the narration in which Muhammad allegedly states that God created himself from horse sweat, the master critics would base their critique on flaws in the hadith's transmission history—identifying personal or professional flaws in the hadith's reporters or fabricated links between two scholars whose ages and/or locations meant that they could not possibly have met each other—rather than offer a personal opinion of its content.[2] The hadith clerics' claim to epistemological supremacy rested on the promise that they did not resort to subjective interpretation but only preserved the Prophet's authentic content through their catalogues of endorsed scholars. At least in theory, a hadith's citational integrity is more compelling to premodern hadith criticism than what it says. Like Deleuze's double-pincered Lobster God, selecting and ordering substances and imposing statistical orders with one pincer and making structures and forms with the other, the hadith stratum is doubled, regulating and stabilizing with substances (corporeal linkages between generations of transmitters) and forms (the coding of relations between these bodies).[3]

While proto-Sunni hadith criticism would come to accept all of Muhammad's Companions as unimpeachable authorities, they also recognized the proliferation of forged reports that had been falsely attributed to Companions and that Companions could be detached from their own words for any number of reasons. Hasan al-Basri often circulated Companions' narrations without attribution, claiming that he avoided naming 'Ali as a source due to the government's extreme hatred for 'Ali.[4] Through the development of transmitter-based evaluation, hadith masters sought to distinguish the most strongly evidenced claims upon the Companions from outright forgeries as well as identify the most (and least) trustworthy experts in their field, theoretically extracting a closed network and homogeneous discourse from an unruly field of stories and storytellers. Defining and policing the boundaries of the aural corpus, they reproduced Muhammad's legacy as inseparable from their scholarship.

Visualizing the isnad to track a hadith's transmission, we typically end up with a flow chart that starts with Muhammad, moves to a Companion who narrates what Muhammad had said or done, follows to one or more of the Companion's students, and from them proliferates into multiple branches as these students become teachers. The isnad produces a vertical genealogy that would send Deleuzians running: it's a *tree*, after all, and Deleuze and Guattari tell us that they're "tired of trees."[5] The tree model upholds an ahistorical vision of traditions appearing as self-evident centers with branches that become increasingly marginal with their growing distance from the trunk, taking for granted a logic of mainstream orthodoxies and peripheral heterodoxies.[6] By definition, this mapping of legitimacy and power names the arborescent function of the isnad, which promises to measure the connections between particular branches and the prophetic root that they claim to inherit. Rather than ask "what a hadith says," classical hadith scholarship would ask the more Deleuzian question, "How was it made?" Deleuzian hadith projects, like the projects of great hadith masters, start with transmission trees and the territories they make.

Deleuze does not necessarily equip us to answer ongoing debates in academic or popular conversations regarding hadiths' authenticity—the problem of whether isnads can reliably retrieve the historical Muhammad. The authenticity question, whether confronted by Orientalists or Sunni apologists, itself remains arborescent, consumed with the matter of whether a tree's roots are truly what it claims. Uninterested in roots, a Deleuzian hadith criticism resists the tree's genealogical organization of authority and moves beyond questions of origins, authenticity, and orthodoxy.

The hadiths' arborescent chains do not deny the possibility of a rhizome; while ostensibly valorizing rhizomes against trees, Deleuze also tells us that every assemblage possesses both rhizomatic and arborescent tendencies. Rhizomes can become trees and vice versa. A rhizomatics of hadith literature would consider the presence of both tendencies throughout the corpus, investigating entities within this assemblage that open or inhibit movement. To examine hadith transmissions as a Deleuzian assemblage, this chapter follows lines running through the *Musnad* of proto-Sunni hadith master Sulayman Abu Dawud al-Tayalisi (133–204/751–820). In rhizomatic fashion, this collection of nearly 3,000 hadiths, each with a chain of transmitters reaching back to one of Muhammad's Companions, offers as reasonable a point of entry into the greater hadith assemblage as any and can connect us to any other point.

The Companions (al-Sahaba)

The *Musnad*'s title first signals an epistemological investment: musnad, "supported," means that its hadiths boast isnads, documenting the linkages of scholarly bodies through which they traveled to enter al-Tayalisi's archive. The title also calls attention to the mode of arrangement: Collections in the musnad genre were organized not by topic, as in the collections of later canonical status (which themselves were "musnad" in the sense that they provided their transmission chains), but rather by the Companions to whom they were attributed. Compared to topic-based collections, musnad volumes remain significantly inaccessible to nonspecialists: If a Muslim asks, "What did the Prophet say about dogs?" she cannot easily find her answer in a musnad collection unless she already knows which Companions offer hadiths concerning dogs. The musnad mode of arrangement implicitly enforces the Companions' collective integrity, as it presumes the acceptance of Companions who stood on opposite sides of early Muslim factionalisms and strife and would have been considered alternately authoritative or problematic by later networks.[7] Al-Tayalisi's *Musnad* thus speaks to (and participates in) a process of territorialization by which these heterogeneous bodies are grouped together and generalized under a shared identity. On the other hand, the musnad format can also allow readers to remain partisan in their sources, choosing to read 'Ali's narrations while ignoring those of 'Uthman. The later *musannaf* arrangement of hadiths by topic would thus reflect a milieu in which the Companions' collective authority as a class, regardless of their alignments in the early power struggles, had been established.

Without a preexistent unity, the Companions' voices could not have been gathered and homogenized in this way during their lifetimes. By all appearances, the surviving members of Muhammad's movement continued to talk about him after his death, but their acts of remembrance did not take place in a more formal or structured context than seniors telling stories to their juniors. There was not yet a system, blueprint, or organizing power to govern this process or regulate participation within it. The Companions never developed an institution analogous to a church that could declare and enforce a universal "orthodoxy," nor did the earliest dissemination of hadiths owe its origin to a caliphal order from above. Unlike the Qur'an, which the *rashidun*-era caliphate sought to standardize with a state codex and the suppression of alternative codices, prophetic traditions circulated through a highly decentralized process in which hundreds of elder sages, many of whom lived at odds with caliphal power at various points in their lives, shared their memories and opinions in local teaching circles. Neither the precise nature of the material transmitted nor the transmitters themselves were assigned discrete and fixed functions: words that began as one elder's pious maxim could later circulate with attribution to Muhammad's own mouth. The concept of the Sunna as specifically the singular Sunna of the Prophet (as opposed to a multiplicity of *sunan* associated with various Companions and their students) had not crystallized into its recognizable form.[8] Nor could there have been an established theorization of the prophetic Sunna as accessible principally through vetted hadiths, let alone a sophisticated methodology for vetting them or elite experts trained in those methods. In this primordial Islam, there was more than one way to define the prophetic Sunna. While the hadith-based Sunna advocated by Shafi'i triumphed, Malik b. Anas (d. 179/796) and his school resisted the Iraq-centered hadith dissemination networks in favor of a Sunna defined by the collective practice that one could observe in the city of Medina, home to the descendants of the original Muslim community. "The Qur'an was not revealed on the Euphrates," Malik complained.[9]

Prior to the articulation and advancement of these concepts and practices, there would not have been a clear sense of "the Companions" as a privileged class of authorities endowed with universal probity; even generations after al-Tayalisi, the Companions' shared status was not a given. There was not yet a shared "common-sense" definition of what it meant to be a Companion; even if hadiths depicted the Prophet as praising his Companions, the Companions themselves held different ideas of who belonged in the category.[10] Nor can it be suggested that the Companions ever shared a united social or political alignment or set of interests, let alone mutually affirmed custodianship over the prophetic memory. The figures that would later be grouped together as Companions disagreed with each other on important questions, challenged each other regarding the integrity of their narrations (which included, in rare cases, calling each other liars),[11] and even fought each other on the physical battlefield.

In al-Tayalisi's *Musnad* and the broader Sunni hadith corpus, a small handful of Companions dominate the representation of Muhammad. To further explore the al-Tayalisi archive as a series of connections forged between heterogeneous elements, I have chosen to focus on the chains of teacher-student connections that link al-Tayalisi to four Companions: Anas b. Malik, 'A'isha bt. Abi Bakr, 'Abd Allah b. Mas'ud, and 'Abd

Allah b. 'Abbas. Each of these Companions appears throughout the corpus as a prolific reporter. Though al-Tayalisi's *Musnad* traces its material to nearly 300 Companions, the demarcated musnads of Anas, 'A'isha, Ibn Mas'ud, and Ibn 'Abbas account for a combined 641 (25.64 percent) of its 2,890 hadiths.

These four Companions each speak through a particular relation to the Prophet and later communities. Anas b. Malik (d. 91–93/710–12) appears in Muslim traditions as having been gifted to the Prophet as a slave boy by his mother, Umm Sulaym. He would have been roughly twenty years old when the Prophet died, and he spent his later life in the garrison town of Basra, where he gained a measure of prestige as an elder authority and became known as the last Companion to have died in that city. G. H. Juynboll has challenged Anas's Companion status, noting Anas's reported death at an extraordinary age of 103–7 and invisibility as a Companion in the earliest prophetic biographies. Having called attention to the widespread exaggeration of lifespans among traditionists in third-fourth/eighth-ninth-century Iraq, which enhanced their connections to the Companions,[12] Juynboll suggests that Anas was elevated to Companion status by a later generation, in part to bolster the strength of Basran transmitters and their reports.[13]

'A'isha bt. Abi Bakr (d. 58/678) is reported to have married Muhammad while still a child; a disputed traditional timeline would have her younger than twenty when he died in 10/632 after a decade of marriage. Upon the death of 'A'isha's husband, her father, Abu Bakr, became first of the "rightly guided caliphs" (rashidun) and would lead the growing Muslim territory until his own death two years later. In 36/656, 'A'isha raised a failed rebellion against 'Ali's caliphate. After 'Ali's defeat of her forces at the Battle of the Camel, 'A'isha retired to a life under house arrest, during which she became an authority on hadiths, jurisprudence, and Qur'an interpretation. To circumvent gendered restrictions on her social interactions, 'A'isha instructed male students to ingest her sister's breastmilk (most likely a few drops in a bowl), legally transforming them into her relatives by milk kinship and therefore eligible for her teaching circle.[14] Though prominent men among the Companions, such as 'Ali, disagreed with her method, 'A'isha became a mentor to foundational scholars in Medina and the source for thousands of hadiths.

Ibn Mas'ud (d. 32/652) was an early convert who participated in all the Prophet's battles. A decade after the Prophet's death, he settled in the garrison town of Kufa, where he would become treasurer for a time and venerated as a local sage. An important jurist in the development of Kufan legal thought, he was also held in high esteem for his knowledge of the Qur'an. When 'Uthman imposed his caliphal codex of the Qur'an as the official standard version, Ibn Mas'ud maintained his own codex, which had been popularly accepted in Kufa for ritual use. 'Uthman denied Ibn Mas'ud his pension for three years; before passing away, Ibn Mas'ud expressed a wish that 'Uthman not lead his funeral prayer. Ibn Mas'ud's prestige as a Qur'an expert finds illustration in the *hadith* sources, which depict the Prophet teaching him *suras*, praying for God to endow him with knowledge of the revelation's meanings, and endorsing him as a reliable teacher of the Qur'an for others.[15]

Ibn 'Abbas (d. 68/687–88) was the Prophet's patrilineal cousin and thirteen to fifteen years old when the Prophet died. He fought in 'Ali's army against 'A'isha's rebellion, and 'Ali appointed him governor of Basra. After a dispute with 'Ali over taxes, Ibn 'Abbas moved to Mecca with appropriated funds from the Basran treasury, retiring to a life of scholarship. In Muslim intellectual traditions, Ibn 'Abbas became widely associated with reports of the Prophet's heavenly ascension as well as Qur'an interpretation. In his image as an authority on the Qur'an, Ibn 'Abbas appears as the local Basran tradition's parallel to Ibn Mas'ud's role in Kufa. Ibn 'Abbas's scholarly prestige was magnified by his significance as the eponymous ancestor of the 'Abbasid dynasty, which overthrew the 'Umayyad caliphate in 132/750 with a claim to power that emphasized its link to the Prophet's family. Examining the promotion of Ibn 'Abbas in 'Abbasid propaganda to compete with proto-Shi'i claims upon 'Ali, Herbert Berg argues for the isnad as a politicized instrument of cultural memory.[16]

Among Anas, 'A'isha, Ibn Mas'ud, and Ibn 'Abbas, we encounter consistencies and departures. With the exception of Ibn Mas'ud, none of these Companions were older than twenty at the time of the Prophet's death. They all survived him by at least two decades, enabling them to become privileged custodians of sacred history in a culture of oral tradition. While teaching younger generations, they did not operate as extensions of caliphal power in a vertically ordered production of knowledge. They just as often spoke from the margins of empire. At the very least, their careers had ups and downs: Anas was tortured by an oppressive governor; Ibn Mas'ud was deprived of his pension; Ibn 'Abbas turned to scholarship after getting pushed out of his government job. 'A'isha could have spoken with an institutionally privileged voice as the first caliph's daughter, but she was barely twenty years old when her father died after a short reign of two years, and her famed students were not yet born. Her full authority as a teacher, jurist, Qur'an exegete, and embodied archive of prophetic knowledge came decades later, when her rival 'Ali held the caliphate, and she lived under house arrest as a defeated insurgent.

Without form and totalization imposed by a shared relation to the state or a unifying category, the Companions taught largely within the bounds of their respective geographic locales and social networks. These multiple teacher-student assemblages intersected, even at the level of exchanges between the Companions themselves, but (contrary to the logic of the Salafiyya) did not produce a monolithic and united "Companion School" from which post-Companion generations received a shared curriculum. In some cases, transmissions in which one Companion reports from another can read as one circle of students polemically asserting itself against another, as in hadiths that depict 'Ali and Ibn 'Abbas deferring to A'isha's superior knowledge. An entire hadith collection, *al-Ijaba li-Iradi Ma Istadrakatuhu A'isha 'Ala al-Sahaba*, catalogues instances in which A'isha corrects other Companions.[17]

The Successors (*Tabi'in*) and Successors of the Successors (*Tabi' al-Tabi'in*)

Just as the "Companions" did not constitute a coherent category in their own lifetimes, the generation after them—retroactively labeled the "Successors"—did not gather itself as a united class engaged in a universalizing project. As Successors reported the sayings of those Companions to whom they had access, each Companion-centered network took on a distinct character. As the elder sage of Basra, Anas spoke in al-Tayalisi's collection through a network of transmitters that appeared overwhelmingly Basran. The sage of Kufa, Ibn Mas'ud, spoke through the mediation of an even more locally anchored circle, with transmitters (which can be named and located) exhibiting links to Kufa. A'isha's transmitters were significantly diverse in comparison, more or less evenly divided between Basrans, Kufans, and Medinans. Ibn 'Abbas also spoke through a geographically diverse network, his transmitters balanced between cities of Iraq and the Hijaz. Personal relationships contributed to the teacher-student connections that we see in these transmissions. The most prolific reporter of A'isha's transmissions in al-Tayalisi's *Musnad*, 'Urwa b. al-Zubayr, was her nephew. The most prolific reporter of Ibn 'Abbas's transmissions, 'Ikrima, was Ibn 'Abbas's slave. Among the reporters of Anas and Ibn Mas'ud traditions, we find these Companions' sons and grandsons. The reporters of Anas also include the Sirin client family, who supported him upon his move to Basra—most famously, his secretary Muhammad b. Sirin. It is through the Sirin family connection that Anas narrates to the only woman among his transmitters: Hafsa bt. Sirin, a legal scholar who reportedly led a school of women ascetics in Basra.[18] As shown in Asma Sayeed's isnad analysis, hadith transmission was decidedly a masculinist enterprise. This does not mean that only men acted as transmitters, but rather that gender opened and restricted access. Among these four Companions as they appear in al-Tayalisi's archive, only 'A'isha teaches hadiths to multiple women. Kinship, slavery, patronage, and gender all contribute to the possibilities for entry into these Companion-Successor assemblages.

At the level of Companion-Successor transmissions, the Companions' personal networks have not yet become parts of a larger collectivity. Of 205 unique reporters found at this Successor layer between the transmissions of Anas, 'A'isha, Ibn Mas'ud, and Ibn 'Abbas in al-Tayalisi's *Musnad*, none appear as direct transmitters from all four Companions, only eighteen narrate from two or more, and only two reporters narrate from three of them. All of the overlaps include 'A'isha: thirteen narrators report from both 'A'isha and Ibn 'Abbas, with two narrators additionally reporting from Anas; five report from both 'A'isha and Ibn Mas'ud. That the greatest intersection exists between 'A'isha and Ibn 'Abbas corresponds to their chronological and geographic proximity. Their lifespans run virtually parallel to each other: 'A'isha was roughly a decade older than Ibn 'Abbas and died a decade before him (58/678 and 68/688). In comparison, Ibn Mas'ud died twenty-five years before 'A'isha; at the other end of the timeline, Anas died more than twenty years after Ibn 'Abbas, which makes for sixty years between the deaths of Ibn Mas'ud and Anas. Ibn 'Abbas spent his later years in the Hijaz, where we would also find 'A'isha's circle; while both Ibn 'Abbas and 'A'isha attracted students from elsewhere, Ibn Mas'ud and Anas appear to have been more local to their respective garrison towns.

The Successors in turn transmitted their narrations to the "Successors of the Successors," an additional layer of post-Companion sedimentation. At this level in the isnads, some names are familiar from the previous level; Hijazi transmitter Ibn Abi Mulayka (d. 117/735), for example, reports directly from 'A'isha but also reports her words that he received secondhand from her other students. Additionally, we find Successors who transmitted directly from at least one Companion but relied on fellow Successors for their transmissions from other Companions. This becomes particularly salient in the relations between transmissions from Anas and those from other Companions, again expressing the generational divide between their networks. The foundational scholar Shihab al-Zuhri (d. 124/742) narrates directly from Anas but transmits from 'A'isha through her nephew 'Urwa. More than the other Companions, the students of Anas's students become direct teachers of al-Tayalisi, providing an accelerated track from the Companion into the *Musnad*; only nine of 193 hadiths travel from Anas to al-Tayalisi with more than two nodes between them. If we followed Juynboll's skepticism and suspended Companion status for Anas—whose lifespan extends the Companions' era for this sample by thirty years—it would dramatically impact our sense of where and how these categories begin, end, and become interconnected. If Anas and other Companion teachers to al-Zuhri were not genuine Companions, al-Zuhri and his students would also undergo a change in status. Repeating the issues of Anas, the question has been asked as to whether al-Zuhri stretched his own age; at the very least, al-Zuhri was interested in establishing the earliest birth date for himself possible, which increased the number of Companions that he could have met.[19]

An immeasurably significant figure for the historical school of Medina, the genre of prophetic biography, and early jurisprudence, al-Zuhri has been called "one of the founders of Islamic tradition in the widest sense of the word."[20] Al-Zuhri occupies a liminal moment in the life of hadith transmission, standing between the localized flows of oral tradition in the generations preceding him and the future of hadith as a highly systematic and professionalized field. Though he did not live to see the full flowering of a travel culture in which scholars journeyed far and wide to collect hadiths, al-Zuhri was notably active in multiple hadith centers (Medina and Damascus), thus enhancing the linkages between local networks.[21] He also pioneered two technologies that would further stratify the field: first, the consistent citation of hadiths with full chains of transmission; second, the collection and dissemination of hadiths in writing. Both signaled the accelerating stratification of hadith culture into an arborescent system. Through the isnad, hadith experts could distinguish themselves from storytellers (*qussas*), popular preachers and entertainers who told fantastic stories of the Prophet in masjids and markets. The plane of hadith circulation, which had been a Deleuzian smooth space, an open desert with possible trajectories not yet regulated and restricted by the forces that would make roads, would undergo navigation and mapping that defined routes for its flows.

Al-Zuhri's interventions in hadith transmission were inseparable from his relationship to the Umayyad caliphate. The Umayyads relied on their patronage of scholars, usually from Medina and most famously al-Zuhri himself (who worked in the caliphal administration as a tax collector), to provide materials in support of the caliphate's legitimacy.[22] Al-Zuhri's position in the Umayyad state also informed his embrace of writing prophetic traditions. Expressing concern that the tradition might otherwise perish, the caliph 'Umar II (r. 98–102 / 717–20) commissioned al-Zuhri to collect written hadiths using the Umayyad mail system and compile them in book form, after which 'Umar II ordered copies to be sent throughout the empire. Caliph Hisham b. 'Abd al-Malik (r. 105–25 / 724–43) is also reported to have compelled al-Zuhri to abandon his previous opposition to writing, first in al-Zuhri's tutelage to the caliph's sons.[23] State power would contribute to the gradual normalization of writing, as one of al-Zuhri's students recalls: "We were not intending to write down from al-Zuhri, until Hisham forced him. Then he wrote for his sons. And now people write hadiths."[24]

Echoing 'Uthman's Qur'an codification project, the Umayyad hadith project met resistance in cities such as Kufa, Basra, and Medina, where hadiths had circulated as fluid oral knowledge and the domain of local authorities. It has been argued that as a counter against Umayyad hegemony, transmitters circulated traditions in which the Prophet and Companions discouraged the writing of hadiths.[25] Between this archival enterprise in the government center of Damascus and traditionists' opposition in Iraq and Medina, the hadith assemblage experienced competing pulls between its arborescent and rhizomatic tendencies. The caliphate sought to stabilize this growing body of knowledge under its control, while transmitters defended the rhizomatic flows of oral tradition. However, the transmitters, in their advocacy for an ostensibly ungoverned circulation of hadiths, also defended their own control over the material, as their resistance to writing demanded that hadith transmission occur through face-to-face encounters within their guarded network. The transmitters claimed expert sovereignty over oral tradition, accompanied by the hardening of boundaries around their professional class.

While cities developed their own local schools and bodies of knowledge with unique legal, ritual, and theological positions, chains of hadith transmission show that it did not take too many successive strata for the local hadith circles to become so mutually entangled that they could appear as a single network. At the third level of the isnads, it is not difficult to find a scholar narrating traditions from all four Companions examined here, having received transmissions from numerous scholars of the previous generations while still operating within relatively local milieus. Salient examples appear in al-Zuhri's contemporaries, Basran scholar Qatada b. Da'ima and Kufan scholar al-A'mash (d. 148–56 / 745–52). Both provide transmissions from each of the four Companions with no more than two nodes between the Companions and themselves, and often less (Qatada, for example, reports firsthand from Anas). To chart either of their archives within al-Tayalisi's *Musnad* would somewhat resemble a set of tournament brackets, in which a number of parallel lines become connected and eventually subsumed by a singular final line. Al-A'mash and Qatada represent molar lines that take possession of molecular lines and embody their collective territories. The range of these molar segmentarities remains local: al-A'mash, the leading hadith scholar of Kufa in his time, absorbs Kufan sources, while Qatada's transmissions reveal his close access to Anas as well as linkages between Basran and Medinan transmitters. Qatada and al-A'mash lived in the last generation before the establishment of a widespread travel culture, often dated to the mid-second/-eighth century, through which hadith transmission networks merged into what might be called a "global" network for its time.

From Shu'ba to Musnads

Qatada and al-A'mash, embodying distinct Basran and Kufan constellations, intersect via the lines running through them to their mutual student and al-Tayalisi's most important teacher, Shu'ba b. al-Hajjaj (d. 160/776). Born in Wasit at an equal distance from Basra and Kufa, Shu'ba initially moved to Basra to study with the great Hasan al-Basri (d. 110/728) and gathered hadiths primarily between these two garrison towns.[26] During Shu'ba's visits to Kufa, al-A'mash asked him about transmissions that he had received from Qatada, reconfiguring the student as a node of mediation between his teachers.[27]

Also a student of al-Zuhri, Shu'ba elaborated upon al-Zuhri's concern for the isnad and became the first to systematically vet hadith transmitters.[28] Shu'ba and his contemporaries became formative in the development of transmitter-based hadith criticism (*al-jarh wa-l-ta'dil*) and "the science of men" (*'ilm al-rijal*), the study of transmitters' biographical data and scholarly reputations.[29] The new fields identified a distinct scholarly class and performed stratifications within it, ordering both an external unity and internal hierarchy. These disciplines privileged consistency; reliable transmitters were those whose reports closely corroborated those of other reliable transmitters. In circular self-authorization, coteries of master scholars could thus bolster their collective credentials and regulate their ranks. Despite these contributions to the field's increasing rigor, Shu'ba had a reputation for forgetting transmitters' names,[30] and Juynboll also implicates Shu'ba in the elevation of Anas's status.[31] With or without citational flaws, Shu'ba operates as a superconnected hub that encompasses multiple networks, for which he becomes al-Tayalisi's most crucial point of entry into the system. Overshadowing all al-Tayalisi's other teachers, Shu'ba's presence consistently dominates as the foundation of the archive: Shu'ba provides 35 percent of al-Tayalisi's Anas musnad, 30.7 percent of his 'A'isha musnad, 44 percent of his material from Ibn Mas'ud, and 35 percent of his reports from Ibn 'Abbas.

Beyond Shu'ba's overwhelming share of the material, examination of al-Tayalisi's teachers reveals other multiplicities gathered in the *Musnad*. Al-Tayalisi's Anas informants remain primarily Basran. Many of these Basran scholars are sources for his Ibn Mas'ud transmissions, though al-Tayalisi's unique Ibn Mas'ud sources mostly reside in Kufa, consistent with Ibn Mas'ud's immediate circle of transmitters. Compared to the stars among his teachers as well as his students, al-Tayalisi was not distinguished as a traveler, apparently content to learn from Shu'ba in Basra. Speight argues that when we find non-local scholars in al-Tayalisi's genealogy, it probably indicates that he encountered them as they passed through his area rather than traveling to seek them out.[32] Al-Tayalisi's roster also includes some transmitters with poor ranks as well as undesired sectarian identities with some variance by locale. Transmitters with links to the Basra-centered Qadariyya show up most among his Anas and 'A'isha sources. The Ibn 'Abbas archive includes Ibn 'Abbas's students who were linked to proto-Shi'ism, and al-Tayalisi's Ibn Mas'ud sources include a handful of transmitters that have been branded Shi'i, reflecting Kufa as a hub of proto-Shi'ism. Chris Melchert presents al-Tayalisi's era as the period just prior to a substantial decline of "sectarian" transmitters.[33] Gendered access also shapes the *Musnad*, as all al-Tayalisi's teachers were men.[34]

The lifespans of al-Tayalisi and his teachers witnessed extraordinary changes in hadith scholarship. When Shu'ba died in 160/776, al-Tayalisi was not yet thirty years old. By that time, hadith transmitters were growing in self-consciousness as members of a distinct community that could draw boundaries against other schools and movements, contesting a multiplicity of potential "orthodoxies" that drew their own centers and margins. The primacy of hadiths for determining the prophetic Sunna was not a universal normative given, but one of numerous contenders (such as the nascent Maliki school's prioritization of Medina's collective norms over isolated transmissions from Iraq-centered hadith networks). During the years of al-Tayalisi's career as an authority in Basra, his younger contemporary al-Shafi'i (d. 204/820) would make systematic arguments for the binding legal power of hadiths, confronting schools of Muslim thought that rejected hadiths' authority to varying degrees.[35]

Al-Tayalisi, who boasted of never having to rely on written notes, died at the age of seventy in 203–4/819–20, allegedly after ingesting *baladhur* to improve his memory. Master critics would rank him favorably while recognizing that he sometimes made mistakes and especially praised him as a source for Shu'ba transmissions. His life of teaching extended beyond his body into others and combined with their energies, as his student Yunus b. Habib al-Isbahani (d. 267/881) compiled their teacher-student transmissions as the *Musnad*. The presence of his name in the book's full title, *Musnad Abi Dawud al-Tayalisi*, refers not to an individual "author" but rather the multiplicities that run through him. As compiler of al-Tayalisi's work, Yunus does not merely present raw data; he gives order to the parts and turns al-Tayalisi's assemblage into a new territory. The *Musnad*'s organization reflects the compiler's milieu: in what appears as a pattern throughout Sunni hadith literature, the *Musnad* begins with the ten Companions whom Muhammad had reportedly promised paradise, including both 'Ali and his opponents.[36] Within this roster, the *Musnad* prioritizes the rashidun caliphs by their chronological order. The *Musnad* gathers women narrators together but does not place them at the end as with other collections and concludes with the reports of Ibn 'Abbas.

Lines flowing through al-Tayalisi also pass into his student Ahmad b. Hanbal (d. 241/855), who in turn would become the named "author" for an exponentially larger and more famous *Musnad*. Overwhelming his teacher's collection, Ibn Hanbal's *Musnad* (compiled by his son and student 'Abd Allah) contains approximately 30,000 narrations from some 300 teachers with chains of transmission tracing to more than 700 Companions. Ibn Hanbal's *Musnad* begins with the same organizing principle as al-Tayalisi (the first four caliphs in chronological order, followed by the remainder of the ten Companions who had been promised paradise) and presents women narrators in their own section at the back.[37]

Born in the new 'Abbasid capital of Baghdad, Ibn Hanbal came of age at a time in which Baghdad's superior access to royal patronage led to the city supplanting Basra and Kufa as a center of hadith scholarship where intersections and amalgamations of regional networks could accelerate. Ibn Hanbal entered hadith studies as a teenager in 179/796, the year that the Medinan giant Malik b. Anas died. Among Ibn Hanbal's early teachers in Baghdad, we find figures such as Hushaym b. Bashir (d. 799/183), Ibn 'Ulayya (d. 809/193), and 'Abd al-Rahman b. Mahdi (d. 198–814), a trio with less scholarly and ideological purity than one might expect for his genealogy. Of the three teachers, Hurvitz writes that Ibn Mahdi was the "only early teacher from those years who belonged to the intellectual elite of the traditionist milieu."[38] Ibn Bashir was a respected traditionist, but Ibn Hanbal later criticized him as unreliable.[39] Ibn 'Ulayya, an advocate of rationalist theological speculation, allegedly despised traditionists.[40] After four years of study in Baghdad, Ibn Hanbal traveled to Kufa and sought numerous local masters, including Waki' b. al-Jarrah (d. 814/198), who had succeeded Sufyan al-Thawri (d. 778/161) as the city's leading jurist[41] (it was also Waki' who dubbed al-Tayalisi the "mountain of knowledge"). Most of Ibn Hanbal's Kufan teachers bore association with the Hanafi school, which hadith partisans considered anathema. Waki', who appears in the *Musnad* as Ibn Hanbal's most prominent source for 'A'isha traditions (providing 200 narrations traced to her) and accounts for nearly 1,900 of the *Musnad*'s traditions overall, was himself trained in the Hanafi school and gave rulings in accordance with it.[42] In a further complication of hadith partisan credentials, Ibn Hanbal also studied under Abu Mu'awiyya (d. 185–95/801–11), leader of Kufa's Murji'a.[43] In Mecca, Ibn Hanbal learned hadiths from Sufyan b. 'Uyayna (d. 198/814), despite Sufyan's associations with both Shi'ism and the Hanafi school; while citing Sufyan as a source, Ibn Hanbal would also accuse him of tampering with isnads.[44] The presence of "heterodox" or "sectarian" figures among Ibn Hanbal's teachers—an issue that grows exponentially if we look at *their* teachers—reveals a segmentation in process. Ibn Hanbal's generation of master critics appears to have been less inclusive than that of al-Tayalisi, but still more inclusive than the rigidly organized generations to come.[45]

Ibn Hanbal first arrived in Basra in 186/802; Hurvitz observes that all his early teachers in Basra died within four years of his arrival, suggesting that Ibn Hanbal had prioritized learning from the city's most elderly transmitters.[46] Among Ibn Hanbal's Basran sages, we also find al-Tayalisi. That Ibn Hanbal sought out al-Tayalisi in Basra matches a trend observable in Ibn Hanbal's archive, the ascendency of hadith transmission networks centered on Iraqi cities of Basra, Kufa, and Baghdad, resulting in a *Musnad* whose sources are 86 percent Iraqi.[47] Melchert writes that in particular, "The prominence of Basran shaykhs . . . suggests that we may be dealing rather with a Basran bloc."[48] Despite his prestige among Basran traditionists, al-Tayalisi appears in Ibn Hanbal's *Musnad* as a relatively modest contributor, cited as the source for 261 narrations. In comparison, 'Abd al-Rahman b. Mahdi (d. 198/814) alone taught Ibn Hanbal 10,000 traditions, of which 6,314 appear in Ibn Hanbal's collection.[49] Of Ibn Hanbal's more than 2,000 hadiths with transmission chains tracing to 'A'isha, only seventeen come from al-Tayalisi; Ibn Hanbal cites 'Abd al-Rahman b. Mahdi as his source for 118, placing him in a tie with Yazid b. Harn as Ibn Hanbal's sixth-most-prolific source on 'A'isha.

Al-Tayalisi, while perhaps a minor local node in Ibn Hanbal's massive network, nonetheless helps to connect Ibn Hanbal with the first generation of globalizing master critics such as Shu'ba, who had passed away before Ibn Hanbal was born. Beyond his modest offering of reports that find entry into Ibn Hanbal's more prestigious *Musnad*, al-Tayalisi contributes to the hadith assemblage as one among several thousand bodies that were able to combine their powers and connections into a greater multiplicity. In the third/ninth century CE, when the 'Abbasids embraced the speculative theology of the Mu'tazila and persecuted nonconforming scholars in the *mihna*, this multiplicity would find its embodiment in Ibn Hanbal's tortured flesh. Whipping Ibn Hanbal reached through his own skin into the thousands of hadith masters whose knowledge he preserved and defended, the power grid that connected him to the Prophet and Companions. The prestige of the hadith assemblage supplemented accounts of Ibn Hanbal's persecution with enhanced gravity; to incarcerate him was to jail the embodied Sunna. As his patience and steadfastness on behalf of the Sunna rendered him a grass-roots folk hero, Ibn Hanbal in turn enhanced the power of the assemblage. The lines that flowed through al-Tayalisi's generation into Ibn Hanbal and his contemporaries would pass into Bukhari's generation of canon makers. It was in this post-mihna setting, Melchert observes, that proto-Sunni hadith transmitters completed their "monumental closing of the ranks" in terms of excluding sectarian minorities.[50]

The development of hadith transmission charted here exhibits not only the merging of networks, but also a regrouping of their forces and redrawing of borders. The increasing segmentation of the field and its master experts becomes apparent in its changing vocabulary. Around the turn of the ninth century, transmitters' statements of *haddathani* ("he narrated to me") and *akhbarani* ("he reported to me"), making unambiguous claims of direct face-to-face encounter between teachers and students, begin to wipe out the vague and less committal preposition *'an* ("from").[51] The consolidation and systematization of the field also accompanied a diminishing of the transmitters' heterogeneity. Asma Sayeed has documented a disappearance of women from isnads after the earliest generations;[52] Christopher Melchert observes an intensified marginalization of ideological minorities from the early third/ninth centuries onward,[53] and Lyall R. Armstrong notes a methodological suspicion toward the qussas that intensifies over time.[54] John Nawas demonstrates that the chains of transmission, mirroring the shift of imperial gravity from Syria to Iraq between Umayyad decline and 'Abbasid ascent, also reflect a reduced percentage of Arab transmitters and growing dominance of the field by *mawali* (non-Arab) transmitters, primarily Persian and Transoxanian scholars.[55] Hadith masters among Ibn Hanbal's students and their network who would produce the collections of the "Six Books" canon all hailed from east of the Tigris and Euphrates. By Bukhari's generation, the assemblage established its ideal embodiment as a Persian or Transoxanian man whose professional and theological credentials had been vouchsafed by his peers.

Changes in tools and machines also contributed to the hadith assemblage, perhaps most markedly in the triumph of writing. In 134/751 CE, the year of al-Tayalisi's birth, Chinese prisoners captured after a battle with Arab forces introduced paper technology into Iraq. By 177/793, Baghdad would become home to an impressive papermaking factory; by 287/900, the city boasted more than 100 shops at which books could be transcribed and bound for purchase.[56] While DeLanda observes advances in communication technology chiefly as agents of deterritorialization for their power to blur spatial boundaries,[57] paper in this context also served to reterritorialize prophetic traditions by intensifying their standardization. Whereas the early transmitters opposed Umayyad efforts to domesticize oral traditions as texts, hadith scholars living in a new book culture produced the enormous compilations that would later facilitate the rise of canonical collections and numerous supplementary literatures of commentary and criticism. Early hadith collections of the third/ninth century would attempt to gather and sort their internal heterogeneities through sections on the "virtues of the Companions" (*fada'il al-sahaba*), which provide evidence of Muhammad's endorsement of the Companions as a class, even his praises of specific Companions who would later wage war against each other.[58]

Book culture radically transformed the culture of hadiths. Corresponding to similar developments in other fields of knowledge, hadith scholars produced enormous biographical dictionaries that charted the development of their field, grouping transmitters chronologically according to their *tabqa* (pl. *tabaqat*) and reporting the field's verdicts as to their credentials. Tabaqat translates literally as "strata," which in the Deleuzian lexicon signifies the homogenizing, stabilizing, and reterritorializing forces that close off their antitheses, the creative and deterritorializing lines of flight, "giving form to matters ... imprisoning intensities or locking singularities into systems of resonance and redundancy."[59] The organization of hadith transmitters by tabqa arranges them in tiers of value, with the first and most prestigious tabqa constituted by the original Muslim generation, and contributes to the predictability and measurability of transmissions. The tabaqat and their adjacent methodologies and literatures become precisely the strata that capture rhizomatic hadith flows such as those circulating through marketplace storytellers, self-serving forgers, or sectarian propaganda, and slow down the flows by thickening them with organization, coding, and ranking. "The strata are judgments of God," Deleuze and Guattari tell us, "but the earth, or the body without organs, constantly eludes that judgment, flees and becomes destratified, decoded, deterritorialized."[60]

As hadith scholarship, following other professions and literary genres, relied on book media to theorize itself as a field, sort and rank its practitioners, and preserve its growing archive, it became a territory in ways that the Companions could not have anticipated. Supporting this territorialization was the emerging concept of *'adalat al-sahaba*, the collective integrity of the Companions as a class, which developed gradually, underwent its first explicit articulation more than a century after al-Tayalisi's death (thus two centuries after the last of the Companions passed), and became crystallized throughout the fifth–sixth /eleventh–twelfth centuries.[61] The concept healed communal wounds from conflicts between Companions, countered Shi'i polemics, and empowered the field of Sunni hadith scholarship by granting supreme authority to its foundational tabaqat. Through this construction, Sunni hadith scholars gathered objects and entities within a territory, defended its border against the outside, and named themselves as the territory's rightful masters.

Approaching the hadiths in Deleuze's model of the assemblage, we first situate Muhammad and his Companions on a horizontal axis. At one end of this line, Deleuze imagines "*machinic* assemblages of bodies, actions and passions, an intermingling of bodies reacting to each other."[62] The Companions enter into a new complex with Muhammad by virtue of *physical* presence: they witness Muhammad and accept his prophethood during his lifetime, even if they are only small children when they encounter him. This intermingling can become even more explicitly embodied, as Muhammad sometimes extends his prophetic corporeality by transmitting baraka into Companions' bodies through fluids such as his saliva and sweat. At the other end of the axis, we find "*collective assemblages* of enunciation, of acts and statements, of incorporeal transformations of bodies,"[63] the ordering of bodies through language. An assemblage's expressive or discursive dimension draws from its materiality, gives a name to the intermingling of bodies, and then in turn inscribes its expression upon them—in this case, producing their later designation as "the Companions," retroactively transforming their status. The Companions form connections with other bodies and bring them into the machinic assemblage, which in turn enables the production of concepts such as "the Successors" and later "Successors of the Successors." As this mass of interconnected bodies expands with each generation, the assemblage of enunciation reconfigures them through new discourses. The machinic assemblage consists of gathered corporealities: young al-Tayalisi sitting at the feet of hadith transmitter and fabric importer Hisham al-Dastawa'i, listening to his narrations. The assemblage of enunciation marks change: al-Tayalisi obtaining entry into Hisham's web of connections with deceased authorities of the past. When Hisham himself dies as al-Tayalisi is still a teenager, al-Tayalisi becomes a body through which Hisham's knowledge will reach the bodies of Ibn Hanbal's generation. Through the organization and reworking of bodies by concepts, al-Tayalisi becomes something new.

The horizontal axis of content and expression intersects a vertical axis that represents the opposing arborescent and rhizomatic tendencies within any assemblage, its potentials for territorialization and deterritorialization. As bodies and discourses move along this axis, an assemblage enhances or suppresses its potential for multiplicity and change. Among the first Muslims and their earliest students, hadith transmission was significantly deterritorialized. They did not produce a literary canon or elite coterie of governing experts, but rather a multiplicity of loose assemblages formed between local elders and their teaching circles, occupying a "smooth space" that had not yet been subjected to rigid striation. An assemblage is formed not as an accidental collision of heterogeneous elements, but through agents with power to do the assembling. Local scholarly networks grew increasingly interconnected and developed concepts and methods to further organize and order their bodies, creating tiers of authorized classes: the "Companions," "Successors," and "Successors of Successors"; the isnad, the chain of transmission that could track a textual body's locations in their network; formal grading systems by which isnads and their transmitters could be ranked; exhaustive listings of the thousands of bodies that together comprised a professional field; and polemics against opposing schools, methods, and communities. They consolidated local and molecular entities into a molar mass with greater powers of self-regulation, helping to form the territory that would ultimately come to be called *ahl al-sunna wa-l-jama'a*, Sunni Islam. While *al-jama'a* in this context usually undergoes translation as "the congregation" or "the community," the *j-m-'a* root signifies broader meanings of gathering, combining, and assembling (Bukhari's supremely canonical collection, most popularly known as the *Sahih*, is also referred to as his *Jami'*); one could render ahl al-sunna wa-l-jama'a as "People of the Sunna and the Assemblage."

The other end of the vertical axis represents deterritorialization. Despite its movements toward stasis and control, the hadith assemblage retains what Deleuze calls "lines of flight," destabilizing resources within an arborescent system that can manifest its rhizomatic tendencies. Modern media technologies, rendering the hadith corpus more accessible than ever in mass-printed books, translated editions, and digital archives such as "daily hadith" phone apps or sophisticated hadith databases, complete with color-coded and hyperlinked isnads that redirect readers to transmitters' appraisals in biographical dictionaries, can both territorialize and deterritorialize the hadith corpus via new assemblages. The prioritization of hadiths in contemporary Sunni revivalism reflects these tendencies between the arborescent Salafism of the modern Saudi state and the rootless rhizomatic proliferation of American Salafi communities and concepts in the 1990s.

Considering ways that viral transmissions changed the relationship between baboon DNA and the DNA of some domestic cats, Deleuze suggests that advances in the study of genetics might force an abandonment of "the old model of the tree and descent."[64] Even as the isnad and its supplementary disciplines construct territory through charted genealogies and hierarchical ranks, premodern hadith masters also formed rhizomes with their viruses. Examining hadith transmission as a potentially rhizomatic assemblage means that we look beyond these clearly stated genealogies and consider undocumented and nonlinear connections.

The claim of epistemological supremacy for isnad-based hadith evaluation never became absolute, even by its own terms. The isnad's power to grant canonical privilege to a hadith means that if a potential rupture of the system comes equipped with an impeccable chain of transmission, it can smuggle alternative maps into the canon. According to well-evidenced accounts endorsed in Sunni hadith canon, Companions such as Ibn ʿAbbas affirm that Muhammad can appear in Muslims' dreams and communicate meaning, and Sunni literatures abound with accounts of the Prophet or even hadith scholars such as Ibn Hanbal appearing in dreams to endorse or discredit particular transmitters.[65] While many Muslims speak of hadith evaluation as science, dreams and visions open lines of flight and warp zones in the isnads. Encounters with long-lived jinns, as Anand Vivek Taneja writes, also make warp zones to cut across lineages, "connecting human beings centuries and millennia apart in time."[66] Esteemed eighteenth-century hadith scholar Shah Waliullah (1703–62) achieved the rank of *tabi'un*, relocating him at just one degree of separation from the original Muslim community, by meeting a jinn *sahabi* who had personally met the Prophet more than a thousand years earlier.[67]

The isnad even grants the human body a share of power over it. In the famous "Hadith of Cringing," Muhammad promises that if a hadith brings distress to one's heart—manifested in reactions of the skin and hair—it could not have come from him, thus theoretically empowering one's personal feelings about a specific hadith against the methodologies that vouched for it.[68] Sufi masters have sometimes vetted hadiths not by isnad analysis but their own intuitions, as in the case of Ibn ʿArabi (638/1240) treating a weakly evidenced hadith as authentic because he *sensed* that it was true, as well as receiving direct communications from Muhammad six centuries after the Prophet's death. For contemporary reformist Muslims who seek to decenter the hadith corpus, accounts in which the Prophet and Companions prohibit the writing of hadiths enable the paradox of claiming that hadith texts deny their own authority. Isnads also become possible lines of flight by undermining claims of ideological and methodological purity, revealing presences that would be regarded as unacceptably "heretical" and "deviant" by later standards.

The isnad can shift between territorialization and deterritorialization by reversing the direction of its flows, starting with a "hadith corpus" and going backward to witness its formation. As it disassembles the corpus into differentiated Companion parts, the *Musnad*'s isnad-based organization both territorializes and deterritorializes: while gathering the Companions as a coherent class, it also enhances their potential for difference. Historicizing the Companions' universal probity can fragment the monolith and renew the Companions' individual subjectivities. Depending on which Companions we read, we'd arrive at different possibilities on matters such as Muhammad's vision of God,[69] his continued sentience and bodily integrity in his grave, or even his physical appearance. Isnads also enable us to disassemble each Companion, breaking down the appearance of a singular individual to reveal a multiplicity of bodies and contexts. The textual representation of Muhammad's body itself becomes an assemblage, a composite of heterogeneous memories, networks, forces, and effects. As Deleuze attributes appearances of unity to the achievement of a "power takeover in the multiplicity,"[70] examining hadith literature as an assemblage is not merely to say that this textual body is made of parts, but rather to give attention to territory-making powers that bring corporealities and discourses together as an ordered and organized new entity.

Again recalling the proclamation from Deleuze and Guattari in *A Thousand Plateaus* that each of them was already multiple, making the two of them "quite a crowd," I recognize that the hadith corpus does not produce a singular Muhammad with a singular, consistent theology that can instantly enter into conversation with Deleuze. There remains the question of *which* Muhammad gets to meet Deleuze—rather, which local network of narrators, presenting itself as the voice of a specific Companion who in turn provides our lens for accessing Muhammad. I imagine Deleuze and Muhammad sitting knee to knee, the Prophet discussing the nature of his access to the divine—did the Prophet *see* God or not? Did he see him with the eyes in his head or the eyes in his heart, did he only see a blinding light that may or may not have been God, or was a vision of God impossible? Did God appear to the Prophet in the "best form" and place a tangible hand on his body? Was God the one "intense in power" who descended until he came within "two bow-lengths or nearer" of the Prophet (53:5–9)? That dialogue changes if I rely on the A'isha corpus, which insists that the one "intense in power" was the angel Gabriel and absolutely rejects the beatific vision (citing verse 6:103 of the Qur'an, "No vision can grasp him," to present God as transcendent beyond human perception), as opposed to the reports of Ibn 'Abbas, Anas, and others, which affirm it (while reporters within these circles differ from each other as to the precise nature of Muhammad's vision and the details of God's appearance). It can change if our arrangement of hadiths favors one geographic origin over another, following Basra and ignoring Kufa or vice versa, or whether we limit the investigation to hadiths privileged by Bukhari and the Six Books network or remain open to a more expansive idea of canon.[71] How expansive? Beyond the Six Books canon, we find earlier and later collections at lower tiers of prestige, such as Malik's *Muwatta* or the *Musnads* of Ibn Hanbal and al-Tayalisi, or the especially enormous—because they were less rigorous in their standards?—collections by al-Tabarani and Bayhaqi. Beyond the lower-tier canons lurks the anti-canon opening the BwO of absolute destratification, the collections of hadiths and catalogs of transmitters compiled specifically for condemnation, the archive marked DO NOT READ expressed most famously in Ibn al-Jawzi's *al-Mawdu'at al-Kubra*, the *Great Collection of Fabrications*. Anti-canon is where we find the statement, attributed to the Prophet through a chain of ill-reputed charlatans and heretics, that God created himself from the sweat of a horse; the tradition ironically survived thanks to clerical scholars warning us to reject it.[72] Where does the horse-sweat hadith get you? An Islamic atheism as the self-destroying BwO that went too far? Perhaps the failed and "empty" BwO of which Deleuze and Guattari warn, existing "on the debris of strata destroyed by a too-violent destratification,"[73] an overdosing Nabi without Organs (NwO) that de-organized without keeping enough to put itself back together. The neo-traditionalist's nightmare of the threat posed by "secular" and "postmodern" critical theory: a disintegrated Islam emptied of meaning. "You don't do it with a sledgehammer," Deleuze and Guattari advise; "you use a very fine file."[74]

But if Deleuze guided me through the pages of a hadith collection, he could not pretend that the text offers a coherent subject, "Muhammad," who can speak with one voice and offer a consistent theology; nor do I expect that Deleuze would find such a Muhammad very interesting. The premodern *hadith* masters preserved the Prophet's rhizomicity in their general distaste for *sira*, the enterprise of combining, cutting, and arranging stories of the Prophet to produce a linear and orderly cradle-to-grave biography. In the hadith masters' eyes, sira projects required a dangerous degree of editorial sovereignty over the material. Though sira authors such as Ibn Ishaq (704–68) were hadith scholars themselves, hadith masters such as Ibn Hanbal perceived sira work as a willingness to sacrifice scholarly rigor in the interests of narrative. The foundational imam Malik b. Anas (711–95), eponym of the Maliki school of law, even called Ibn Ishaq a *dajjal* (antichrist) and had him chased out of Medina.[75]

Between the image of Muhammad as a singular human life that could be told in a narratively fulfilling biography and the prophetic assemblage disassembled beyond recognition, we could take Deleuze and Guattari's advice: "Lodge yourself on a stratum, experiment with the opportunities it offers, find an advantageous place on it, find potential moments of deterritorialization, possible lines of flight."[76] The hadith corpus is not a reality of Muhammad's inside, but an assemblage formed by his connection with countless outsides, and those outsides further connecting to new outsides. The hadith corpus does not pull the reader as an *interpreter* to the Prophet's personal interiority; there's no entering Muhammad through his book (or rather, the thousands of books representing him), though the book says that Muhammad can enter you through your dreams. Rather than attempt to "go in" and interpret hadiths, looking instead to the process by which they (and their adjacent machines) were made, I experience the hadith corpus as a series of openings to the infinity of difference that canon-making forces endeavored to suppress.

3 / Beyond Theology: Sufism as Arrangement and Affect

Sufism is a name without a reality, but used to be a reality without a name.
—ABU HASAN AL-BUSHANJI

Teaching in the tenth century CE, al-Bushanji lived during the era in which the term *tasawwuf* (literally "becoming a Sufi"), our basis for the English term "Sufism," underwent increasing crystallization as a discrete accumulation of ideas, practices, social organizations, and identities. But while a construction had grown visible as "Sufism," al-Bushanji lamented that an essence was lost, the work was lost, the true knowledge had decayed, and the formerly nameless reality was now overrun with elite intellectuals treating it as a philosophical abstraction and imposter holy men hustling crowds with fake miracles.[1] Something had changed, causing al-Bushanji to view the Sufism of his time as the degenerated shell of the truer, more "classical" Sufism of an earlier age.

Al-Bushanji's time was more than a thousand years ago.

If we follow his analysis, Sufism was rendered incoherent just three centuries after the death of the Prophet and ceased to meaningfully exist.

If Sufism had received a name and lost its reality by al-Bushanji's era, what can we access as Sufism today? I'm not interested in the power plays of claiming authenticity or latching onto the specific reterritorialization attempted by al-Bushanji. Grounding his argument in an appeal to the superior piety and sincerity of righteous elders from a lost golden age, al-Bushanji's harsh verdict on the condition of Sufism in his age can express an ideological project as much as an empirical observation; but before thinking about a conversation with Deleuze, al-Bushanji's remark is helpful for deconstructing Sufism as a named category. The assemblage is a process, forever forming and organizing and scattering its contents, opening and sealing its lines of flight, adding and cutting strata, allowing and denying connections to its outside. When we encounter "Sufism" today, it cannot signify what tasawwuf meant to al-Bushanji.

We start with recognition that Sufism, both as a material phenomenon of bodies, sites, and artifacts and an expressive or discursive phenomenon (that is, the inscription of a category such as "Sufism" upon the bodies and the incorporeal transformations imposed by these terms and statements), undergoes change across time and space. Al-Bushanji had identified change between the original Sufis (who preceded "Sufism" as a category) and his contemporaries, but we also face the immeasurable changes between al-Bushanji and our age, including developments such as the ongoing development of institutional Sufism, the discursive elaborations by great thinkers and systematizers like al-Ghazali and Ibn al-'Arabi, and eventually the immense impact from European-dominated modernity, through which colonial productions of knowledge recoded the world, added their own layers of strata, and gave us the *modern* category of "Sufism" (along with broader categories of "religion" and "mysticism").

Modern representations of Sufism often forget Sufi bodies (perhaps apart from the decontextualized images of "whirling" dervishes) and the things that bodies do: the ways that these bodies form connections and transform each other through shared performances of movement and recitation (ritual), named relations (i.e., *murshid* and *murid*), institutional histories, and physical space, the Sufi lodges and masjids and shrines, not to mention this intermingling of bodies as it relates to other forces, such as nation-states and transnational networks. In terms of the Deleuzian assemblage model's horizontal axis, uniquely modern constructions of Sufism eliminate the machinic assemblage and reduce the tradition to a narrowed idea of Sufism's enunciative or expressive assemblage, its "acts and statements" and "incorporeal transformations attributed to bodies."[2] Along the vertical axis, the territorial sides (reterritorialization) and cutting edges (deterritorialization), the former are all but forgotten to favor a vision of Sufism as absolute deterritorialization. Sufism becomes presented as "Islamic mysticism" or Islam's "mystical dimension," an individual's adventure of pursuing direct, unmediated knowledge of God, personal "spirituality" in direct contrast to Islam as "religion." Recoded as a spirituality without bodies, Sufism signifies all of the "good stuff"—love for God and humanity, feelings of union with God and/or the universe, attachment to the essence of the tradition with or without the formal strictures of law, transcendence beyond all religious divisions, boundaries, and bigotries—without the "bad stuff," namely "religion" clerical hierarchies, obsessive construction, and enforcement of communal boundaries, fixation on correct ritual, and uncritical surrender to the law. This image of Sufism expresses a tracing of Western European histories and prejudices. As acknowledged earlier, Orientalist scholars sometimes racialized Sufism's relationship to broader Islam, mapping their anti-Jewish prejudices and notions of oppositional "Aryan" and "Semitic" essences onto Islam. In these logics, Semitic religion (Judaism and Islam) was defined by spiritually dead laws, rituals, and undeveloped anthropomorphic theologies and rendered obsolete by Aryan spirituality (Christianity and Sufism). In the Aryanist-informed framework, just as Christianity flourished in Europe as an "Aryanization" of Israelite religion, a translation of unsophisticated Semitic monotheism into higher Aryan spirituality, Sufism was treated as not "really" owing its development to anything internal to Islam. Instead, Orientalists perceived Sufism as the product of an Arab religion's encounter with the brighter lights of Iran (i.e., Aryamehr, "Land of the Aryans").[3] The racialized taxonomy of Islamic thought enabled a cutting away of Sufism from Islam, a simultaneous privileging of Sufism as Islam's highest expression and reduction of Sufism to "borrowing" and "outside influence" for which Islam could receive no credit. Orientalists reterritorialized Sufism as Persian, not Arab; Aryan, not Semitic; and an amalgamation of Christian gnosticism, Manichaeism, Buddhism, Zoroastrianism, and Hinduism disguised by a veneer of Islam, but not genuinely Islamic.[4]

This is not to say that everyone who takes part in constructions of Sufism as a purely individualized spirituality is immediately a white supremacist; nor does it mean that a Muslim who identifies with Sufism through a rubric of "spirituality vs. religion" has been hopelessly colonized away from Muslim consciousness; nor does it mean that that such a construction is necessarily a terrible "misreading" of "real" Sufism and can find no legitimate support in "classical" Islamic tradition—and even if it did signal a misreading, that shouldn't necessarily make it less useful. This modern vision of Sufism beyond religion has been immensely useful for countless people, including Muslims with antiracist and anticolonial interests, and it's not my project to cut away the "New Age" stratum only to accept an equally troubled and ahistorical stratum of neo-traditionalist revival in which all "legitimate" Sufis are assumed to have been "orthodox" and *fiqh*-compliant 'ulama. Neo-traditionalists stratify their own modern reconstructions of Sufism in which the mysticism and uneasy theological ambiguities are blocked off to leave essentially a spiritualization of etiquette. Every version of the Sufism assemblage has its strata and cutting lines. The construction of Sufism as individual spirituality in opposition to "organized religion" can destratify some assemblages but also restratify others, as seen in the projects of modern states building their own narratives of apolitical Sufism as antidotes to networks that they have marked as the "bad" Muslims (which different states will define on different terms).

If we're trying to read Sufism through a philosopher, it could seem intuitive to reduce Sufism to a philosophy, abstracting it from the world and limiting ourselves to Sufism as it might appear through the tradition's elite intellectuals and poets: Read a Deleuze system against an Ibn al-'Arabi system and see if the two systems can agree on something. But Sufism is not only (or even primarily) a literary corpus of great minds theorizing on divine names; more than theologies and cosmologies, it is also an arrangement of bodies and space. To look at Sufism through a Deleuzian lens could certainly ask how Deleuze and his uses of the great thinkers that comprise his toolbox, such as Duns Scotus and Spinoza, might read alongside great Sufi thinkers outside his toolbox, such as 'Ayn al-Qudat or Suhrawardi; but it would also need to think about marriages and lineages and successions, the *pir* as a hereditary position, pirs (both living and dead) as mediators between tribes, shrines' relations to feudal lords and rural tribe economies, flows of money and control over land,

FIGURE 4. Hazrat Pir Asghar Ali Chan Pir Sarkar (*seated*) with Amir Haydar Chan Pir (*standing*), pocket-sized laminated card. Author's collection.

the patronage of shrines by rulers and elites as political acts, dances of power and baraka transactions between lodges and kings, and the way that Sufism undergoes modern recodings by theocratic and secularist regimes alike. Deleuzian Sufism would concern itself not only with doctrines and concepts, but also with the forces that arrange corporealities within a category, subject them to a discourse's incorporeal transformations, and enhance or diminish their powers. Yes, the discourse is there, but the discourse needs bodies; it does its work within and through and between bodies. Sufism is the stack of small laminated cards that I collected in my visits to shrines in India and Pakistan, bearing images of pirs and masters, portable baraka satellites connected to sites such as the Chan Pir shrine in Pakpattan.

I engage Deleuzian Sufism both as someone who reads Deleuze and classical Sufi masters all alone in his office and as someone who physically visits Sufi shrines, holds initiation in an order, and keeps material baraka transmitters on his person.

Order and Assemblage

Early in Islam, personalities known for their exceptional piety, asceticism, virtue, knowledge, the eloquence of their teachings, and rumored miracles attracted students and followers. Neither the personalities nor the people clustering around them were necessarily "mystics" or practitioners of "mysticism," whatever those terms could have signified here. Nor was it self-evident that these nascent assemblages of charismatic renunciants and their devotees had pursued a line of flight out of Islamic law or theological "orthodoxy." In fact, there was significant overlap in early Islam between proto-Sufi renunciants and proto-Sunni scholars of *hadiths* and the law. Early biographical dictionaries cataloging great Sufis of the past counted the pious jurist Ibn Hanbal, a foundational figure in the development of Sunni Islam, among Sufi ranks—the same Ibn Hanbal who denied the potential for esoteric openings in the Qur'an and who, from a certain reading of history, could be called the great-great-grandfather of the ideological foundation for the modern Saudi state, which adheres to the Hanbali legal and theological school bearing his name. The martyred ecstatic mystic poet Mansur al-Hallaj, prototype for heretical Sufi passion at odds with the strictures of the law, used to spend his nights at Ibn Hanbal's grave; after al-Hallaj's execution, the Baghdad Hanbalis—the same folks who threw rocks at al-Tabari's house and overturned the gravestone of a responsible theologian like al-Ash'ari—were so outraged at his death that they apparently rioted in the streets.[5] The Hallajian Abstract Machine and the Hanbali Abstract Machine each constructed a "real that is yet to come, a new type of reality";[6] even if those realities represent polar antitheses in modern imaginaries, their historical entanglements speak to shifting limits of the thinkable. Sufis looked to Ibn Hanbal, a paragon of so-called fundamentalism and austere legalism as an elder within their own genealogies. Al-Hallaj, a "drunken Sufi" famous for allegedly calling himself by God's name and dancing to his execution, viewed the jurist's grave as a locus of supernatural energies and was sufficiently admired by the Hanbali "fundamentalists" that they would burn down the neighborhood in his name.

By the eleventh century CE, Sufi lodges were transformed by a growing drive toward institutionalization, which included emphasis on the relationship between master and disciple and the argument that tutelage under a master was necessary for the seeker.[7] Contrary to the popular modern image of Sufism as existing outside "organized religion," focused entirely on the individual's unmediated relationship to God and thereby devoid of earthly institutional hierarchy, Sufism's medieval success came through its crystallization into structures—namely, the orders (*tariqas*) rigidly organized under the transcendent authority of their masters, to whom dervishes pledged their loyalty and obedience. The Sufi orders were not disconnected from politics, but rather deeply embedded in complex power relations with rulers. Sufi masters legitimized rulers through the bestowal of baraka upon them while receiving social capital through their close proximity to the ruling elite. Rulers also legitimized themselves as pious Muslims by building and financially supporting Sufi lodges and the tombs of Sufi masters. In Mamluk Egypt, Saladin not only founded his own khanaqah but also established a paid government position of "Chief Sufi," a parallel to the post of Chief Judge.[8] The fact that rulers saw it as favorable to their interests to support and appropriate Sufi orders resists another popular assumption—namely, that Sufism is reducible to visionary esotericists and their marginalized followers, whose subversive theologies and nonconformist behaviors place them at odds with established religion. Sunni rulers fostered connections with Sufi orders in part to perform their faithful commitments to Sunni Islam precisely because the masses regarded these Sufi orders as authentic Sunni institutions. Sufi orders participated in the construction of "orthodoxy" and contributed to daily lived religion in Muslim-majority societies.

This does not mean that all Sufi figures and groups enjoyed favorable relations to the state. Rulers intervened in disputes between Sufi groups and could demonstrate their Islamic authenticity by persecuting orders deemed heretical. When a Sufi faction with strict commitments to the

Shafi'i school of jurisprudence objected to the burial of a rival Sufi at al-Shafi'i's shrine in Cairo, charging that the Sufi subscribed to anthropomorphist theology, Saladin acquiesced and ordered the body exhumed and dumped in the Nile.[9] In Damascus, Saladin's son famously ordered the execution of Suhrawardi, whose provocative statements (such as claiming equal rank to the prophet Hermes, ostensibly asserting prophethood for himself) led local clerical scholars to charge him with claiming prophethood.[10] The Mamluks also reportedly executed an excessively "orthodox" Sufi who, having grown incensed at local Muslims offering sacrifices to the Sphinx, took it upon himself to destroy the Sphinx's nose. The Ottoman ruling elites relied on cooperation with Sufi masters, whose constituencies proved instrumental for the coherence of the political order. Sufism's integration into the imperial assemblage produced rearticulations of the caliphate in Sufi terms and models of mystical kingship as well as a construction of the theologically provocative Ibn al-'Arabi as "patron saint for the Ottomans."[11] However, "deviant" dervish groups such as the Bektashis, Qalandars, Haydaris, and others faced state suppression under the Ottomans, either gradually disintegrating or negotiating with the pressure to become "legitimate" Sufi orders.[12] With the dissolution of the Ottoman Empire and rise of secular Turkey, the government abolished Sufi orders altogether. Shi'ism had spread throughout Iran as the official state orientation through the triumph of a sixteenth-century Sufi war machine, the Safavids, whose teen master Shah Isma'il I (d. 1524) rose to power, adopted Twelver Shi'ism as the new state confession, and persecuted Iran's Sufi orders (especially Sufi orders with Sunni commitments), destroying saints' graves and targeting living masters as well. One Sufi order, the Nimatullahis, had flourished amidst the Safavid anti-Sufi campaigns, in part by reorienting itself toward Shi'ism and achieving intermarriage between the order's leadership and the royal family. When people expect Sufism to remain forever removed from politics and marginalized from official orthodoxy, I like to bring up that the most important Sufi of the twentieth century, without argument, was the Ayatollah Khomeini, who studied classical gnosis ('irfan), including the works of Ibn al-'Arabi, and composed his own mystically tinged poems loaded with al-Hallaj references: "I have departed from myself, beating the drum of 'I am the Haqq'; I have become like Mansur [al-Hallaj], a buyer of a hanging rope."[13] Nonetheless, the revolution made for uneasy relations between Sufi orders and the new state. The Nimatullahi order, which had survived centuries earlier by adapting to the Safavid program, fled Khomeini's Iran in 1979 and became a Western order in exile.

The Nimatullahi order was established roughly five centuries after al-

Bushanji's diagnosis of Sufism as a name without a reality, though the founder held chains of transmission that traced his knowledge back to 'Ali. After spending time at the order's San Francisco khanaqah, I received the invitation to become a dervish. Adhering to the order's script, I came to the khanaqah on the appointed night with a specific assortment of gifts: a white cloth, a coin, a ring, rock candy, and nutmeg. These material artifacts paid my price of admission with the symbolic values inscribed upon them. The white cloth represented Islamic burial shrouds, because initiation into the order was something of a death and resurrection. The coin signified wealth, or more precisely the attachment to wealth. The ring signified slavery. As the local shaykh's assistant who walked me through the process explained, "When you are a slave to God, you are truly free." The rock candy symbolized joy, and the nutmeg was a symbolic stand-in for my head.

My gifts to the order were wrapped in the white sheet. As I held them in my left hand, the shaykh's assistant led me by the right hand to a room with Persian rugs and cushions, the walls bearing the portraits of past masters. The *shaykh* sat alone on a mat beneath two axes crossed over an animal skin. I kissed the floor, then prostrated myself in front of him, a perfect reproduction of the *sajdah* that I had performed repeatedly each day in my previous life as a Sunni Muslim, but a dramatic rewiring of the posture's meaning. In my five-daily-prayers era, I held very clear and non-negotiable ideas about what constituted proper Islamic monotheism—one of those ideas being that Muslims do not offer sajdah to anyone but God. And now I had given it to a man. The shaykh and I shared the order's handshake: we kissed the back of each other's hands, saying *Ya al-Haqq* as we touched our foreheads to each other's hands.

With the white sheet bundle between us, my hand still on it, he instructed me to repeat his words. With the oath of initiation, a short speech act had transformed my body into a dervish body. Then he taught me the order's formula for remembering God: saying "Allah" as I inhaled, "Hu" as I exhaled. "Allah represents the attributes of God," he told me; "Hu is the essence of God. When you breathe in, you contemplate the attributes. Then you exhale the essence." I was to repeat this process fourteen times each morning, followed by one silent repetition.

The khanaqah's dervishes entered the room. The shaykh said, "Ya al-Haqq," as he handed each dervish a piece of the rock candy that I had brought. The shaykh asked everyone present to remember his own moments of entry into the order. Then he sat down, a cue for the dervishes to sit. The lights went off, a recording of dhikr and stringed instruments played, and we lost ourselves chanting in the dark. I was now a Nimatullahi dervish.

The shaykh was the leader of the local khanaqah, but his body symbolically represented the Master several thousand miles away, so my performance of sajdah before him signified my submission both to the shaykh as my teacher and to the hierarchy at large. As much as its project expresses a longing for God, historical Sufism also marks relations between flesh-and-blood bodies on the ground. It was popularly understood that to embark on the Sufi path, one needed a teacher: a widespread truism attributed to Abu Yazid al-Bistami holds that if you have no shaykh, your shaykh is Satan.[14] It would be shocking for many, given popular assumptions about Islamic monotheism and Sufi spirituality, that dervishes often seek a meditative union with their order's masters, who can serve as corporeal signifiers and stand-ins for the Prophet and/or God.

Authority comes from genealogy: the critical document of a Sufi order was its *shajara*, its vertically charted lineage, naming the chains of masters connecting the order's present master through the ages to a figure (usually 'Ali) who had received his knowledge and mantle directly from Muhammad. Prostrating to the shaykh and entering into a new relation with the Master through him, I put myself under an authoritative lineage of masters reaching back to the order's eponymic founder, Sayyid Nur al-Din Shah Nimatullah Wali, and through him to his master, 'Abd Allah al-Yafi'i, who held initiatic chains traceable through generations to *the* al-Ghazali's brother, Ahmad al-Ghazali, who in turn inherited authority from a lineage of masters tracing back to the famed ascetic Hasan al-Basri, who was born just ten years after the death of the Prophet and had been nursed by the Prophet's widow, Um Salama, and received the Prophet's baraka through her milk. Hasan al-Basri was himself a disciple of the paragon of discipleship, 'Ali, of whom the Prophet said, "I am the city of knowledge, and 'Ali is the gate."[15]

Often memorized by dervishes and displayed on shrine walls, the shajara is how a Sufi order legitimizes its master's credentials and establishes its embodied link to the Prophet and the sacred past. Through its shajara, the Nimatullahi order can document its "official" origin with Shah Nimatullah Wali in fifteenth-century Iran, but also claim its true origin in the Prophet's teachings to 'Ali. Shah Nimatullah Wali was also apparently a *sayyid*, a direct descendant of the Prophet through the Prophet's great-great-great-great-grandson Isma'il b. Ja'far (eponym for Isma'ili tradition). Within the Nimatullahi order, the authorizing lineage was both institutional and biological: Shah Nimatullah Wali designated his son Burhan as his successor, and for the next three centuries, leadership of the order was restricted to Shah Nimatullah Wali's direct descendants, supporting the order's coherence and centralization.[16] While the Nimatullahi order went through substantive transformations across shifting historical contexts—starting with a Sunni orientation, moving toward Shi'ism with the rest of Iran in the Safavid era, and ultimately moving away from formal Muslim identity after 1979, when the order's leadership fled Khomeini's revolution and reterritorialized in London as a Western tariqa—the shajara upholds a sense of continuity. Because the master inherits a transcendent authority from the masters who preceded him, the genealogy could matter more than a specific doctrinal point or praxis. Like the isnad that authenticates hadith transmissions, this should set off Deleuzian alarms: the Arabic shajara literally translates as "tree," and shajara charts are typically stylized and ornamented to look like trees. The Sufi order is a hierarchical structure that derives its vertical power through privileged access to the transcendent unseen and a literal drawing of a tree. If initiatic, tariqa-based Sufism looks like a purely arborescent assemblage with all power located in the master at center, where's the rhizomatic Sufism with horizontal anti-genealogies?

We can first insert a disclaimer from Deleuze regarding the nature of assemblages—that they are never finished but always in motion and that every assemblage contains "lines of *deterritorialization* that cut across it and carry it away"[17]—as well as its forces of reterritorialization. Chains of initiation create the order as a territory but can also deterritorialize, as when a master passes away without leaving a clearly designated successor, sometimes resulting in the proliferation of new lineages. From the fifteenth to eighteenth centuries, as the Nimatullahi leadership recentered in India, a separate lineage developed in the Yazd region of Iran.[18] New shoots such as the Kawthariyya and Shamsiyya became orders distinct from the Nimatullahi, which itself could have been considered a Qadiriyya shoot. The Nimatullahi order in which I received initiation actually represented one of three Nimatullahi lineages that had developed after the master Rahmat 'Ali Shah's death in 1861, each of which grew in a distinct direction. The Gunabadi lineage, which survives in Iran today, maintained a close relationship to Islamic law and clerical establishment Shi'ism. The Safi 'Ali-Shahiyya lineage became the Andjuman-i Ukhuwwat (Society of Brotherhood), moved from a classical Sufi model with a singular master to a "pseudo-masonic lodge" led by a twelve-man committee, and disappeared after the death of leader 'Abd Allah Intizam in 1982. The third Nimatullahi lineage followed the successors of Munawwar Ali Shah and itself splintered after the death of Mirza (Munis) 'Ali Shah in 1953 into no less than thirteen competing factions, each favoring a claimed successor. One of those thirteen candidates, Dr. Javad Nurbakhsh, became immensely successful in part for his publishing output, much of which placed classical Sufism in conversation with his training as a psychiatrist.[19] It was Dr. Nurbakhsh who deterritorialized the order from Iran and followed a line of flight from overt Shi'ism into an almost "spiritual but not religious" construction of Sufism; as part of this move, he changed the dervish greeting to "Ya al-Haqq" from its earlier "Ya 'Ali." Dr. Nurbakhsh passed in 2008; my initiatic pledge was to his son and successor, Dr. Alireza Nurbakhsh.

The Nurbakhsh structure is what most seekers outside Iran experience as *the* Nimatullahi order. The "official" in-house biography of the late master reorganizes the rhizome to present a pure tree, erasing the split histories and imagining a singular line that flows smoothly from Munis 'Ali Shah to the Nurbakhsh family. The biography acknowledges internal tension with some resentful elder dervishes and external hostility from "fanatical, exoteric mullas"[20] but never invites consideration of Nimatullahi Sufism having a multiplicity of authentic lineages, rival factions, or competing narratives.

An abundance of trees, each claiming to represent the center, can destabilize the center and scatter authority, but does not itself undo arborescence. Perhaps a more effective rhizomatic appears in the criss-crossing of genealogical chains through dervishes holding simultaneous initiations in multiple orders. In her study of early Sufi shaykhs and their companions, Laury Silvers observes that only a minority of companions were attached to just one shaykh, and provides the remark of al-Hujwiri: "It is allowable for a disciple to associate with five or six or more directors and to have a different station revealed to him by each of them."[21] Al-Yafi'i, the master who initiated Shah Nimatullah Wali, possessed chains of initiation in several orders and founded his own Yafi'iyya lineage of the Qadiriyya.[22] Shah Nimatullah Wali's disciples (and even his descendants who became leaders of the Nimatullahi order) often belonged to multiple tariqas. In his *Shambhala Guide to Sufism*, Carl Ernst mentions the example of Muhammad al-Sanusi al-Idrisi (1787–1859), an Algeria-born revolutionary who boasted initiations in forty distinct Sufi orders (and founded his own, the Sanusi tariqa). Al-Sanusi wrote a book, *The Clear Fountain on the Forty Paths*, articulating the dhikr practices of these forty orders, a few of which Ernst describes as "theoretical"; it seems that al-Sanusi made a special effort to number his initiations at exactly forty, conforming to an established genre of authors discussing their forty initiations.[23] Al-Sanusi's "theoretical" orders reflect chains of transmission connecting his knowledge back to particular figures, even if these figures did not establish formal orders: so he mentions the Hallajiyya (named for the ecstatic martyr al-Hallaj) and Hatimiyya (linked to Ibn al-'Arabi); he even names a Muhammadiyya path for the Prophet. The roster includes paths that are better described as tendencies or trends than institutionally coherent organizations, such as the Malamatiyya, the "blameworthy" Sufis who regarded fame as celebrated "holy people" to be a spiritual trap, so they deliberately cultivated bad reputations; and the Qalandariyya, the famously antinomian dervishes of south and central Asia. Among his forty connections, al-Sanusi also claimed an Uwaysiyya transmission, the mode of linkage with the greatest deterritorializing power, since it opened a route to authority beyond the intercorporeal connections that usually constituted a Sufi lineage. Named for Uways al-Qarani, a man from Muhammad's lifetime who never met the Prophet but communicated with him telepathically, the Uwaysiyya signifies a connection obtained through incorporeal encounters with teachers from the unseen, such as deceased Sufi masters from previous generations, Muhammad, and Khidr, the enigmatic teacher of Moses.[24]

When claimed by the master who founds a new order, a multiplicity of lineages can consolidate territories and enhance the master's credentials. The master forms connections rhizomatically but gathers these connections together and combines their forces to make a new authorizing whole. The murshid's mode of stratification, however, can become the murid's destratification. When a dervish takes initiation into more than one order, upholding simultaneous pledges to multiple masters and their respective genealogies, each initiation can deterritorialize from the others and de-organize the shajaras from their centralizing functions. There is no singular center for the dervish's meditation but instead a multiplicity of possible centers, each conceivably having its own lineage, doctrinal and ritual commitments, theories of sainthood, preference for loud or silent dhikr, relationship to music, khanaqah and shrine cultures, attachment to a particular legal school, and even Sunni or Shi'i orientation. Dervishes open themselves to heterogeneous connections and become Sufi rhizomes.

Even while authority theoretically exists at the top, bodies of the machinic assemblage enact change upon the order. When Javad Nurbakhsh deterritorialized his Nimatullahi tariqa out of Iran and formal Shi'ism and reterritorialized himself as a Western spiritual teacher in exile, appealing to a post-revolution Iranian diaspora as well as non-Muslim seekers of a New Age orientation, his literature sought connections in a Western metaphysical marketplace. Nurbakhsh's *Jesus in the Eyes of the Sufis* compiles commentary on Jesus from throughout Sufi tradition, reterritorializing Jesus as a Sufi for readers coming from Christian backgrounds; his *Dogs from a Sufi Point of View* resists the trope of dog revulsion as a universal Islamic norm, presenting Sufi traditions in which the dog's uncritical love, loyalty, and servitude are treated as positive models for the dervish path. He even published *The Great Satan "Eblis,"* a compilation of classical Sufi materials in which Satan was recoded as a paragon of self-effacing love for God.[25] He also produced a sixteen-volume encyclopedia on symbolism in Sufi poetry and literature, recoding the canon.[26] Bawa Muhaiyaddeen, the Sri Lankan holy man who became a foundational figure for North American Sufism, attracted a following that included both Muslims and Hindus, as well as dervishes who sought a contemporary "spiritual but not religious" position (and even within the dervishes self-identifying as Muslims, one found a diversity of views as to how Sufism related to larger Islam and questions of "orthodoxy"). Prior to modern nationalist constructions of Islam and Hinduism as entirely self-contained and mutually antagonistic religions, as Dominique-Sila Khan demonstrates in her work on religious reifications in South Asia, such Muslim-Hindu assemblages were a historical norm.[27] The bodies in the room, the form of content, were not only affected by the form of expression but also affected its power of incorporeal transformations. After Bawa Muhaiyaddeen's passing, the heterogeneity of religious orientations within his order led to deterritorializing lines of flight between factions that reterritorialized with their own respective priorities.

Despite al-Bistami's warnings that if you have no shaykh, your shaykh is Satan, not all experiences of Sufism fall neatly into formal affiliation with tariqas and the master-disciple model. South Asian shrine cultures have grown around the graves of numerous holy people who were not known for links to a specific order. Besides the masters who had no masters or who received their initiations in telepathic and visionary modes, Sufism also deterritorializes from formal tariqa structures through its materialization in physical space: one does not have to be initiated into an order or even be a Muslim to visit a shaykh's tomb and access the beneficent energies flowing from/through it.

The shrines become sites of multiple and promiscuous connections. In Lahore, the shrine of Shah Jamal (1588–1671), a saint with Qadiriyya and Suhrawardiyya affiliations and a reputation as a defender of orthodoxy against the emperor Akbar's new religion, had become the center for local live music with Pappu Sain and his *dhol* players every Thursday night. Through these weekly performances, the shrine had also become the center of the neighborhood hashish trade. The shrine and surrounding masjid were packed on those Thursday nights. The crowd included *malangs* with red henna dreadlocks, people only there for the music, people coming for the drugs, tourists, and young people attaching love-magic (or love-prayer) padlocks to the shrine. The pursuits of beneficent energies at a holy man's grave, ecstatic spirituality, music, drugs, and Islam were by no means mutually exclusive to each other—and I'm not the one to decide where the mystical drug adventure ends and recreational drug adventure begins—but this multiplicity of forces exposed a polysemy for Sufism in that specific intermingling of bodies. This was lived Sufism in bodies on the ground, not a spiritless academic systematization of concepts. The shrines of Sufi masters are part of Muslim popular culture and in fact historically "mainstream" Islam.

Everyday people who visit shrines for whatever reason, along with the rulers and states that build shrines and fund their maintenance, are *doing* Sufism, connecting themselves to Sufism and, through these connections and combinations of their affects, transforming the possibilities for what Sufism can do. The overwhelming majority of people who *do* Sufism, the ones who make a Sufi world, are not mystics or esotericist theologians, but "regular" Muslims (and sometimes non-Muslims) for whom the shrines and adjacent institutions remain meaningful in daily life.

Sufi Affects

Sufi lives are stories of transformative encounters—corporeal, visionary, telepathic—in which bodies and their powers become radically altered by interacting with other bodies. When Indian saint Tajuddin Baba (1861–1925) was just six years old, he was discovered by Qadiri shaykh Syed Abdullah Shah at the madrassa. Shah recognized him immediately. The shaykh chewed on a piece of sweetmeat and then shared it with the child, then told the boy's teacher that he required no more instruction, since he was "already well-taught in his previous life." He instructed Tajuddin to read the Qur'an "as though the holy Prophet Muhammad has descended upon you." The encounter with Syed Abdullah Shah impacted Tajuddin to such a degree that he cried nonstop for three days, left childhood play behind, and preferred studying and contemplating Sufi masters in his solitude. Tajuddin grew up to become a *majdhub* saint, a "holy fool" whose absorption in God gave the impression of mental illness. The British colonial authorities locked him up in their Nagpur sanitarium, but word of his status as a genuine knower of God continued to spread, and during his institutionalization he continued to receive visits from growing masses of followers. His shrine in Nagpur persists as a destination for pilgrims, Muslim and Hindu alike.[28]

Tajuddin Baba, six years old, shares sweets with the Sufi master, bringing the two bodies and their flows of energy into connection. Syed

Abdullah Shah's body is already connected to a Sufi power grid populated with bodies of his own order, the Qadiriyya, nodes of extended corporeality reaching beyond their networks to multiplicities of holy bodies and ultimately linking to the Prophet. These connections enact a transformation upon young Tajuddin, who becomes an extension of the entire grid's collective energy, and whose tomb becomes a site at which devotees gather for transformation in his ongoing presence. Deleuze would call it "affect." Building on the distinction between *affectio* and *affectus* in Spinoza, Deleuze gives us affection, the body's condition in relation to the changes imposed by bodies around it, and affect, the variation that affectio causes in our power to act—but the energy can find definition in Islamic vocabulary as baraka. Muhammad spits in the tired camel's mouth, and it then runs at full power to the next village. Waves and fluxes of energies bring bodies' powers of action up or down. The energies flowing between bodies in a room create differences in what those bodies can do.

Something happens to me at Sufi khanaqahs: a transformation under the skin. During the peak moments of an intense vocal dhikr in a dark room, we get worked up with the repetitions of *Allah-hu, Allah-hu* that eventually become just *hu, hu, hu, hu, hu,* our bodies pushing out the syllable faster than we can think it, concepts leaking out of our heads, the dial going all the way up—and then it goes down, the dhikr slows down, the lights come back on, and we return to the world. But the world doesn't feel the same. Everything moves slower. My breath has slowed down. We're quiet with each other and take soft steps on our way out. My sensitivities have changed, my posture has changed. There has also been a change in my powers to change other bodies, as I leave the khanaqah with my altered post-*majlis* energy and carry it to other places.

When we envision "Sufism and philosophy" projects purely as dialogues between a mystic's theosophy and a philosopher's concepts (in this case arranging Deleuze's literary buggery with a classical master), lived Sufi experience disappears. We do more with our religious materials than simply believe or disbelieve in them, and Deleuzian Sufism has more interesting priorities than reconciliation with supernatural figures. The energy of Sufi bodies is real. Baraka is real, whether one thinks of that in terms of transcendence as a divinely allotted energy descending into the world from the top of a chain of being or in terms of immanence, as a social force produced through bodies acting upon each other: baraka as a secretion of atheist energies? To think of Sufism as Islam's "mystical dimension," a pursuit of *unmediated* experiential knowledge of God, demands that we erase an extraordinary historical abundance of mediators: the Sufi order, the institutions of shrine and lodge, the living masters and shaykhs, and the dervishes who create a Sufi environment with their presence. Sufism consists of bodies acting upon bodies, creating mutual transformations into Sufi bodies. Deleuzian Sufism, or at least a Deleuzian lens through which to engage Sufism, would look beyond textual canons and think about flesh-and-blood bodies in collision and energy exchanges between them.

By the time I first encountered the Nimatullahi order, the pure Sunni faith of my teen adventure at an Islamabad madrassa had been stretched out. For most of my Muslim life, I've wandered without a stable 'aqida by which I could demarcate the limits of acceptable Islam to measure my own "orthodoxy" or that of others. Some Muslims would accept the Nimatullahi theological heritage as legitimate, others would not. The Nimatullahis could be categorized as a wujudi order informed by the theology of Ibn al-'Arabi (Shah Nimatullah Wali even wrote commentary on Ibn al-'Arabi's *Fusus al-Hikam* that he claimed had been a revelation from the unseen, like the *Fusus* itself), but initiation did not require that I study theology or a new interpretation of the Qur'an. "We don't advocate reading the Qur'an," the shaykh told me during my first visit. My reassembly as a dervish came through connections to places and bodies and sensations that enacted change upon my body, producing a new dervish body. I came to the khanaqah and shared in the dervish greeting, took a seat on the floor in the right posture and with correct hand placement (right hand on left leg, left hand on right wrist), accepted tea from the dervish appointed to serve us, and entered into my own self with silent reflection or dhikr or a book from the shelves. I followed both the silence and sounds, taking in the visual environment—the artifacts on the walls, the postures of the dervishes, the cupbearer's coned hat, photos of the Master and his father—that turned this room into a Sufi space, responding in my body when the lights were turned off and the formal majlis began in complete darkness. When the lights came back on, my breath and heartbeat had changed, and the energy between our bodies in that room had changed. The affect of the room and my adherence to bodily scripts amounted to a technology of the dervish self. At the khanaqah, I plugged myself into a tasawwuf machine—as well as to my larger sense of being Muslim, even if other dervishes did not share in that concern with the same meanings attached, or at all—as a materiality, something that I could see, hear, smell, touch, and taste. The Nimatullahi shaykh also told me, "We don't advocate reading namaz," meaning the five daily prayers that I had once performed consistently. Those prayers, too, produced an Islamic affect, but one from which the tariqa had severed itself.

This emphasis on bodies doesn't mean that the Nimatullahi tariqa was absent of discourse or claims to transcendence. After all, the khanaqah did have books on the shelves. I had been drawn to the order through Javad Nurbakhsh's publications and eventually collected the entire sixteen-volume *Sufi Symbolism*. The shaykh described the master as "seeing with God's eyes" and asserted that we were always in the master's presence "because . . . well, I'll let you figure that out." But at the khanaqah, learning a doctrine and believing it to be factual felt less significant than the praxis of adab through which bodies could resonate with each other and produce a shared Sufi affect with our breaths and silences and postures and scripts. *The assemblage is the theology.* Even after I became an unacceptable deviant by every Muslim rubric possible, I would still participate in fiqh-normative prayers, standing shoulder-to-shoulder and foot-to-foot with my brothers (and in progressive Muslim spaces, with my sisters and non-binary Muslim siblings) to cultivate changes in my body that I understood to be *Islamic* affects. In whatever Islamic space I found myself, the secrets of my prayers would not have been acceptable to everyone else in the room; but Muslim prayer is not only a private appeal in the heart. It is also an act of the body, a script of positions and movements that intensifies its power when performed in collaboration with other bodies. The "Islamic" nature of my prayer was not dependent on whatever I perceived to be my prayer's object. The morning after my ayahuasca quest, in which dimethyltryptamine and monoamine oxidase inhibitors carried the Prophet's daughter Fatima az-Zahra across my body's blood-brain wall of endothelial cells into my central nervous system, all I wanted was to visit a *masjid*. Still groggy from the power of last night's medicine and visions that flew off all "orthodoxy" maps, I stumbled in from the desert to the Islamic Center of Los Angeles, performed the ritual ablutions (*wudu*) without interference from any concepts or thoughts, just adhering to the body script, and then performed a prayer in the Hanafi mode that I learned as a teenager. My prayer was slow and clumsy, but its secret was Fatima az-Zahra, Fatima the Radiant, the Lady of Light. The script carried me through when my brain moved at half speed. What was Fatima az-Zahra at this point—did I need her to be a supernatural creature blessing me from beyond this world, or the voice of the ayahuasca vine that so many men appeared to witness in goddess form, or just a chemical reaction in my head? The post-ayahuasca prayer had no doctrine, no 'aqida, and could uphold no orthodoxy beyond the fact of my prayer physically looking like other prayers. The setting of the *masjid* and the movements of my body, along with the aural environment produced by Muslims nearby, produced an internal condition. I wouldn't call it "faith," exactly. To borrow a phrase from Brian Massumi, translator of *A Thousand Plateaus* and pioneering scholar of affect theory, I could call it "memory without content."[29] The prayer was an act of my arms and legs and head—and I don't mean my head as in an abstracted mind holding certain cognitions to be true or false, I mean my brow touching the carpet—in the physical space of the masjid, loaded with visual, aural, and olfactory cues changing my body's powers. I have an automatic corporeal plan to guide my movements in that condition, along with words to eject silently—words that most of the planet's Muslims recite in a language other than their own, since only a third of Muslims grow up speaking Arabic. The words are not "words" at that point, but movements of the mouth. The words carry an act of prayer through the standing and kneeling and prostrating and sitting, but do not have to convey an idea. The movements and breaths and words did something to my body that might have been empirically measurable to an outside observer; I don't know. But my body was changing into a Muslim body through these changing postures and recitations, a feeling of a Muslim body and a Muslim body's connectivity to this masjid space along with the other bodies that it contained, with or without a coherence of doctrine. So what can dervish bodies do? Without values sent down from the unseen, what are a dervish body's political and ethical consequences? The collapse of theological transcendence doesn't have to mean deconstruction into amoral chaos and self-centeredness with no sense of community or commitment. The tradition is fragmented and fissured, but so is the individual, his/herself a product of intersecting forces and environments and intensities, defined not as a self-contained singularity but instead by its encounters and connections to other bodies. As Rosi Braidotti has argued, Deleuze's sense of the subject as a rhizomatic set of ongoing and fluctuating interrelations and mutual affectations with others, rather than as a self-contained rational consciousness, can open us to a "nomadic ethics."[30]

Put the dervish bodies in a room together, turn off the lights, start the dhikr and find out.

Conclusions

Thinking about the possibilities for a Deleuzian Sufism, I prioritized assemblages and affects over theology. Calling attention to Deleuze's assemblage reminds us that there's more to this work than extracting concepts and theorizations from great minds of Islam such as Ibn al-'Arabi, al-Ghazali, or al-Ghazali's cooler queer poet brother in order to read them as "systems" or "schools" with or against Deleuze.[31] Rather, when we talk about Sufism, we're talking about *bodies* and the ways in which these bodies organize with each other both discursively and physically (such as the assemblage of a master-centered tariqa or the culture surrounding a shrine), enhancing each other's powers for entering into new conditions. When I think, "Sufism," and consider this construct's possible resonances with a Deleuzian toolbox, I turn to bodies and affect. Jenna Supp-Montgomerie, writing on the salience of affect theory for the academic study of religion, draws upon Deleuze (and in turn, Deleuze's use of Spinoza) to discuss the importance of corporeality and materiality to religion, momentarily decentering "faith"/"belief" as religion's definitive element.[32] When I'm in a khanaqah with chanting and breathing multiplicities or at a shrine between a special dead multiplicity and the living multiplicities searching for baraka transmissions, my experience of the baraka field cannot be reduced to faith in a set of theological claims. Deleuze calls theology "the science of non-existing entities, the manner in which these entities—divine or anti-divine, Christ or Antichrist—animate language and make for it this glorious body which is divided into disjunctions."[33] God can exist or not, or have an existence that transcends *this* mode of being or not, or occasionally descend from the highest tier of transcendence to a lower one, but the bodies and flows are *here*, making affects with their vocalizations of God's names or proximity to baraka-transmitting graves. Baraka is *here*: the energy between bodies, the vibe of the khanaqah, the circulation of forces intensifying or dissolving my sense of a body and self, separate from these other bodies and selves. We recite the names of a nonexistent entity and our bodies change each other, forging a new condition. Neither dhikr nor ayahuasca ever gave me a system; nor did I have a system before opening my body to them. With or without chemical enhancements, when I really get *there*, I don't have doctrines; whatever's happening in my heart rate and breath and frontal lobes and neural pathways has shut down any chance for theology. This is why premodern Muslim jurists argued that when ecstatic mystics such as al-Hallaj enter into states of spiritual "intoxication" and fly off the map—such as, in the Hallajian hagiography, apparently self-identifying with God—you can't hold them accountable until they've had a chance to "sober up" and clearly articulate their beliefs.[34] The mystic's corporeal technology of affect enables connections beyond responsible public theology and the limits of its vocabulary—al-Hallaj's outburst could require regulation to protect the social order but isn't *wrong*, exactly—even if the ecstatic line of flight that he provides must circle around and land you back inside the structure. Theorized in diverse ways throughout Islamic theological, legal, and aesthetic traditions, these drunken heresies ejected from Sufi bodies provoke the recognition that formal articulations of "orthodoxy," bound in the limits of representation, remain inadequate and that articulations of blasphemy could paradoxically be more "true" (or rather, equally true, but true on a higher level, as the privilege of a special class of knowers) than the Islam of common understanding. It is at this point, with Islamic transcendence demanding that language must ultimately fail and thus accelerating toward a theological self-destruct button, that an Islamic atheism leaks from the love for God.

4 / The Immanence of Baraka: Bodies and Territory

> *I take this for the baraka that exudes from you.*
> —UMM SULAYM, collecting Muhammad's sweat in a bottle

Beyond Mecca's city limits, the pilgrim finds Jabal al-Nur, the "Mountain of Light," where Muhammad is believed to have first encountered the angel Gabriel. In a small cave at the top, Muhammad's prophetic career began when he received the first verses of what would become the Qur'an. At the foot of the mountain, before starting upon the rugged and narrow footpaths leading up to the cave, a large sign in multiple languages discourages visitors from treating the mountain as anything special:

> Brother in Islam!
>
> The Prophet Muhammed (PEACE BE UPON HIM) did not permit us to climb on this hill, not to pray there, not to touch its stones and tie knot on its trees and not to take anything from its soil stones and trees.
>
> The good deed is to follow the path of the prophet Muhammed (PEACE BE UPON HIM) so do not oppose that. Allah said "Indeed in the Messenger of Allah you have a good example to follow for him." [AL-AHZAB:21].

It could strike some as paradoxical that the Saudi state imagines a pilgrim's visit to the Mountain of Light as an un-Islamic or even *anti*-Islamic act. The conflict is one between Islam's historical diversity, characterized by a multiplicity of traditions and authoritative voices, and the Saudi state's commitment to a severely narrowed archive as the intellectual repository of "true" Islam. Of course, the long lines of visitors hiking up the mountain, many with significant physical struggle, along with the reverential but rough decorations with which non-state actors had ornamented the cave, reveal that multitudes of Muslims disagree with the official state position. If the state had sought to deterritorialize this mountain away from what some would call "folk" or "popular" Islam, its project has not been completely successful.

The Islamic holy cities or *haramayn* of Mecca and Medina are teeming, as one might expect, with important sites that provide linkages to the sacred past. The meanings and values of these sites, however, remain contested between various interpretive traditions. The Saudi state has grown infamous for its efforts to "correct" popular practices and transform lived conceptualizations of the "Islamic," most notoriously through demolishing such sites or otherwise discouraging their veneration. Through its control over these sites and policing of their visitors' practices, the state constructs and enforces a vision of Islam in which the Saudi kingdom itself becomes the authorized center, illustrating the Saudi rulers' self-conception as "custodians" of the two haramayn.

Since the founding of the Saudi state, these conflicts have reached special intensities at Jannat al-Baqi, a cemetery in Medina that has become a site of international controversy due to the state's demolition of its domes and raised tombs. Bringing the issue of Jannat al-Baqi into conversation with the Deleuzian model of assemblages engages both its arborescent and rhizomatic tendencies, emphasizing the stakes in power struggles over such sites for the Saudi state's self-legitimation and global engagement. Jannat al-Baqi's history also renders it a battleground in a definitive issue for the "Deleuze and religion" conversation—namely, the tension between atheist immanence and theist transcendence—and offers Islamic conceptions of *baraka* as a possible point of entry for engagements of this tension from Islamic archives.

Jannat al-Baqi

Jannat al-Baqi, also known as Baqi' al-Gharqad or simply al-Baqi, is the oldest cemetery in Medina, and lies nearly adjacent to the Masjid al-Nabawi where Muhammad, Abu Bakr, and 'Umar are buried. Al-Baqi hosts the remains of thousands of Companions and various luminaries of early Islam, including A'isha and the other wives of the Prophet (excluding Khadija and Maymuna); Muhammad's daughters; his son Ibrahim, who died in infancy; his grandson Hasan b. 'Ali, the second Imam of Shi'i tradition, along with the fourth, fifth, and sixth Shi'i Imams; Muhammad's aunt Safiya, mother of Zubayr; Fatima bt. Asad, mother of 'Ali; and Muhammad's uncle 'Abbas b. 'Abd al-Muttalib, epnonym of the 'Abbasid dynasty. It was in al-Baqi that ʿAli constructed a "house of sorrow" in which his wife, Muhammad's daughter Fatima, could privately mourn her father's death; though Fatima is also believed to have been buried in al-Baqi, her precise location in the cemetery remains contested, as she had reportedly asked ʿAli to bury her at night so that Abu Bakr could not find her grave. ʿUthman b. ʿAffan, rehabilitated in Sunni historical memory as the third rashidun caliph but exceedingly unpopular at the time of his assassination, was initially denied burial at al-Baqi by his opponents and subsequently buried in the adjacent Jewish cemetery. The caliph Muʾawiyya, who belonged to the same Umayyad lineage as ʿUthman, later merged the two cemeteries, bringing ʿUthman's grave into the bounds of al-Baqi.[1] In succeeding generations, al-Baqi would receive the bodies of notable scholars and pietists, such as the early Medinan jurist Malik b. Anas, eponym of the Maliki school.

An account of the first Muslim buried at al-Baqi, ʿUthman b. Mazʾun (d. 624), speaks to the tensions that have characterized Muslim cemetery practices as far back as the original community. The Prophet himself reportedly marked the grave with a rock so that he could remember ʿUthman b. Mazʾun by it. A few decades after the Prophet's death, however, Medina's governor (later the fourth Umayyad caliph, r. 684–85), Marwan I, noticed the rock and removed it, provoking a local controversy. As Leor Halevi observes, the episode may or may not be historical, but nonetheless serves as an expression of ongoing conflicts over the culture of graves. From virtually the start of Muslim interpretive traditions, communities witnessed a multiplicity of opinions among jurists as to whether (or how) graves could be marked, while various governments took part in both the construction and demolition of monuments.[2]

Traditions of *ziyarat* (pilgrimage, literally "visitation") to specific graves developed in the early centuries, along with their opposition. While Sunnis popularly engaged in grave veneration, some Sunni intellectuals condemned ziyarat as a form of idolatry and flagrant rejection of the Prophet's message, additionally linking ziyarat to groups that they deemed heretical—namely, Shiʾi Muslims—and what they perceived as heretical expressions of Sufism. Ziyarat met its most famed opponent in the Damascene Hanbali jurist Ibn Taymiyya (1263–1328), who regarded the practice of tomb veneration as a reprehensible innovation that he traced to the Shiʾi empire, the Fatimids. According to Ibn Taymiyya, popular practices surrounding the graves of holy people amounted to "imitation of the ways of the polytheists" and betrayed the example of the Companions, who did not build a domed shrine over Muhammad's grave or perform pilgrimages to it. In Ibn Taymiyya's view, Muslims should greet the Prophet with peace if they happen to find themselves at his grave, but traveling to Medina with an intention of visiting the Prophet's grave constituted a sin and could invalidate one's pilgrimage to Mecca. Grave visitation was only acceptable for the purpose of reminding oneself of death and of growing fearful of God, not because one believed that prayers were more effective at a specific grave or that the grave's occupant held powers of intercession with God.[3] At least in his own lifetime, Ibn Taymiyya's efforts against shrine pilgrimage and tomb veneration failed; his position on ziyarat led to his imprisonment in Damascus just two years before he died, and ziyarat remained definitive of what might be called "orthodox" or "mainstream" Islam, supported in governmental and scholarly establishments as well as "folk" practices, throughout Muslim-majority societies.[4] However, Ibn Taymiyya's thought experienced a renaissance in modernity, most notoriously with the Sunni revivalist phenomenon of the Muwahidun, pejoratively known as "Wahhabism." This movement began in the eighteenth-century Hijaz, when Hanbali scholar Muhammad b. ʿAbd al-Wahhab (1703–92) preached for a return to what he presented as authentic and original Islam and targeted ziyarat as this pure, primordial Islam's chief antithesis. Ibn ʿAbd al-Wahhab's opposition to ziyarat rested on two fronts. First, his particular construction of monotheism denounced the engagement of any other supernatural agents, such as deceased holy people, as polytheism. Second, his construction of Islamic authenticity disqualified any practice that could not find an authorizing precedent in the Salaf (who are popularly conceived as the generations of Muhammad's Companions, their students, and *their* students). For Ibn ʿAbd al-Wahhab, to erect a domed shrine over a grave or visit that grave with hopes for its occupant's intercession constituted base idolatry and flagrant defiance of Islam.[5]

Ibn ʿAbd al-Wahhab's alliance with the al-Saʾud family led to the spread of his ideology and the development of a new tribal confederacy, the first Saudi state. During this state's seven decades, Ibn ʿAbd al-Wahhab's followers secured control of the holy cities and destroyed numerous historic sites, such as the shrine for Muhammad's tooth that was broken at Uhud, and including the domes and other structures at Jannat al-Baqi and other cemeteries. Visiting Medina shortly after the end of the first Saudi state, Johann Lewis Burckhardt described al-Baqi as "perhaps the most dirty and miserable burial-ground in any eastern town the size of Medina.... The whole place is a confused accumulation of heaps of earth, wide pits, and rubbish, without a single regular tomb-stone."[6] The cemetery was in such disarray that Burckhardt, while noting the "ruins of small domes and buildings," refused to believe that only the "Wahabys" were responsible, insisting that it had always been neglected.[7] The Ottoman defeat of the first Saudi state in 1818 enabled a series of reconstructions and renovations to the memorial landscape. The Ottoman restoration projects included new monuments for the celebrated occupants of al-Baqi, such as a large domed shrine that covered the adjacent graves of the second, fourth, fifth, and sixth Shi'i Imams and the alleged grave of their matriarch, Fatima.[8]

Amidst the disintegration of the Ottoman Empire, the early twentieth century saw the rise of a new Saudi state that would recapture the Hijaz. On April 21, 1925, the nascent Saudi regime demolished the domed tombs in Jannat al-Baqi and even destroyed the cemetery's greenery. The destruction of Jannat al-Baqi and other sites was met with widespread condemnation from Sunni and Shi'i scholars alike, and the date's *hijri* anniversary (Shawwal 8) is remembered in contemporary Shi'i communities as Yaum-e-Gham, the Day of Sorrow.[9] Throughout the second half of the twentieth century, the Saudi government continued to demolish historical and sacred sites, as in 1998 when it bulldozed over the grave of the Prophet's mother Amina and poured gasoline upon the rubble.[10]

Though Medina holds no formal significance for the rites of hajj, and despite Ibn Taymiyya's condemnations of ziyarat to Medina, it remains a popular convention for pilgrims to Mecca to spend a portion of their trip in Medina, visiting the Masjid al-Nabawi and other sites, such as Jannat al-Baqi. Approaching the cemetery's gate, visitors encounter a large blue sign instructing them as to the Prophet's way of visiting graves ("The Prophet has forbidden to perform salah toward the graves.... The Prophet has forbidden addressing supplications to the dead and asking them to procure for us what is good and ward off what is evil"). Inside the gate, men (the entire cemetery is off-limits to women) encounter a dirt lot with scattered stones that bear no markings to identify the graves' occupants. Stone walkways direct the visitors' paths and determine the graves to which they can have the closest proximity. Though the occupants of the graves are unidentified, 'Uthman's grave is distinguished from other graves by the stones outlining its perimeter, the construction of a raised stone pathway around it, and another blue sign prescribing "correct" behavior. State-employed scholars linger throughout the cemetery to discourage what they regard as inappropriate ritual practices, which sometimes leads to heated arguments with pilgrims. The area of the cemetery hosting the graves of the Shi'i Imams and (possibly) Fatima has been fenced off, preventing Shi'i pilgrims from accessing them. This area includes yet another blue sign reminding pilgrims that the Prophet prohibited prayers to the dead.

In *What Is Islam?*, Shahab Ahmed suggests that the holy cities' twentieth-century transformation expresses "the cognitive and imaginal condition towards which modern Islam as a whole is tending as regards the meaning of the environment of its past." A modern Muslim in Mecca or Medina will "not be able to *locate the terrain* in which his predecessors walked ... a modern Muslim if shown an image of pre-Wahhabi Mecca or Madinah will not *recognize* the townscape."[11] Ahmed describes the Saudi transformation of its sacred geography as a material repudiation of Islam's historical "philosophical-Sufi amalgam" and accumulated archive of interpretive traditions and resources. Ahmed's analysis presents Mecca and Medina in terms of removal, erasure, and restriction, a coercive severing of modern Muslims from historical Islamic tradition in favor of an imaginary "Year Zero."[12]

Jannat al-Baqi as Territory

The Deleuzian assemblage model would present Jannat al-Baqi on two axes.[13] The first axis lies between content and expression, or between a machinic assemblage and collective assemblages of enunciation. The content or machinic assemblage consists of the material, corporeal artifacts, "an intermingling of bodies reacting to one another."[14] The content, in this case a cemetery, obtains its meaning through transformation by incorporeal modes, the dimension of expression or collective assemblages of enunciation. Changes can be made to the physical content—domes are built and destroyed, and the spatial limits of the cemetery have been expanded multiple times—but the content also undergoes discursive change by statements made upon it. In the case of 'Uthman ibn 'Affan's grave, the physical act of changing Jannat al-Baqi's boundaries to incorporate his body, which was initially denied burial at al-Baqi, corresponds to the discursive construction of al-Baqi's value. The collective assemblages of enunciation acting upon the physical content would include a prophetic tradition in which Muhammad prays specifically for those buried at al-Baqi.[15] In another tradition, Muhammad names himself as the first human who will be resurrected, followed by the caliphs buried next to him, Abu Bakr and 'Umar, followed in turn by the bodies buried at al-Baqi, who will be gathered with him.[16] The expansion of al-Baqi's physical perimeter brought 'Uthman's body into an improved symbolic arrangement in relation to the Prophet, better reflected his rank as a rashidun caliph in relation to Abu Bakr and 'Umar, and privileged his grave over that of 'Ali, who was buried several hundreds of miles away in Iraq.

Deleuze conceptualizes the content of an assemblage as having form as well as substance. In his work on Foucault, Deleuze illustrates the assemblage with the example of the prison, in which the content's form is prison and its substance consists of the prisoners.[17] In Jannat al-Baqi's content, the form is the cemetery as a defined space, a territory with borders, walls, and a gate that regulate access from the outside, internal pathways that determine the flows of visitor traffic, stones that mark the locations of graves, frames of brick or cement that distinguish some graves from the others, fencing that obstructs access to specific graves, and dirt. Before the rise of the Muwahidun, the content's form also included raised tombs and domed mausolea. In terms of the substance, we are thinking literally about physical bodies, first the bodies buried at the cemetery, as well as living bodies: the visitors, the state-employed scholars patrolling the pathways, and the guards who control the gate. Inside the gate, all these living bodies belong to men and boys.

At the other end of the axis, the assemblage of expression or enunciation, the bodies buried at al-Baqi undergo incorporeal transformations through which these graves are discursively ordered and receive meaning. The expression, like the content, includes both form and substance. What Deleuze would call the expression's form corresponds to what Ahmed presents in *What Is Islam?* as the Islamic "Con-Text," the archive of resources—textual canons, historical norms, sectarian identities, schools and modes of thought—through which Muslims make meaning in Islamic terms.[18] Ahmed distinguishes the Con-Text *in toto*, the entire "universal lexicon" of Islamic tradition as it remains *potentially* available, and the Con-Text *in loco*, the specific pool of materials that are *actually* available within a given setting.[19] Avicenna, for one example, appears as a crucial ingredient in the Islamic Con-Text in some times and places but does not operate as such for all Muslims everywhere. The Con-Text *in loco* determines the discursive field of recognizable Islamic tradition—its center, margins, and modes for assessing authenticity and authority—with which Muslims can inscribe meanings upon the field of bodies at Jannat al-Baqi. The form defines the shape and limits of the substance, a specific construction of "Islam."

On the axis of content and expression, Jannat al-Baqi appears as an organization of bodies and set of possibilities for deciding what the bodies mean and how Muslims should properly relate to them. Muslim historical consciousness marks the bodies at al-Baqi as some of the most significant figures in early Islam, though they differ greatly in the values assigned to them. Muslims measure these bodies differently—that is, they inscribe diverse expressions upon the cemetery's content. The cemetery houses the bodies of a third of the Ithna Ash'ari Shi'i imamate—four of the twelve infallible Imams—but it also contains the body of A'isha, the Prophet's wife, who has been reviled in Shi'i historical consciousness for her opposition to 'Ali's caliphate, as well as 'Uthman, regarded in Sunni interpretive tradition as a "rightly guided" caliph but seen in Shi'i traditions as a usurper. These graves are coded by the discursive supplements that one chooses for understanding the Prophet, identifying those in closest proximity to him, and interpreting relations among the first Muslim generation. The question of how to correctly engage these graves within the bounds of "Islamic" codes also depends on which Islamic archive gets to speak. The destruction of tombs at al-Baqi and elsewhere draws justification from a hadith in which Muhammad, speaking from his deathbed, curses Jews and Christians for having turned their prophets' graves into masjids. This narration, however, appears specifically in *Sunni* hadith canon, with attribution primarily to A'isha and Abu Hurayra, neither of whom is regarded as authoritative sources in Shi'i hadith scholarship, while Shi'i hadith literature extols the virtues of ziyarat to the Imams' graves. Multiple forms of expression compete to define the substance ("Islam") at al-Baqi and thus determine the meanings of the bodies that it contains. On this axis, content and expression inform and transform each other. Assemblages of enunciation perform incorporeal transformations upon the machinic assemblages, but these incorporeal transformations also produce material change, as the form of expression that successfully inscribes itself upon the graves also decides whether the graves will have domed tombs.

The axis of content and expression intersects with a line that represents the spectrum between reterritorialization and deterritorialization, the assemblage's tendencies to enable or resist change. It is tempting to imagine reterritorialization and deterritorialization as antitheses locked in a zero-sum battle against one another, and even to assign them competing moralities in a contest between good and evil. One might expect that forces of deterritorialization are always on the side of "good," seeking liberation from the authoritarian repressions of reterritorialization. But Deleuze does not treat all deterritorializations as positive events or inevitably the opposite forces of reterritorialization, since deterritorialization can ultimately lead to reterritorialization. Deleuze's treatment of these tendencies calls for recognition that as arborescent and rhizomatic structures can turn into one another, each assemblage contains elements of both reterritorialization and deterritorialization.[20]

Prior to the Saudi takeover, Jannat al-Baqi was territory in an Ottoman imperial milieu. The Ottoman Empire identified itself as officially a Sunni regime, but "Sunni Islam" in this milieu was characterized by a considerably positive relation to the tradition's historical diversity and permeated with potential lines of flight. Ottoman rulers gave patronage to Sufi orders and maintained the tombs and shrines of Sufi masters. In the early sixteenth century, Sultan Selim even gave imperial endorsement to the controversial Ibn al-Arabi, constructing and maintaining an elaborate shrine and masjid at his tomb in Damascus.[21] The permeation of Sufism in the Ottoman regime—reflected in educated elites holding positive views of Sufism,[22] rulers framing their power in Sufi-informed terms, and Sufi orders and masters becoming significant political actors[23]—does not in itself contradict claims of Sunni identity, at least not in historical (that is, pre-Wahhabi) Sunni traditions. Sufism is not a sectarian "third party" separate from Sunnis or Shi'is, though modern discourses (both favorable and antagonistic) have often constructed Sufism as a distinct category at (or beyond) the margins of Sunni tradition.

Similarly, the Ottoman construction of Sunnism would appear to some contemporary Sunnis, following an increasingly reified modern demarcation between traditions, as infused with Shi'ism. Ottoman rulers upheld veneration for the Prophet's family (*ahl al-bayt*), maintaining not only the domed tombs of Shi'i Imams at Jannat al-Baqi, but additionally giving patronage to Shi'i holy sites in Iraq when shrine cities such as Najaf and Karbala came under Ottoman rule in the sixteenth century.[24] As in the case of Sufism, Ottoman support for shrines dedicated to the Prophet's family was not itself a departure from historical Sunni tradition, though the Saudi state and compatible forces and networks would seek to purge such practices from Sunni Islam and recode them as distinctly Shi'i. Finally, Ottoman constructions of "Islamic law" would not satisfy the reification of shari'a seen among modern Sunni revivalists. While privileging the Hanafi school, the Ottomans gave patronage and authority to four schools of Sunni jurisprudence—instituting a "four *madhab*" model of Sunni law that has persisted through the centuries since—and adhered to a conception of "Islamic law" that incorporated fiqh, the rulings of jurists, in negotiation with *qanun*, Sultanic law.[25] As an archive to determine Islam's nature and limits, the Ottoman imperial Con-Text includes what Ahmed calls the "Sufi-philosophical amalgam,"[26] patronage of shrines for the ahl al-bayt, theories of the caliphate informed by models of sacred kingship and Sufi cosmologies, and legal thought that incorporated allowance of historical custom and gave official government recognition to multiple Sunni schools. It is not that the Ottoman Empire was measurably "less Sunni" than the Saudi state (though some Sunni revivalists would make this charge); the Ottoman Empire was in fact more *comprehensively* Sunni, reflecting a greater diversity of historical Sunni thought and practice.

One of the schools of jurisprudence recognized by the Ottomans, the Hanbali madhab, represents the tradition from which the Muwahidun or so-called Wahhabiyya emerged. The resurgence of the Saudi state on the margins of a disintegrating Ottoman Empire consisted of a fragment of the Con-Text, extracted and deterritorialized, that carried the Hijaz out of the Ottoman assemblage. The demolition of al-Baqi's tombs, read in this light, does not mark a straightforward return to "original" or "fundamentalist" Islam, but the expression of a portion extracted from a larger archive, a narrowed version of the Con-Text in loco that provided a line of deterritorialization. The new Saudi regime cut itself away from the Sufism-infused, Shi'ism-appropriating, legally pluralistic Hanafism of the Empire with a dome-smashing, shrine-plundering expression of Hanbalism that promised a return to the primordial Islam of the Salaf and valorized the act of takfir (charging other Muslims with apostasy) upon those who transgressed its boundaries.

Saudi deterritorialization constituted a movement out of empire that became a "negative deterritorialization," meaning that it blocked its line of flight and created a new system of reterritorializations.[27] The destruction and redesign of al-Baqi shut down potential for multiplicity in the Con-Text, erasing possible linkages to Shi'ism and Sufism and concretizing borders between these constructs and Sunni Islam, not to mention denying an internally diverse Sunni tradition. The Saudi project, in Ahmed's analysis, cuts away so much of Islam's historical Con-Text as to deprive modern Muslims of Islamic tradition's resources for engaging complexity and contradiction.[28]

On the content-expression axis of the Jannat al-Baqi assemblage, the graves (content) are reinscribed to signify the Salaf, of whom, Ahmed writes, "no significant physical memory is allowed to remain."[29] The Salaf remains a distinctly Sunni historical category, in which the Prophet's Companions hold universally authorized truthmaking power as a monolithic class, which in turn authorizes the two generations that follow them. Modern Salafiyya oppose the attempt to formulate Islamic theology through Platonism, but still present a historical Platonism in a hierarchical ordering of Muslim generations by their proximity to an unattainable pure template (the Prophet and his Companions); with each successive generation, the copies of copies further degrade, until the end times in which Muslims are nothing but simulacra with no legitimate claim to represent the Sunna.

Shi'ism offers its own pure template in the infallible Imams descended from the Prophet; but in Shi'i historical consciousness, the Companions cannot be imagined as a singular category with shared status, since some Companions supported the Prophet's family while others marginalized, arrested, tortured, assassinated, and waged war against it. For the fullness of its consequences, the destruction of the tombs constitutes a Sunni sectarian assertion even when also inflicted upon tombs for Sunni-specific figures. Though Jannat al-Baqi's pre-Saudi landscape of shrines honored not only the Prophet's descendants but also Companions who were significant for Sunni interpretive traditions, such as A'isha, the domes supported a culture of ziyarat that would privilege some graves over others. The physical transformation of the terrain corresponded to an incorporeal transformation of the bodies and their meanings as demanded by the Saudi regime, which named the Sunni hadith canon (and Hanbali intellectual strategies for engaging it) as Islam's center. On the axis of deterritorialization and reterritorialization, the demolition at Jannat al-Baqi deterritorializes the land from its Ottoman history, erasing mausolea that had been built, rebuilt, renovated, or ornamented by Ottoman sultans, and manifests a Hanbali line of flight out of the Sufi-Hanafi territory of the Empire. Jannat al-Baqi undergoes reterritorialization, however, as the Saudi Con-Text in loco closes lines of flight and connections to other Islamic Con-Texts, both Sunni and Shi'i. Finally, the flattened cemetery expresses a logic that reterritorializes the Saudi kingdom as a natural center of gravity for the transnational Islamic world.

There is a global stake in Jannat al-Baqi's destruction. If ziyarat is legitimately Islamic, the Hijaz cannot claim an exclusive right to pilgrimage, since shrines and tombs of exemplary Muslim figures can be found throughout the world. If constructing domed shrines and performing pilgrimage to the graves of holy people is disqualified, the Saudi project effectively denies alternate centers of gravity across the map of Islam—rich cultures of enshrined saints and local holy places found in cities such as Damascus, Cairo, Touba, Karbala, Najaf, Lahore, and Delhi—and preserves Mecca as the singular, exclusively authentic "holy place" for Muslim pilgrimage.

Jannat al-Baqi serves as a snapshot of a global conflict in modern Muslim communities over the correct system of doctrines and practices surrounding graves, which is more broadly a question of how one properly engages Islamic tradition in all its diversity and historical fragmentations. Throughout Muslim-majority societies, the construction of shrines and veneration of the dead appear as fully "mainstream" practices, covering the expanse of what Ahmed calls the "Balkans-to-Bengal complex" and beyond.³⁰ In historical Islam, veneration of shrines and tombs have been significant components of Muslim life, with or without "official" permission from jurists. But from the mid-twentieth century onward, the modern Saudi state has been exceptionally empowered to position itself as authoritative (for its physical custodianship over the holy cities) and export its ideology (due not only to its gravity as a global canter of Muslim pilgrimage, but also to its oil wealth and significant U.S. support) across the world, while its particular Sunni revivalism has cross-pollinated with other Sunni revivalist movements. As a result, traditions of tomb veneration in numerous settings have been challenged, and Islamic mausolea dedicated to holy figures have been bulldozed, bombed, or discursively recalibrated. Beyond Saudi borders, the most famous incidents in recent years have involved groups such as al-Qaeda and ISIS detonating or bulldozing tombs of pre-Islamic prophets, Sufi shrines, and other Sunni and Shi'i structures deemed heretical by their standards. In Pakistan, Sufi shrines fall under state administration. While violent attacks against the shrines continue from non-state actors, the government has negotiated between Sunni revivalism and traditional "folk" practices by reforming shrine practices and recalibrating the significance of the graves' occupants. State regulation of the shrines actually began prior to Pakistan's independence, as seen in the Music in Muslim Shrines Act (1942) and Female Singers' Prohibition Act (1943) under British rule, and the Muslim League's project to cultivate a uniform and universal sense of Muslim-ness in order to claim the foundation for a state. In 1959, the government began taking over Sufi shrines, replacing traditional caretakers with state-employed managers, appropriating shrines' revenue, and recoding the bodies to erase local variation and fluidity under a modern standard Islam.³¹ The tombs are not materially destroyed as in Saudi Arabia, but rather subjected to a new state imaginary in which entombed Sufi saints become reconstructed as "orthodox" clerical scholars and the potentially "heretical" aspects of their thought are swept aside.³²

Conflict over the veneration of graves and shrines can be read in Deleuzian terms of the assemblage as taking place on an axis between reterritorialization and deterritorialization. Examining the question globally, tensions such as those observed at Jannat al-Baqi can also speak to the Deleuzian tension between transcendence and immanence, which a growing scholarly conversation has pinpointed as the definitive question of Deleuze's relationship to religion.³³ Theologies of transcendence are supreme forces of reterritorialization insofar as they nourish the establishment of arborescent, hierarchical orders, naming natural centers and straightforward chains of command. They impose unity on multiplicity, build structures that resist change, and guard against future fragmentations. Of course, they can also enable lines of flight and break away to form new assemblages, but in the case of the Saudi state, deterritorializing away from Ottoman mystical kingship only produced a more intensely reterritorialized Wahhabiyya regime. Theologies of transcendence inform both the rulers who construct elaborate mausolea for God's friends and the rulers who tear them down in the name of purging Islamic monotheism of historical corruptions. However, I would suggest that these theologies of transcendence differ from each other in the possibilities that they allow for immanence. To explore this idea, I give attention to the notion of baraka as it connects to both the Ottoman and Saudi orientations.

In conflicts over the veneration of tombs and shrines throughout Muslim contexts, we find two competing models of baraka: one that favors transcendence, the other immanence. In the case of the former, baraka undergoes conceptualization as a system of points or credits that a divine sovereign dispenses among human beings from beyond the clouds. Baraka becomes a gold star that God awards for obedience. In this model, the efficacious means of winning *baraka* is to properly understand and carry out God's commands as clearly laid out in a specific collection of texts—namely, the Qur'an, canonically privileged *hadith* collections, and the corpii of supplementary literatures by authoritative experts and commentators. According to the Sunni revivalist version of this archive, building domes over graves and treating them as places of worship have received the most severe condemnation from the Prophet himself. To destroy such sites could thereby be seen as an earning of *baraka* credits. This is the relation to *baraka* furthered by the likes of Ibn Taymiyya, who could be considered an ideological grandfather to the modern Saudi state.

However, the "point system" model is not the only way of thinking about *baraka* and its flows. *Baraka* tends to unfortunately appear in both popular and academic translation as "blessings," betraying its complex meanings in Muslim lives. But as an alternative to "blessings," G. S. Colin's definition accounts for baraka's historical complexity, presenting baraka as a "beneficent force, of divine origin, which causes superabundance in the physical sphere and happiness in the psychic order."[34] Joseph Meri likewise conceives of baraka as an "innate" and "emotive" force that can be located in physical space, chiefly the bodies of prophets and saints and relics or sites associated with them. Baraka exists as a force that can be accessed through things of this world, including not only graves but also shrines devoted to relics such as the Prophet's hair or footprint, the places where a particular prophet or saint prayed, or even the site at which such a figure appeared in a vision.[35] In his treatment of ziyarat, Ahmed writes, "The idea of the cosmic economy of *barakah* proceeds directly from the Neo-Platonic logic of emanation that underpins the Avicennan cosmos,"[36] though I object that baraka's rhizomatic messiness, given the multiplicity of societies in the "Balkans-to-Bengal complex" and beyond that could read baraka through their own indigenous concepts, defies tracking through a singular genealogy. There's even an atheist route to baraka, since lots of Muslims and non-Muslims alike believe in vibes and energies without depending on a god to disseminate them from the great supralunar beyond.

The imaginary of baraka as force informs the logic of ziyarat, as tombs and shrines become baraka transmission towers. Baraka thus becomes an immanent flow, threatening to decenter textualist constructions of Islam and their elite coteries of authorized experts. If visiting the local shrine can spiritually repair us through the transmission of baraka, we might have less need for the prescriptive guidance of scholars and their canonical citations. In Muslim contexts throughout the world, local holy sites offer resistance to a globalizing Sunni textualist revival powered by flows of Saudi resources and networks. When the tombs are destroyed and have been denied their capacity for transmitting baraka through spatial proximity, the scholars take over and reterritorialize baraka as strictly an award that God grants to obedient servants. If baraka exists immanently in the world, it can become accessible independent of the Saudi state's scholarship machine and the exceedingly narrow sense of Islam's historical Con-Text that it's willing to accept. Shrines and tombs become immanent baraka's choke points that, once closed, reposition baraka as accessible strictly through a top-to-bottom flow from the transcendent to the world, thereby empowering textualist hegemonies over Islamic thought and practice.

I would not draw too absolute a binary between textualist transcendence and the immanence of baraka found in shrines and tombs. Rulers have ordered and funded the construction of mausolea to forge their own links to the transcendent, authorizing themselves through relation to unseen forces beyond earthly power. Control over physical spaces such as graves can establish hierarchies and centralized institutions no less than control over textual meaning. Baraka itself can become territory, a powerful currency in negotiations between politically engaged Sufi orders (a historical norm, despite modern portrayals of Sufism as removed from politics) and sultans. "Baraka is, as much as anything else, about power," Omid Safi argues; "the spiritual power of the saint, the power of the saints to interact with mighty rulers, and the power to lend them legitimacy."[37] Sites of immanent baraka remain assemblages defined by power (and power struggle), and Deleuze warns of the ostensibly arborescent "despotism and hierarchy" that can exist within a rhizome.[38] Nonetheless, Sunni revivalist projects have targeted the immanent model of baraka in part because this construction of baraka enables the power to remain local and molecular, resisting the global molarization favored by modern pan-Islamists.

By no means do I suggest that Muslims who favor baraka's immanence are deniers of God's transcendence and supreme agency over baraka, somehow less pure in their monotheism, or neglectful of divinely revealed commands and prohibitions. But as these are precisely the charges levied against many such Muslims by Sunni revivalist discourses, perhaps the immanent model of baraka does enable a cutting across the molar lines and upending the vertical model of "blessings" that rules over the territory.

Conclusions

The conversation between Deleuze studies and Islamic studies remains largely undeveloped, but I hope that a cursory look at Jannat al-Baqi opens portals on both sides. On the Deleuzian side, assemblage theory provides a compelling and possibly fruitful framework and vocabulary for thinking about how a tradition and its various artifacts, whether cemeteries, textual canons, mystical orders, or schools of law, become constructed, deconstructed, and rebuilt. On the Islamic studies side, the history of Jannat al-Baqi and modernity's broader recalibrations of Islamic traditions on a global scale provides a salient site for watching assemblages undergo reterritorialization and deterritorialization. Deleuzian assemblage theory, acknowledging the coexistence of arborescent tendencies and reterritorialization along with rhizomatic tendencies and deterritorialization—in the case of mysticism, think of Teresa of Avila (d. 1582) supporting the Inquisition[39]—complicates the popular reduction of Jannat al-Baqi's destruction to entirely an act of "fundamentalist" repression and hatred for multiplicity, reminding us of the imperial power from which the Saudi state first deterritorialized. Finally, framing the Islamic controversy over shrines and tomb veneration, a historical dispute that has dramatically intensified over the previous century, in terms of *baraka* invites consideration of resources within Islamic tradition to rethink a binary opposition between immanent atheism and transcendent religion.

5 / Arm Leg Leg Arm Head: Five Percenter Theologies of Immanence

> *A specifically philosophical concept of immanence brings with it a specifically philosophical "danger": pantheism or immanence. . . . It makes man commensurate with God.*
>
> —GILLES DELEUZE, *Expressionism in Philosophy: Spinoza*

> *If I'm not Allah, who is?*
>
> —ALLAH

The Allah quoted here was born Clarence Edward Smith in Danville, Virginia, in 1928, and became Clarence 13X when he dropped his "slave name" as a member of the Nation of Islam. His eventual self-identification as Allah did not come with a claim to preexist the material universe, shoot lightning out of his hands, or serve as the earthly vessel in which a higher abstract spirit could incarnate itself. He arrived at his godhood in the 1960s, as an attritioned former member of Harlem's Mosque No. 7 and student of Malcolm X, through an interpretation of the Nation's theology. He spread his teachings throughout New York, founding a movement of young Black men who denied the existence of a supernatural creator god outside the world and, in the absence of such a god, took Allah as their name and claimed attributes of the divine as immanent in their minds and bodies. Whether this amounts to Islamic atheism depends on how you define both "Islamic" and "atheism."

While telling us, "There is always an atheism to be extracted from religion" in *What Is Philosophy?*, Deleuze and Guattari suggest with some confidence that Christianity "secretes" atheism more than any other religion.[1] Why Christianity? F. LeRon Shults confesses that it would be hard to measure Christianity's atheism in comparison to what other traditions can secrete,[2] but he traces the Christian secretion of atheism to a tension between theologies of the transcendent Absolute and human projects of representation. God exists beyond representation, but human beings still need to represent him within the limits of their concepts and language. Shults explains that because "not much can be said about a wholly transcendent, infinite Person," humans inevitably resort to imagining "anthropomorphic and socially relevant supernatural agents."³ Christianity thus secretes its atheism from the crisis of affirming a god's existence when our worlds of reference fail to make that existence comprehensible. In Christian intellectual traditions, this crisis can inform a mystical adventure that seeks to encounter God beyond the inadequacies of representation and/or projects of apophatic or "negative" theology that seek to "un-say" God's attributes and liberate God from the constraints of human language. For Shults, the crisis provides an opening for a "hammering" of Christian theology, an "iconoclastic theology" that extracts Christianity's atheism from within.⁴

If Christianity secretes atheism from the problem of representation, I would ask how Deleuze and Guattari might compare its atheism with possible secretions from Islam, in which we also encounter the tension between representation's impossibility and its necessity. The short answer is that in their naming Christianity as the prime atheism-secreting religion, Deleuze and Guattari have privileged the tradition most familiar to them. Rather than accept their verdict as a natural given and ask how Christianity indeed excels at secreting atheism more than any other religion, we can take the shock of Deleuze and Guattari's language—the suggestion of overtly theistic religions producing interior atheisms that can be *extracted* from them—as a provocation for thinking about the atheistic secretions that can be extracted from Islam.

With this chapter, I am not trying to smuggle a transcendent god past Deleuze's guard, but rather to launch from Deleuze to think about a resource *within* Islamic tradition for an atheism that still makes its meaning in Islamic terms, an atheism that can even present itself as Islam's secret. The tradition offers a diversity of potential lines to that point, but my own routes lead me through "classical" Islamic traditions to land at 1960s Harlem, where a man named Allah reprocessed Islamic theology without reference to supernatural outsiders. If we follow Deleuze's definition of theology as "the science of nonexisting entities,"⁵ Allah was not a theologian; or we could say that Allah offered an Islamic ontology of pure atheist immanence. Regardless, Allah did find his divine name by doing work within a theological tradition, and his intellectual heirs deploy a wide range of Islamic theological resources to erase what they call the "mystery god" from Islam and manifest themselves as the true and living gods of the universe.

The Islam of Islamic Atheism

"Islamic atheism" might logically read as the most excessive contradiction possible; once atheism is achieved, how could it preserve its status as "Islamic"? If one essentializes Islam in terms of a monotheistic faith confession, defined first by a necessary condition of belief, it inflicts a major shock to the system to suggest that Islam could lose or even reject this condition and remain recognizably itself. But the full impact of that shock depends on what we perceive as the possibilities of Islamic theology and the historical range of meanings that it has already covered. To this end, I argue that a Deleuzian approach to the question, before entering into abstractions based on a view of "Islamic theology" as a homogeneous unity with clearly drawn and "natural" limits, would search a stratum for "potential movements of deterritorialization, possible lines of flight."[6]

To think about how Islam could contain lines of flight to its own atheism and how exactly a departure into atheism could remain Islamic, we first have to define the word "Islamic." Pursuing the secretions of Islamic atheism means exploring not only critical tensions in canonical sacred sources and the voices upheld by gatekeepers of "orthodoxy," but also rejected and forgotten archives and voices at the edge of orthodoxy-making power. As much as it belongs to the textualist revivalisms fostered by modern states, Islam also belongs to the minor, marginal, and condemned; as much as these modern states and transnational forces desire a hegemonic, monolithic, self-contained, and historically consistent Islam, the tradition remains disordered and capable of unpredictable connections both within and beyond its borders, which themselves remain in motion. I should say again that I don't personally like using terms such as "orthodoxy," "heterodoxy," and "heresy," for two primary reasons. First, without enclosure in quotation marks, reference to "orthodoxy" suggests that orthodoxy might be a reliably observable thing in the world, an empirical fact of the religion in its correct form, rather than the product of historically specific power struggles. Second, these terms all come from Christian histories, with limited usefulness for thinking about the Islamic constructions and disputations over theological boundaries.

The Qur'an can secrete an atheism but never stands alone, regardless of the modern phenomenon of self-identified "Qur'an-only" Muslims. The Qur'an becomes accessible through the reader's tools for working on it, and some of these tools can be deemed unacceptable by particular orthodoxy-machines. If we're not limiting ourselves only to legitimate connections with proper experts and prestigious canons, we can more creatively explore Islam as a historical tradition that offers a wealth of internal "heresies" and "heterodoxies." Bringing them into this conversation necessitates a reflection on their status as "Islamic" when all responsible Islamic establishments crash down upon them as illegitimate and despicable.

For the construction of a heterodoxy-positive Islam, a useful resource with loads of academic gravitas appears with Shahab Ahmed's *What Is Islam?* The late Dr. Ahmed was very much a classicist and not interested in some of the traditions that I will discuss here, but his effort to assemble Islam's vast heterogeneity and multiplicity into a coherent artifact—what is it, after all of this difference and diversity, that pulls together an assemblage under the category of "Islamic"?—nonetheless provides an opening. *What Is Islam?* gives a case study on its front cover, which includes an illustration of a Mughal coin on which the emperor Jehangir appears holding a wine cup. Ahmed aims to establish that even if Muslim jurists would have condemned wine as beyond the pale of acceptable Muslim behaviors (and Muslim legal conversations about wine's legality are surprisingly complex), Jehangir's wine cup remains an inherently and inescapably *Islamic* wine cup. Muslims and non-Muslims alike popularly assume that Islam forbids artistic depictions of the Prophet, but we also have a rich tradition of Muslims making Muhammad images (even with a fully depicted face) as devotional Islamic art for Muslim eyes. Some Muslims will assert that Muhammad himself prohibited stringed instruments, but Islamic music also includes praises of the Prophet made with them. And regardless of what Islam can be read to "say" about wine, we have Islamic wine cups. Historically, the tradition is characterized not by an uncompromising unity, but rather by fragmentation and paradox. Even the ideal of ijma, clerical scholarly consensus as a basis for determining the Islamic, fails to determine the limits of the assemblage, in part because the clerics have not produced a consensus as to what "consensus" means. Moreover, the notion of ijma imagines creative and authority-making power as resting entirely in the hands of the clerics, and historically, this is a monopoly that has never existed: Islam has always had a life beyond the jurists' reach.

As discussed in Chapter 4, Ahmed's framing of Islam's definition as Pre-Text, Text, and Con-Text, while not beyond critique, allows for a sense of the Islamic that includes margins (while also recognizing that what could look "marginal" in one context, such as mysticism, could be fully "mainstream" and the Islam of privilege in another), multiplicities, and contradictions. This comprehensive view of the Islamic Con-Text in toto (that is, the full archive of historical Islam), allowing for recognition of the Con-Text in loco (the specific pool of materials accessible as

Islamic in a given setting), leads to a different view of the tradition, a decentered, productively incoherent, rhizomatic Islam with local molecular weirdnesses waiting to be recovered and new connections to be forged.[7]

Representation and the Divine Body

Shults centers his exploration of Christianity's atheist secretions on the problem of representing an infinite creator god in relation to a finite created world and argues that the human inability to meaningfully discuss an infinite and transcendent being leads theological imaginaries into anthropomorphism. While his schizoanalytic treatment of religion only meaningfully investigates Christianity, Shults allows that theologians in other traditions (such as Islam) can face their own versions of this problem.[8]

The Qur'an does not self-evidently offer a solution to the problem of anthropomorphic representation but produces a world in which both absolute incomparability and description by likeness are true and yet regulated by each other. The Qur'an affirms God as supremely transcendent, relatable to nothing in the universe, existing far beyond comparison with created things, and promising that nothing can resemble him (42:11, 112:4). But the Qur'an also describes God in highly corporeal and anthropomorphic terms, referring to his body parts and the chair in which he sits (2:255). The Qur'an preserves ambiguities as to how this seemingly corporeal God might be perceived or accessed by humans. In the first verses of the 53rd sura, the Qur'an mentions an unidentified *shadid al-qawwa*, one "intense in power," who descends to meet Muhammad at the horizon, drawing near to Muhammad until they are "two bow-lengths or nearer" (53:5–18). While some schools regard the verses as describing an encounter with God, more privileged interpretive traditions defer the theological tension by identifying the shadid al-qawwa as the angel Gabriel. The hadith corpus intensifies the Qur'an's anthropomorphism, with detailed accounts of God appearing to Muhammad in the "best form." These accounts vary in the strength of their transmission chains, canonical privilege, and intensity: some offer disclaimers that Muhammad saw God with the "eyes of his heart," not the eyes in his head, or clarify that the vision took place in a dream, softening its consequences; but other hadiths describe God explicitly as a beautiful boy, in some versions with details of his curly hair, crown, veil, robes, sandals, and furniture. The boy god even touches Muhammad between the shoulders with his cold hand, causing Muhammad to feel the coolness between his nipples—at his heart, as the divine hand achieved a transmission of knowledge from God into Muhammad's body.⁹ While numerous Companions of the Prophet reported versions of the theophanic encounter, Muhammad's wife A'isha resolutely denied that Muhammad saw God. She insisted that her husband only saw Gabriel and offered a verse from the Qur'an as proof of God's transcendence: "No vision can grasp him, but his grasp is over all vision" (6:103). A compromise tradition, popularly attributed to Abu Dharr, allows that Muhammad simply saw a "light," without clearly confirming or denying a vision of God.¹⁰

Beyond corporeal anthropomorphism, the Qur'an and hadith literature also depict God as performing actions and feeling emotions in ways that speak to anthropocentric frames of reference, with or without a body. The friction between these necessities—a need for God to stand completely outside the created universe, alongside a need for God to successfully involve himself in its affairs, communicating to believers and describing himself in terms that make sense within the limits of their own experience—finds expression in vocabularies of Islam as a spectrum between *tanzih* and *tashbih*. The former signifies "transcendence" or "incomparability"; the latter represents the drawing of similarities, or in this theological context, anthropomorphism. The historical struggle for many Muslim intellectuals has been to allow that each side of this spectrum is true and "Islamic" while locating the perfect point of balance between them, avoiding the extremes of *tajsim* (corporeality) and *ta'til* (negation). While the former stands as a charge wielded by rationalists and speculative theologians against those who appear to interpret scriptural anthropomorphism literally, the latter serves these ostensible literalists against those who seem to call God a liar for claiming in his Qur'an to have hands and feet and a chair.

In a theology without tanzih, God's nonnegotiable supremacy over material reality becomes compromised, and Muslims take to worshiping a god that they made themselves, a conceptual idol if not a physical one. The intuitive move for many Muslims, particularly in modernity, would be to favor tanzih, proclaim that God exists completely beyond any human comprehension, and flatly reject all tashbih as a transgression against tawhid. But absolute tanzih, while affirming *some* verses of the Qur'an, threatens to deny others—namely, the verses in which God tells you about his attributes, actions, and feelings. Without tashbih, God is denied the power to speak for himself and describe himself in the terms that he chooses, because human readers with their theological projects rush to impose speculative allegories upon his words. Without tashbih, we lose more than a man-shaped god sitting in his chair; God cannot have emotional states such as mercy or compassion or perform god functions such as creating, loving, or forgiving, at least not in any way that can have meaning to human readers. While tanzih upholds God's abstraction from the world, tashbih enables God to actually say things and have compelling content. Pure tanzih treats the Qur'an's account of God as a veil of language and concepts that obscures his essence and activates verses such as 112:4—"and is nothing comparable to him"—as eject buttons that necessarily launch a theology beyond the Qur'an's limits, a search for theologies outside the Qur'an that still depend on the Qur'an as their first points of departure. Pure tashbih shuts down the speculative theologian's lines of flight, demanding that "hands" must always mean "hands," but can also deterritorialize the Qur'an away from those scholarly elites and mystical masters who would impose their own strata and hierarchical tiers of knowledge over the text's "plain sense" meanings.

Moving along the spectrum between tanzih and tashbih, which direction leads to Deleuze's absolute positive deterritorialization of the Body without Organs? Rather than imagine one theology as the plane of consistency and the other as the strata, we could draw this line intersecting with the axis of reterritorialization and deterritorialization, creating quadrants in which every theological construction also becomes bound in a relation to power. For some, the most obvious quadrant is the theology moving in the direction of both tashbih and reterritorialization, concrete assemblages offered by the modern Saudi state and its related Sunni revivalisms. In this quadrant, high (but not absolute) tashbih signifies not a strict literal reading of the Qur'an and canonical hadiths, but interpretation by means of anti-interpretation—God has hands because God says that he has hands, and we don't know what "hands" really means when he says the word (this supposed refusal to interpret is the mode of engagement with which Deleuze and Guattari essentialize the Qur'an's entire history). At the diagonally opposed quadrant, we have movement toward tanzih and deterritorialization, a negative theology that deconstructs God's named attributes and self-descriptions; or perhaps the modern popular imaginary of Sufism as entirely individualized "spirituality" that transcends religion, a one-on-one mystical pursuit of direct experience of God with no mediating institutions or hierarchies of human authority. In contrast to this modern individualized Sufism, at the quadrant of high tanzih and high reterritorialization we'd find "classical" premodern Sufism with its hierarchical orders centered on masters who boast lineages of authority and privileged access to the unseen, both imitating and contributing to Islamic models of sacred kingship.[11] Reterritorializing tanzih gives us sophisticated theological abstraction and centralized authority, as in the Isma'ilis, charged with ta'til by their Sunni adversaries. Then we arrive at the fourth quadrant, the movement toward tashbih and deterritorialization: stateless anthropomorphisms, local theologies on the fringes of imperial scholarly "orthodoxies," *hululi* incarnationisms, *ghulat* traditions deifying the ahl al-bayt and perhaps, surprisingly enough, the Salafiyya. When the proto-Sunni hadith scholars of Ibn Hanbal's time faced state persecution at the hands of a Mu'tazila-reading caliphate in which they were mocked as anthropomorphists and crude literalists, a refusal to interpret away the Qur'an's anthropomorphist implications became the line of flight out of a philosopher-king's despotic regime. Centuries later, the medieval Hanbali grandfather of modern Sunni revivalisms, Damascene jurist Ibn Taymiyya (1263–1328), found himself at odds with the empire and was even jailed for his acceptance of anthropomorphist hadiths such as the "Hadith of the Goats" (which describes the goats supporting God's throne, even providing their physical measurements and distance from this world—meaning that God can be located in physical space and measured at least speculatively for his dimensions).[12] As reterritorializations can begin with absolute deterritorializations that remain stratic, even the so-called Wahhabiyya first appear as a deterritorialization, a line of flight from the mystical Ottoman imperium that eventually graduates from a Deleuzian war machine into a full state.

In modern Muslim discourses, it remains popular to assert that "true" Islam flatly rejects all anthropomorphist theology; the abstracted tawhid that would have circulated among high-end intellectuals in the premodern world has become today's popular, "mainstream" tawhid. Whether or not this tawhid of anti-anthropomorphism is "really" anti-anthropomorphist, I wouldn't say that Islam flatly opposes theological anthropomorphism, first because Islam is not an autonomous agent who *says* and *does* things apart from the sayings and doings that humans project upon it. There's no "real Islam" hovering above the fray of humans who argue with each other over what this "real Islam" advocates. Instead, Islam, as far as I can access it, is only what Muslims throughout history have said about it, and Muslims frequently disagree with each other over where and how to demarcate this "real Islam" from the flawed products of human interpretive traditions. Even if *all* Muslims *everywhere* collectively named tawhid as the absolute essence that made Islam "Islamic"—that Islam is *nothing* if not an uncompromising monotheism, surrender to a singular God with no partners or co-gods—Muslims in all their historical diversity would still lack a universal definition of what monotheism actually meant, its nonnegotiable characteristics, or the line of the unthinkable at which its limits were transgressed. Muslims might have produced a "universal" declaration of monotheism with the first half of the shahadah—*la ilaha illa Allah*, there is no god but God—but reciters of this testimony have accused each other of violating its conditions for fifteen centuries.

Even after necessary disclaimers to resist generalizations and essentialisms about a specific theology as Islam's "heart" or "core," I can say that problems of representing the divine infinite, particularly the matter of somehow evading anthropomorphist representation while doing so, have fueled dominant theological anxieties in historical Islam. It's not a given that this tension secretes an atheism, because at numerous points in Islamic traditions, we find celebrations of paradox and confusion in the attempt to know God. But this could also mean that the secretion of atheism leads to an *Islamic* atheism, an atheism made in terms of Islam.

Noah and the Mothership

"It is obvious that a triangle, could it speak, would say that God was eminently triangular," Deleuze writes in *Expressionism in Philosophy*, warning of a "subtle anthropomorphism, just as dangerous as the naive variety."[13] Muslim theological traditions have struggled with the crisis of anthropomorphism, caught between God's transcendence above all human reference points and God's own self-description in anthropomorphic terms (sitting in a chair, having anthropomorphic body parts, etc.). Canonical sources present Muhammad explaining that God created Adam "in his form"; in some versions, Muhammad connects the statement with a prohibition against striking humans in the face. While hadith masters wary of anthropomorphic implications suggested that the pronoun in "his form" referred to Adam, not God—as in "God created Adam in *Adam's* form"—scholars such as the giant Ibn Hanbal favored a more plain-sense read that it was God's form, while reading the tradition with a bi-la kayf resistance to speculative interpretation.[14] The suggestion of a resonance between divine and human faces supported mystical projects that the hadith masters could not have expected, as early mystics in pursuit of divine beauty took to staring at its earthly expression, beautiful human beings. The notorious practice of *shahidbazi*, "witness play," consisted of homosocial contemplations of beauty, with (male) dervishes meditating upon the faces of handsome beardless youths. This was the "best form" in which Muhammad saw his lord; it followed a kind of sunna, imitating Muhammad's experience, though the Prophet's beardless youth was not of this world. Shahedbazi was widely criticized and condemned for its dangerous proximity to both illicit theologies and illicit sexualities but was linked to luminaries such as Ahmad al-Ghazali.[15]

One of the most famous and controversial treatments of tanzih and tashbih in Islamic tradition appears in Ibn al-'Arabi's *Fusus al-Hikam* (*Bezels of Wisdom*), a text that Ibn al-'Arabi claimed to have received from Muhammad himself in a vision. Each chapter of the *Fusus* represents the *fass*, the bezel that holds a gemstone of a specific prophet's wisdom.[16] While the *Fusus* serves to express Ibn al-'Arabi's unique concepts that earned him the competing titles of Shaykh al-Akbar (Greatest Shaykh) and Shaykh al-Akfar (Most Blasphemous Shaykh), this work grew especially notorious for its chapter on Noah, in which Ibn al-'Arabi disparages Noah's spiritually immature grasp of the balance between tanzih and tashbih. Ibn al-'Arabi's depiction of Noah as a failed prophet, along with other offenses in the text, led to jurists attributing the *Fusus*'s origin not to Muhammad but to Iblis (Satan) and calling for all copies to be destroyed in order to guard believers from the danger of Ibn al-'Arabi's thought.[17]

Ibn al-'Arabi points to a verse in the Qur'an (42:11) that declares transcendence ("There is nothing like him") and anthropomorphist immanence ("he is the Hearing, the Seeing") simultaneously, upholding both that God transcends creation and likens himself to it. But paradoxically, it is when God speaks of himself in terms of transcendence, denying his comparability to creation, that he in fact compares himself to creation and thus "makes himself two," while his declaration of immanence makes him "transcendent and united."[18] In the same verse ("even in half a verse," as Ibn al-'Arabi notes), the Qur'an likens God to creation but places God above all likeness. The paradox within 42:11 amounts to the Qur'an making "two calls" to God, one rooted in transcendence, the other in immanence.

To recognize only one of the Qur'an's two calls amounts to a restriction of God and selective acceptance of revealed knowledge. In Ibn al-'Arabi's view, this was the failure of Noah, whose version of monotheism favored tanzih to the absolute exclusion of tashbih. Because Noah only offered half of the religion, his people "thrust their fingers into their ears" (71:7); if he had combined the two calls and offered a more comprehensive tawhid, Ibn al-'Arabi argues, they would have accepted his message.[19] In the chapter's most provocative claim, Ibn al-'Arabi (or the Prophet dictating the text to Ibn al-'Arabi, as it were) reveals that because Noah could not recognize divine immanence, he failed to accept that the "idols" worshiped by his people—Wadd, Suwa, Yaghuth, Ya'uq, and Nasr" (71:23)—were not "false" gods, because these gods still represented the Real, which is "reflected in every worshiped god, whether one knows or does not know."[20] According to the *Fusus*, God's command "You should worship none but him" (17:23) is not a request or instruction to humanity, but a statement of natural fact: God has made the worship of others impossible, as "in every object of worship it is God who is worshiped."[21] Both lovers and opponents of Ibn al-'Arabi could read his treatment of the divine names as an opening to Islamic pantheism: nothing but God can be worshiped because nothing but God truly exists.

In the *Fusus al-Hikam*, we have an Islamic text, presented as a revelation from Muhammad himself to his greatest saint, that apparently sides with polytheists against a prophet. As advanced knowers of God's immanence who comprehend God's names through things of the world, these "unbelievers" surpass Noah in their grasp of divine secrets. As for the punishment that falls upon Noah's people, the *Fusus* offers an esoteric read: Noah's people were drowned and burned in "the knowledge of God, which means perplexity." The Qur'an's note "Except for God, they found none to help them" (71:25) means that God was indeed their helper, and that they were "annihilated *in him* forever."[22]

Noah's denial of divine immanence could secrete a kind of atheism if he has stripped God of attributes and descriptions to such a degree that God dissolves as a knowable entity, losing all power to describe himself and take hold in believers' imaginations. Some triangles need a triangular god. In his Noah commentary, Ibn al-'Arabi acknowledges that scriptural presentations of God, while grasped more comprehensively by elite knowers, offer "easily understood meanings to the common people."[23] This is a lesson in the famous "Hadith of the Slave Girl," in which Muhammad proclaims freedom for a woman when he asks her, "Where is God?" and she simply points *up*, which would trouble some theologians for Muhammad affirming the apparent location of God in physical space. Theologians and prophets work with different priorities.

On the other (and perhaps more instantly recognizable as "Islamic") hand, exclusive tashbih can open another secretion of atheism, since it reduces God to his descriptions *within* human language, rendering God a product of human knowledge and experience. Even without a material "idol," God becomes a conceptual idol because believers only worship representations. Whether or not Islam "inherently" opposes theological anthropomorphism, historical Islamic theology shows Muslims of competing interpretive camps weaponizing the charge of anthropomorphism against each other as the nuclear-level polemic. Rationalists who insisted that mentions of God's hands and feet must be interpreted allegorically charged scriptural literalists with crudely anthropomorphizing God; but literalists threw the charge back at them, arguing that a literal reading did not require God's hand to resemble a *human* hand, while rationalists were ironically the true anthropomorphists, since they were the ones who demanded that "hand" necessarily signified a human hand unless read as allegory. While mistaken for literalists or "fundamentalists," some Muslim interpreters chose a path of anti-interpretation, arguing that a verse ostensibly discussing God's body parts must not be read literally *or* allegorically—as *both* were unjustified speculations on God's words—but accept them bi-la kayf, "without asking how," allowing no explanation of unclear verses beyond whatever the Prophet offered to his Companions. If you needed any knowledge of a verse beyond its own words, goes the bi-la kayf argument, Muhammad would have provided it to his Companions; if he didn't explain the verse to them, or the Companions did not pass this information to the next generation, it's not required knowledge for reaching your afterworld. The Qur'an does not tell you the nature of God's hands; Muhammad did not explain what he meant when he said that God has no left hands, but both of God's hands are right hands. You accept divine revelation and transmitted prophetic knowledge without imposing your subjectivity on the words.

The gradual formation of Sunni and Shi'i traditions crystallized a variety of theological resistances to anthropomorphism, some more resistant than others, and sought middle positions between the extremists who denied God's attributes and those who imagined God to be a corporeal being locatable in time and space. But while various Muslims argued over which faction had truly resorted to anthropomorphism, there were in fact Muslims who did not see the problems of divine anthropomorphism or corporeality as actual problems. Some Muslims who would distinguish between anthropomorphism and corporeality denied that God had a body like human bodies, but accepted God as having *some* kind of body and even offered speculations as to its shape and powers. In the eighth century, Dawud al-Jawaribi conceptualized God as having a mouth (because God speaks) and a heart (the locus of cognition in the ancient world), but not a digestive system, since God does not need to eat or drink. Hisham al-Jawaliqi held that God had a body made of light, with his hair made of black light, and only one eye and ear because he had no need for organs in pairs; Hisham ibn al-Hakam envisioned God as having a body of light that bore a closer resemblance to geometric shapes than the human body, complete with tentacles of light through which God touched things and engaged the world.[24] These thinkers understood themselves as Muslims and their theologies as Islamic. In one of the more famous and outrageous cases of corporeal Islamic theology, universally reviled and condemned by all responsible scholarly clerics, a forged hadith depicts Muhammad as claiming that God created himself by first creating a horse, causing it to run until it sweated, and then creating himself from the sweat. The hadith appears in no canonical source, and premodern hadith scholars attacked it both for its transmission (exposing its origin from disreputable transmitters and sectarian fringes) and as a claim so absurd that it could be dismissed without attention to the chain. But even in the recognition that Islamic theology could *have* such edges, we find a moment of opening, a productive instability. Islam secretes an atheism through its historical multiplicities, since a historicized Islamic theology reveals fragmentations and power struggles. The horse-sweat hadith reveals greater creative possibility for our theologies than the winners of that struggle would allow. Even if the words of the Qur'an come from a source that transcends the created universe, the Qur'an cannot regulate the flows that traverse its words. The text has produced a seemingly infinite diversity of answers to its difficult questions and unclear verses. For Ibn al-'Arabi, the Qur'an's boundless capacity for meanings is not a crisis, but a proof, because God knew and intended all interpretations of the text.[25] Some of these answers receive greater support than others, whether in terms of the faithful masses or intellectual establishments or imperial patronage, and become privileged with markers such as "mainstream," "orthodoxy," and so on. Orthodoxy-machines have ways of pushing out unacceptable and unthinkable theologies and imagining themselves as representations of a consistent and unbroken Islamic tradition. They offer the presentation of an arborescent Islam with a clearly identifiable trunk ("mainstream" interpretive tradition) that emerges as a straightforward manifestation of the roots (the Prophet and his Companions) and from which grow major and minor branches. Historically, what gets called "orthodoxy" in a tradition is more the result of the tree model turned upside down: the branches precede the roots and compete with one another for the chance to define the roots and take on the appearance of the trunk, the natural center. Or the tradition is a naturally rootless rhizome that falls to the arborescent tendencies internal to itself but preserves its openings to bodies without organs that already exist in the strata if only we're willing to look.

Muslim Gods

In addition to intellectuals speculating as to the nature of God's body and its parts, Islamic theology also includes mystical theosophers and sectarian leaders identifying *themselves* as God. The paradigmatic case in Islamic tradition appears in Mansur al-Hallaj allegedly proclaiming, "I am the Real" (*Ana al-Haqq*) and sentenced to death for it. Apart from the question of whether al-Hallaj actually said the words or was really executed for building a replica Ka'ba in his yard, Muslim thinkers responded to al-Hallaj's execution in diverse ways. Some defended al-Hallaj against the charge with theorizations of what his proclamation actually signified as well as an argument that the blasphemous utterances of mystics during their states of ecstasy should not warrant a legal penalty until they had a chance to "sober up." The tradition also produced a view, in harmony with an Islamic affirmation of paradox and perplexity as essential to the path, that both the mystic and his killers were correct. Yes, al-Hallaj *was* the Real, at least in a mode that seekers of a particular spiritual insight could understand; but to protect the masses who were incapable of grasping his gnosis, the state was obligated to regulate ecstatic mysticism and justified in its elimination of the Hallajian threat.[26]

In her scholarship on early Islamic Iran, Patricia Crone provides a survey of leaders and groups who upheld theologies of *hulul*, "indwelling" or "incarnation." The followers of al-Muqanna, "the veiled one," believed that he was the latest in a long line of human bodies occupied by God; whenever God appointed a prophet, he entered the man's body. The Khidashiyya and Minhaliyya believed that God could change shapes and forms, even appearing as animals and plants.[27] Ghulat ("exaggerator") communities such as the Mukhammisa believed that God appeared in the forms of Muhammad, 'Ali, Fatima, Hasan, and Husayn; the followers of 'Abd Allah ibn Mu'awiya believed that God had circulated through the bodies of prophets and 'Alid imams, all of whom were gods.[28] In his discussion of antinomian Sufism, Ahmet T. Karamustafa gives attention to figures such as Otman Baba, whose understanding of wahdat al-wujud constructed God as "manifest in everything and particularly in every human being," including himself,[29] and the Hurufiyya, which held the human face as "the locus par excellence of the continuous theophany of the Divine in human beings."[30] Muslims who hold a stake in the idea of an unchanging Islamic "orthodoxy" (again, with awareness of these terms' limitations) could of course choose to ignore groups that had been disqualified and erased from history by that orthodoxy's authorized enforcers. But in a Deleuzian theology, "orthodoxy" should read as stratification and reterritorialization. Orthodoxies, however defined and elaborated and institutionalized in a specific historical setting, work as the "acts of capture" that "consist of giving form to matters, of imprisoning intensities or locking singularities into systems of resonance and redundancy, of producing upon the body of the earth molecules large and small and organizing them into molar aggregates."[31] The strata impose coding and capture upon the schizoidic rhizosphere of prophetic experience, imprisoning the energy of revelation—prophethood has no "system"—and turn it into sustainable, predictable *tradition*. How do you take Muhammad's angelophanic shamanic ecstatic experience in the cave and recode it into "schools of jurisprudence"? Orthodoxy is the stratum that protects stasis and restricts the tradition's potential for internal multiplicity, unpredictable connections to external forces, and change. Orthodoxy striates the heterogeneous smooth space, cutting lines through the forest to make worn trails and paved roads and direct your thinkable possibilities for movement. The scholars name consensus among themselves (ijma') as a compelling source of Islamic law, though they have not achieved consensus on a definition for consensus.

If orthodoxy is stratification, heterodoxy is theology's destratifying line of flight to the BwO. Presenting subordination to the One as its demand and false promise, orthodoxy gathers and regulates the intensities under its power, directing the flows in their proper channels and slowing them down to manageable speeds. An opening to heterodoxy means a positive relation to difference and multiplicity, an Islam that invites experimentation, unpredictability, and change. Even more vital for a Deleuzian engagement of Islamic theology than what a "Deleuzian theology" might actually say about God is a Deleuzian attention to Islam's destratifying abstract machines, resources that already exist within the tradition for thinking beyond prior limits and creating new realities. Deleuze refers to the strata in multiple places as the "judgments of God," precisely the truthmaking power and privilege claimed by orthodoxy machines. *It's not us, it's simply what the Tradition says.* The assemblage of Islam stands between forces of stratification and the Body without Organs, capable of moving in one direction or the other. An Islamic attainment of the BwO would be reached not by a specific theological school or doctrinal point, nor even by belief or disbelief in specific unseen beings, but instead by a relation to the earthly forces of orthodoxy machines and their projects of imposing "the judgment of God, the system of the judgment of God, the theological system"[32] and *organ-izing* Islam to regulate and inhibit its flows. Deleuzo-Islam looks for an escape from that system.

These hululi Muslims and related groups move Islamic theology toward immanence insofar as they locate the divine in a material body within this world but preserve transcendence insofar as these loci of the divine retain privileged connections to something beyond the world, operating as concentrated incarnations or manifestations of an unseen power outside creation. Whatever is deterritorialized by the ostensible compromise of tanzih undergoes a quick reterritorialization by whatever is imagined to hide behind the god-man, but the god-man does open the exit from the territory. One can read Muhammad's ascension into the heavens not only as a mark of the Prophet's special place in the universe, but as a template for what humans can do, even non-prophets, as a deep library of Islamic mystical ascensions illustrate. Al-Hallaj calling himself by God's name does not lead to the worship of al-Hallaj as the singular al-Haqq, but instead opens up a new world, a Hallajian tradition through which dervishes can understand their own stations. A fifteenth-century polemicist reported that when Ibn al-'Arabi's books reached the city of Zabid in Yemen, Zabid's "ignorant Sufis" began to regard their leader as a comprehensive embodiment of the divine names. Not only did local Sufis call him Allah, but they began claiming divine union for themselves and each other, recognizing everyone in their brotherhood as Allah.[33] My primary concern is not whether the Sufis of Zabid "correctly" read Ibn al-'Arabi and faithfully upheld his system or criminally misrepresented him; Ibn al-'Arabi opened a world for a local circle of fringe dervishes, expressing divine names in their persons, to circulate a theomorphic anthropology of radical immanence.

For its representation of God as a man with a physical body, the Nation of Islam is typically dismissed as a gross departure from "classical" Islam, which is imagined as having a universal and standard theological orthodoxy that imagines God with only uncompromising transcendent abstraction and no space for anthropomorphism. We've seen here that historically speaking—thinking in terms of what Muslims do in real life, rather than Islam as a theorized orthodoxy floating above the fray—it's not hard to find Muslims representing God in various degrees of anthropomorphism and corporeality and seeing the divine in their master teachers. The Nation's deification of its founder, Master Fard Muhammad, does not depart from Islam as a transhistorical totality or essence, because Islam is already too heterogeneous and multiple to have an essence. The Nation might exist outside the bounds of a particular territory, a city of self-identified "tradition" overwritten with striations that deny the existence of a smooth space beyond its limits, seals off the lines of flight that lead to the desert or sea, and constructs a fantasy of its outer reaches as the final edges of the world. But this territory has never held the exclusive ownership of Islam that it claims. Islamic heterogeneities do exist outside the city, wherever one locates the lines at which the city begins and ends (not always so obvious), and the Nation could construct an authorizing genealogy for itself from so many other Islamic flows that have traversed the smooth space outside.

Master Fard Muhammad arrived in Detroit on July 4, 1930, named his origin as the holy city of Mecca (adding that people had not yet seen him in his "royal robes"), and taught from an eclectic archive that included an all-Arabic Qur'an, Jehovah's Witnesses radio sermons, and books on Masonic symbolism. From this selection of intensities he produced a radical liberation theology that flipped the racial codings of theology in a white supremacist regime: Blackness was God, whiteness was devil, and the devils' time to rule this earth had run out. As the Prophet, Fard Muhammad had taught for nearly four years when, after repeated run-ins with the police, charges of human sacrifice, and travels in secret between Detroit and Chicago, he disappeared forever. In his absence, the movement splintered into factions. The group that ultimately triumphed and became the "mainstream" Nation of Islam was led by his minister, Elijah Muhammad, who intensified the absent Fard's transcendence by elevating him from the Prophet to Allah. In turn, this shift elevated Elijah's own status to that of Allah's Messenger and confirmed his claim to power by positioning him as Fard's most gifted student: among all of Fard's followers, only Elijah possessed the spiritual insight to recognize him as Allah, and Fard advised Elijah to keep this knowledge a secret because the rest of the community was not yet ready. The earliest academic work on the Nation, Erdmann Doane Beynon's 1938 *American Journal of Sociology* article on the "voodoo cult," notes that the Nation had become increasingly amorphous since Fard's disappearance and describes Elijah's followers as "an even more militant branch than the Nation of Islam itself" that deified Fard as Allah and elevated Elijah to prophet level.[34] With his theological intervention, Elijah succeeded in establishing a new pyramid of authority, ultimately gathering the molecules of the community together and reterritorializing the Nation under his own power.

Scholarship on the Nation of Islam tends to misrepresent Elijah Muhammad's theology by presenting the divinity of Master Fard Muhammad in terms of "manifestation" or "incarnation," as though Allah relates to Fard as a transcendent, unseen spiritual entity that occupies a physical body. Similarly, discussing the Nation in Sunni community spaces, I have often encountered the objection that Elijah Muhammad's chief offense against Islamic orthodoxy was hulul, "incarnationism." Hulul would be tamer than what Elijah actually taught: in Nation theology as it developed under his leadership, Allah is not a spirit that becomes "incarnated" in a body, because there is no spirit to incarnate: Allah is a living man with a physical body. Master Fard Muhammad does not operate as the corporeal vessel for an immaterial spirit; there is no spirit. Nor is Fard the idealized image of a transcendent being that otherwise exists beyond representation: Fard *is* Allah. Does this take the Nation out of Islam? If the Nation had emerged just a few centuries earlier, it could have been positioned as a Sufi order centered on a "complete human" (*al-insan al-kamil*) who had mastered the actualization of divine names in perfect harmony and accordance with Allah's sunna. During a visit to Cairo in the 1990s, Farrakhan articulated Fard Muhammad's divinity in *al-insan al-kamil* terms, presenting Fard's arrival in Detroit as a perfect performance of Allah's attributes.[35] Shah Nimatullah Wali, a fifteenth-century *wujudi* master who founded the Sufi order to which I had pledged, toyed with these theological ambiguities in his poetry. With verses such as, "Others have seen God through his grace, but we see the grace of God through him," "The grace of God appeared like a light: take a look, behold, it is love," and "Do you want to reach the grace of God? Then leave both annihilation and permanence behind,"[36] the master opened a multiplicity of relations to "orthodoxy": Writing "the grace of God" in Arabic gets you the master's own name, *ni'mat Allah*.

In the decades following Fard's disappearance, the Nation's corporeal anthropomorphism did not express a rejection of transcendent theologies. The Nation developed from 1934 to 1975 as a rigidly hierarchical, arborescent structure, with meaning disseminated top-down from an absent Allah (Fard) to his appointed Messenger (Elijah) to the community. While the Nation officially denied transcendence via unseen supernatural beings, it upheld transcendence through claims to a knowledge outside the world: hidden councils of scientist-imams who control the weather and who will redeem the world through technological marvels, most famously the Mothership. But the Nation also secreted its own atheism from specific tensions within its own archive: The Nation's initiatory Supreme Wisdom Lessons, denying the existence of an unseen mystery god, proclaim God to be the Asiatic Black man. It appears that early in the Nation's history, divinity was located in Black people as a collective. Fard Muhammad's secretary, Burnsteen Sharrieff Muhammad, would later write that in her prayers to Allah, she imagined masses of Black people. Despite Elijah's reterritorialization of Fard as Allah, the Lessons preserved Fard's pre-1934 theology: in the Lessons, the Black man is God, Fard is a prophet. In Nation theology as it developed under Elijah's leadership, all Black men were to see themselves as gods, but affirm Fard as Allah, the supreme god, "best knower" of his time. Farrakhan has linked Fard's mission in America to the Qur'an's explanation for how Jesus could be born without a biological father: just as God says "Be" and it is, Fard came to America to say "Be" and create a nation of gods from people who had been reduced to nothing.[37] The Nation's secretion of atheism emerges from reading Fard's rejection of an unseen "mystery god" decades after Fard himself had disappeared and become a mystery: his face on the wall is both the center of the territory and the opening to its outside.

The Lessons also secrete a possible atheism when they present God as the Black man in an apparently general sense while the Nation as an institution upholds Allah as a specific man of mysterious origins who referred to Black men as his "uncle." In/around 1964, a Muslim named Clarence 13X grew estranged from the Nation in part for his own readings of these tensions. Why would God pray to God's nephew? Outside the *masjid*, he dropped his X and renamed himself Allah. Again, within the specific theology in which he found the name, Allah did not mean that he claimed to be a higher entity's incarnation or manifestation. The divine name signified his mastery over the Lessons. To call him Allah is not a confession of faith in the former Clarence 13X as a transcendent being; the mayor of New York addressed him as Allah because that was his name. As Erykah Badu, an artist well versed in Five Percenter tradition, demands in "On and On," "If we were made in his image, *then call us by our names*. Most intellects do not believe in God, but they fear *us* just the same."[38] According to a Five Percenter *hadith*, Allah once held up a plate and said, "The maker of this plate is the god of this plate."

As Allah, the former Clarence 13X began disseminating his message among young Black men in Harlem and Brooklyn, developing a movement that became known as the Five Percenters. While teenagers in police custody claimed that their community's name identified them as "the five percent of Muslims who smoke and drink," the name actually referred to the Lessons' designation of "poor righteous teachers" who sought to liberate the minds of the masses (85 percent) from the lies and manipulation of the priestly bloodsuckers and slavemakers (10 percent), who maintained their privilege and power through false religions centered on the unseen mystery god of transcendence. Teaching Black men to reject the white mystery Jesus and recognize themselves as righteous gods, Elijah Muhammad would have understood his own Nation of Islam as this enlightened "5 percent," but by the 1960s, the Nation had developed its own "10 percent": Elijah himself and his inner circle, growing wealthy through a community's devotion to the absent god that he represented. Allah (the former Clarence 13X) is said to have viewed his own position as that of a "five percent *within* the five percent."

So we have a man on New York street corners in the 1960s, calling himself Allah and telling Black teenagers that they are gods. Shortly into his preaching mission, Allah was institutionalized after an altercation with police in front of the Hotel Theresa, site of Malcolm X's post-Nation organizations. Five Percenter legend claims that in the summer of 1965, Allah proclaimed from a Bellevue window, "My Five Percenters are not Muslims, and they will never be Muslims," meaning that he had pursued a line of flight out of Mosque No. 7, the intimidation of its Fruit under

Captain Joseph X, the hierarchy under Elijah Muhammad, and surrender to an unseen Allah who had disappeared in 1934 and now existed only as a portrait, the Face for a signifying center. The new Allah of immanence, the former Clarence 13X, had escaped the system and ventured into the desert, where he formed a new assemblage with young Black men who had not been initiated into the *masjid*. Later in the year, Allah was found unable to comprehend the charges against him and was sent to Matteawan State Hospital for the Criminally Insane; he was also added to the FBI's Security Index, a catalog of feared subversives who could be snatched up and placed in prison camps in the event of a national emergency. The list included figures such as Dr. Martin Luther King Jr. and John Lennon. Released from Matteawan in spring 1967, Allah returned to the city and found a swelling movement of gods. New York's then-mayor, John Lindsay, scared shitless by this power, reached out to Allah and engaged him as a respected community leader. On the night of Dr. King's assassination, Allah walked arm-in-arm with Lindsay through the streets of Harlem while his teen gods served as security and became hailed as a "moderate" Black voice by the same local media that had demonized him as a violent extremist just three years earlier.[39]

On June 13, 1969, Allah was shot down by unknown assassins in an elevator. The movement seemingly dispersed for a year, but gradually reterritorialized itself as young Five Percenters on playgrounds and in projects began telling stories about the man named Allah, teaching what they had been taught to a new generation of gods, and ultimately producing New York's first hip hop generation and so many of its "golden age" MCs, such as the Wu-Tang Clan (RZA's name stands for Ruler Zig Zag Zig Allah) and Rakim, who promises, "It even tells us we are gods in the holy Qur'an."[40]

During his lifetime, Allah stood at the center of his movement like a standard despot-god, sending meaning out in concentric circles through the movement. But before his assassination, he liberated the divine name from his control and shut down the routes by which his power could undergo reterritorialization by self-proclaimed successors. Rather than repeat a tension in Nation theology—that all Black men are gods but must recognize Master Fard Muhammad as the "highest" god—Allah scattered the power throughout his community. When Allah instructed his followers to abandon their "Muslim names" and create new names for themselves drawn from Five Percenter culture, a young man known as Bilal changed his name to Allah Born God (ABG for short). Some of his contemporaries became outraged that Bilal had claimed the divine name as his own, but the senior Allah told them that all Black men had to be their own gods and thus had a right to his name. Today, it is convention for Five Percenter men to use Allah as a surname. Allah, the former Clarence 13X, dispersed the power of the divine name, scattering it among a nation of gods rather than preserving himself at the end of a vertical chain as the distant original cause.

During his institutionalization from 1965 to 1967, Allah mentored a white teenager named John Kennedy who had been dumped at Matteawan for stealing a car. Young John had been beaten into a coma upon arrival, and as the hagiography goes, regained consciousness to find Allah standing over him.

"You are a righteous man," Allah declared.

"Well, you must be God," John Kennedy answered. Allah told him that yes, he was Allah, and he took in John as his disciple. Allah named him Azreal, after the Islamic angel of death. In the forty years that followed, Azreal remained in Allah's nation, received with respect and affection by the gods as an elder from the sacred past, sometimes even acknowledged as a god himself. Early in my encounter with the Five Percenters, I met Azreal in Harlem and became his student. During our time together, Azreal named me Azreal Wisdom, meaning "Azreal #2" in the Five Percenters' sacred algebra (he also told me that in the future, he might adopt the name Albino Unicorn Allah). Life as an American Muslim provided my point of entry into this territory; the Five Percenters' location *within* Islamic tradition was what provided the point of our linkage. I would pinball between the Nimatullahis, a 500-year-old Iranian wujudi Sufi order with a lodge in downtown Manhattan, and the Five Percenters' "Allah School" uptown in Harlem, and from their overlaps and resonances pulled together my own Islamic assemblage.

"Islamic" does not always mean the same in this context as "Muslim." Five Percenters tend to claim Islam as a "way of life" but reject self-identification as Muslims (with the rationale that Muslims submit *to* Allah, but a Five Percenter *is* Allah), though some factions and schools of thought within Five Percenter tradition have pushed back against this, either by aligning with Farrakhan's Nation of Islam or participating in Sunni communities (as with the elder First Born Prince Allah) or engaging the paradoxes and complexities of classical Sufism. In the settings of American Islam, Five Percenters have contributed to the Con-Text in loco as part of the contextually specific archive; Five Percenter tradition adds to the available pool of resources through which seekers can make meaning of themselves and their worlds *in terms of Islam*. Universal Shamgaudd Allah, one of the earliest Five Percenters in Brooklyn (and designer of the community's Universal Flag), had reported that the Father allowed his Five Percenters to pursue any religion, so long as they denied that religion's theological transcendence and understood their own immanence as the highest force in that religion. Universal Shamgaudd Allah also claimed that the Father instructed Five Percenters interested in the Qur'an to pursue Yusuf Ali's translation for its positive relationship to Sufism and notes on the Qur'an's disconnected "mystery letters" (bearing in mind that this was in the 1960s, before Saudi media forces edited all unacceptable content from Yusuf Ali's commentary). Whether or not the historical Father "really" offered such prescriptions is beyond my scope (Universal Shamgaudd Allah, while revered in the community's historical consciousness, operates as a bit of a hagiographical "hadith factory" along the lines of Abu Hurayra in classical hadith canon), but this Five Percenter hadith has become a deterritorializing line of flight, encouraging the tradition's capacity for rhizomatic connections and permeable borders. There's not much in terms of a prescription for what exactly "God" means here: Five Percenters can treat their personal divinity as a matter of mystical pantheism or connection to a living conscious universe or read it entirely in a materialist criticism of religion and spirituality, an anarchist "no gods, no masters" replaced with "I Self Lord Allah Master" (the Five Percenters' reinscription of I.S.L.A.M.). If you're Allah, you are *rabb al-'alamin*, lord of all the worlds, meaning that you can enter into thought-worlds such as Christianity and recenter yourself as Christ, or become a Buddhist if this means becoming Buddha. You are the maker and owner of Islam, the object of your own surrender. Like First Born Prince Allah, nicknamed the "Sunni god," who was washing for prayer when he glanced at the mirror and recognized himself as the secret of his prayer, you can pray as a Sunni Muslim in the Sunni masjids and yet submit to your own divine self. Some Five Percenters engage the Nation of Islam, some join Sufi orders or otherwise construct a Sufism of immanence through bewildering quotes from al-Hallaj, Ibn al-'Arabi, and the Punjabi poet-saint Bullhe Shah, and some have no interest in Islamic tradition whatsoever. Some are Buddhists, and some realize that they are Allah through an esoteric study of pre-Islamic Egyptosophy. As Allah, you can experiment on your own smooth space, forging connections between multiple planes of consistency, patching together your book of life from the resources most useful to you. Hip hop artist Vast Aire of Cannibal Ox, for one example, builds as a Five Percenter with the righteous name Vishnu Allah. The Five Percenters are rhizomatic in their capacity for linkages, each Allah making a new universe of meanings, and yet preserve sufficient territoriality and coherence as a Five Percent *Nation* through the strata of shared history and sacred founders, internal vocabularies, collective identification with a culture and flag, and a mutually accepted canon of intellectual resources (the Nation of Islam's Supreme Wisdom Lessons and Allah's alpha-numeric keys for unlocking them). The most important stratum is affirmation of the Black man as God, though even this stratum contains room for movement and negotiation, both in determining the precise meaning of "God" and who can enter the category. As noted earlier, the question of how the Five Percenter assemblage should relate to other assemblages, such as the Nation of Islam or Islam more broadly, receives diverse answers. Gender and race also undergo diverse recodings by major and minor voices: though the community tends to favor a patriarchal view of the Black *man* as God, some Five Percenters recognize women as gods (a view that Allah favored in at least one case). While Five Percenters generally embrace a global vision of Blackness (in which everyone who's not "white" is Black, thus God), some have also accepted white Five Percenters as gods. The Five Percenters resist many destratifications commonly associated with religion but have not performed the radical destratification that leads to a "demented or suicidal collapse": their Body without Organs remains a body.[41]

Five Percenters recalibrate the meanings and functions of "religion," which cannot be totalized as a system of rituals for engaging supernatural agents if the rituals remain after the supernatural agents are gone—as in Elijah Muhammad performing the pilgrimage to Mecca in the 1950s, kissing the Black Stone: "So there I was kissing the sign of myself and I didn't want to tell the Sheik, This is Me you are talking about here."[42] Or First Born Prince Allah continuing his ablutions in the sink after realizing the truth, washing for a prayer to *himself*. Many Five Percenters indeed object to the label of "religion," but wouldn't think of their tradition as "atheist" because even as they deny the existence of unseen "mystery gods," they remain gods themselves. They do possess a theology, but one without interest in nonexistent entities. As the Supreme Wisdom Lessons report, "The Son of Man has searched for that mystery god for trillions of years and was unable to find a mystery god. So they have agreed that the only god is the Son of Man. So they lose no time searching for that which does not exist."[43] Transcendence is absence. The ethical and political consequence of the former Clarence 13X's project is that the value of Black life does not depend on judgments from outside; power to manifest the value of Black life does not depend on a distribution of power from above. These values and powers are immanent in Black bodies, not as promises to be interpreted in a top-down scripture.

Five Percenter tradition offers an Islamic atheism (or an Islamic theology of pure immanence) when Five Percenters envision their knowledge of God-as-self as the hidden heart of Islam, a truth that they locate within

FIGURE 5. Five Percenter pin bearing Allah's portrait. Author's collection.

the Islamic archive. Their godhood is the reality for which al-Hallaj was killed, the secret jewel buried under the masjid, the meaning of the prophetic hadith, "He who knows himself knows his lord" (a rendering of the Delphic Maxim as words of Muhammad with no isnad evidence as an authentic transmission, though Ibn al-'Arabi sensed in his gut that it was legitimate).[44] Many Five Percenters, while vehemently rejecting supernaturalist theologies, support their pure immanence with citations from the Qur'an, classical Sufi masters, Isma'ili esotericism, and theories of the Imamate, along with teachings of the Honorable Elijah Muhammad. In his lyric, "It even tells us we are gods in the holy Qur'an," Rakim hammers theology from within, as an Islamic theologian himself, with a hammer that the masjid provided.

The triconsonantal Arabic root signifying prayer, s-l-w, also signifies blessing. Prayer is salat; and when Muslims call for blessings (salawat) upon the Prophet, they say, Salla Allahu alayhi wa salam or Salli 'ala Muhammad wa ale Muhammad. We do salat and ask for God to do salat. We bless and God prays.

With the secretion of its atheism, the Qur'an might expire itself. If interpreting a text creates its author, and the Qur'an "tells us we are gods," who wrote the Qur'an? Who's the Allah giving away his name? If the

Qur'an tells you that you are a god, do you still need the Qur'an, or has your reading freed you from reading? In the Supreme Wisdom Lessons, Master Fard Muhammad asks about the Qur'an's author. The Qur'an and Bible were written by the original people, his student answers, and will expire in the year 25,000. Elijah Muhammad fabulated unrecognizable future Muslims yet to come with his promise of a coming book to render both the Qur'an and Bible obsolete. The Lessons also appear to treat "Qur'an" as interchangeable with "history"; the "wise man of the East" writes his Qur'an/history in advance and makes it equal to his planet's circumference, 25,000 years as (approximately) a year for every mile. Allah, the former Clarence 13X, deciphered the Supreme Wisdom Lessons with his alpha-numeric systems of Supreme Mathematics and Supreme Alphabets, in which every number and letter signified an attribute. Digit-summing the Qur'an's expiration date, we get 2+5+0+0+0=7, which corresponds to God in both systems: in Supreme Mathematics, the number 7 signifies God; in Supreme Alphabets, the letter G also signifies God and happens to be the seventh letter. In Supreme Mathematics, one could read the equation as Wisdom (2) added onto Power or Refinement (5) and three Ciphers (0) *borns* God (7). In *a* Five Percenter reading of the Lessons—not *the* reading, because the gods continually draw up new science from the text—the expiration of the Qur'an and start of a new one correspond to knowledge of self as God. When you're washing for prayer and look up at yourself in the mirror and it hits you that you are the god of immanence, the year 25,000 has come and scripture has expired. In the Nimatullahi Sufi order, where dervishes greet each other with "Ya al-Haqq" (O Reality), calling each other by the name of God for which al-Hallaj reportedly tasted martyrdom, a shaykh told me, "We don't advocate reading the Qur'an here." Though Allah, the former Clarence 13X, supposedly preferred Yusuf Ali's translation of the Qur'an (because, an elder god claimed, Allah liked Yusuf Ali's Sufism-compatible appendices and interest in the Qur'an's "mystery letters"), we have no record of Allah quoting from the Qur'an or citing it in an argument. Interpretosis is the disease of priests, not gods.

Conclusion: The Seal of Muslim Pseudo

> *Your only choice will be between a goat's ass and the face of the god, between sorcerers and priests.*
> —GILLES DELEUZE AND FELIX GUATTARI, *A Thousand Plateaus*

I have pushed the idea that pursuing a Deleuzo-Islamic theology would not simply become a matter of reading Deleuze against the Qur'an or a foundational thinker such as al-Ghazali and asking whether one's ontology of immanence and atheism could find common ground with the transcendent theism of the other (though I have also indulged in that search, looking for pockets of immanence in Islamic traditions). More urgently, I argue that Deleuzo-Islamic theology starts not with the problems of transcendence and representation, but the question of how Deleuze's concepts change the journey. Look at the tree and ask how it can be turned into a rhizome; expose the opportunities it offers for escape and creative transformation. Ask how the assemblage has been made, what forces collected and organized it in resistance to mixture and change, and then locate the lines of flight, the secret passages and underground tunnels that allow for movement. In conversations of Muslim jurisprudence, we see the running opposition of *taqlid* (consistent adherence to a legal school) and *ijtihad* (independent reasoning). Ijtihad could act as a tradition's self-destruct button and even the escape from transcendence, or it could enforce transcendence with new intensities by closing the lines of flight opened by centuries of legal thought. In Western discourses, ijtihad often appears as the "liberal" or "progressive" line of flight from conservative strata of tradition; but ijtihad can also produce the severe reterritorialization claimed by Salafiyya networks asserting that they can cut through all the strata and warp-zone across history to restore the primordial Muslim society in absolute conformity to transcendence, freed from all pollution of human subjectivity. Depending on the priorities of the *mujtahid*, ijtihad can get you a transgender-affirming fatwa or a prohibition of women driving cars. While progressive Muslims might think of ijtihad as affirming every believer's personal agency, conservatives maintain a sense of scholarly prerequisites needed to qualify a mujtahid; it's not a tool that just anyone can use to break the system, but a clerical privilege that can absorb new challenges and keep the system intact. Just as any assemblage contains both rhizomatic and arborescent tendencies, taqlid and ijtihad are bricks that either build houses or go flying through windows, depending on the moment.

Some years ago, I attended a weekend seminar in Calgary taught by Yasir Qadhi. During one of his lectures, Qadhi referred to what many would consider the definitive controversy in early Islamic theology, the question of whether the Qur'an was created or uncreated. Qadhi represented what has been established as the Sunni "orthodox" position for more than a thousand years: that the Qur'an, as God's speech, preexisted the universe and that it was essentially unthinkable for a legitimate Muslim to believe that the Qur'an had been created. Moreover, he took it for granted that everyone in the audience, presumably "orthodox" Muslims in more or less the same universe of Sunni Islam that he inhabits, shared in this doctrinal point as one of the universal Islamic postulates that go without saying. But in a later Q & A session, someone asked how one could possibly say that God did not create the Qur'an, if God was indeed the creator of all things. Qadhi answered the question with patience, but the moment revealed a disconnect between Qadhi's training as a professional theologian and scholar of Sunni intellectual history and the multiple "commonsense" theologies that occupied the lecture hall. The person asking the question was not, as far as I expect, speaking from a sectarian fringe or "heterodox" identity, but rather asked as a self-identifying "normative" or "mainstream" or "orthodox" Sunni Muslim who had never heard of the Mu'tazila or their premodern controversy and thus took it as a natural given that, "according to Islam," God created *everything*, which would obviously include the Qur'an. Qadhi's line-drawing ultimatum made no sense in the questioner's Sunday-school monotheism, which could teach "true Islam" without a need to historicize it or even mention the Mu'tazila.

Islamic traditions do contain spaces for the notion that knowledge and comprehension are accessible at different levels to different classes. For both the interests of personal salvation and social order, in a classical opinion, the masses should stick to the most straightforward, plain-sense grasps of Islamic theology without exploring the complexities of difficult verses. When the Qur'an says that God sits in a chair, the masses should accept God's self-description without trying to decode what it "really" means, while trained theologians and philosophers explore the revelation's interior. In the modern world, we can observe a theological bottleneck effect in which ideas that had been the premodern domain of elites now circulate as "mainstream" and "universal" Islam for many communities. But these waves and flows and moments of rupture between scholarly clerics and "average" Muslims establish the impossibility of Deleuzo-Islamic theology, if such a project requires Islam to stand still for Deleuze to capture it. There is no singular "Islamic theology." It is always multiple, always heterogeneous. To deny the instability and incoherence of Islamic theology and simply read Deleuze against elite Muslim thinkers would deprive us of a prime Deleuzian tool, the assemblage.

In the early 'Abbasid caliphate, as the new capital of Baghdad became a cosmopolitan world city equipped with a vibrant book market and populated with an extraordinary diversity of Muslim groups that included philosophers, speculative theologians, occultists, astrologers, and astrolaters and a variety of charismatic fringes, all working in constant exchange with non-Muslim communities, a network of clerical scholars reterritorialized itself as the *ahl al-hadith*, the People of Hadith (often called "Hadith Folk" or ahl al-sunna, People of the Sunna). Though enjoying grass-roots populist support, the network was less favorably viewed by intellectuals and even underwent persecution at the hands of a philosopher-king caliphate on the point of the Qur'an's uncreated nature (which turned these grass-roots clerics, at least the ones who refused to capitulate, into folk heroes). The People of Hadith outlasted the Mu'tazila platform that had targeted them and ultimately triumphed as the deterritorialized fragment that formed a whole new assemblage, or rather took over the assemblage from which it had taken flight, becoming a seed for later "mainstream" or "classical" Sunni Islamic tradition.

The ahl al-hadith's scapegoat, its despised counterbody, consisted of the philosophers, speculative theologians, proto-Sunni schools, proto-Shi'is, ascetics, and mystics, everyone who sought to negotiate with or navigate around the hadith-defined Sunna, whether by means of their allegorical interpretations of difficult verses and *hadiths*, training in Hellenic literature, or allegiance to transcendent masters and Imams. These groups were derided collectively as *ahl al-rayy*, the People of Opinion; or *ahl al-ahwa*, the People of Desire; or *ahl al-bida'*, the People of Innovation. Bida' survived through the centuries as the antithesis of Sunna and potent disqualifier of any practice, concept, or community that could not ground itself in the most explicit and self-evident reading of sources and methods that the Sunna's custodians had determined to be authentic.

The trilateral Arabic root *b-d-ʿa* appears four times in the Qur'an: two in which the root expresses a positive meaning, two with a negative connotation. Both positive usages appear as descriptions of God in the context of anti-Christian polemics. In 2:116–17, the Qur'an scoffs at the suggestion that God has a son, since God is the originator (*al-badiʾi*) of the heavens and earth and wills things into existence simply by saying "Be." In 6:101, the Qur'an again dubs God "originator of the heavens and earth" and asks how he could have a son when he does not have a wife and is the creator of all things. In traditions of God having ninety-nine names derived from descriptions of him in the Qur'an, al-Badiʾi finds inclusion as a divine attribute. Conversely, the two instances in which the *b-d-ʿa* root appears with a negative connotation refer to human beings. In 46:9, the Qur'an instructs Muhammad, "Say: 'I am not a new thing (*bidʾan*) among the messengers.'" In 57:27, the Qur'an gives a favorable account of Jesus's followers as characterized by their mercy and compassion, but also mentions "monasticism which they innovated" (*rahbaniya abtadʾawha*) without receiving such a command or permission from God. In these four appearances of the root, the Qur'an praises God as the one who does *b-d-ʿa*, tells Muhammad to deny that he does *b-d-ʿa*, and criticizes Christians for doing *b-d-ʿa*. The hadith corpus further enforces the condemnation of human bidaʾ, "innovation," as a reprehensible departure from the template of perfect humanity set by the Prophet. Numerous reports in the canonical Six Books, passed down through multiple Companions, present Muhammad warning of innovation or condemning the innovator. The Prophet tells us, "Every bidaʾ is a *dalalatun*"—that is, an error, misguidance, delusion.[1] Hadith canon demonizes bidaʾ more intensely than the Qur'an because the two literatures reflect their different historical milieus. The Qur'an, immanent in Muhammad's own plane, speaks as though the Hour will come any second, not even anticipating that the world could outlast its immediate audience. Developing across generations from the original Muslim community into the early medieval period, the hadith corpus expresses a more intense concern with the community's long-term historical consciousness, preservation of the Prophet's legacy, legitimate connections to the sacred past and its superior generations, and the problem of distinguishing authentic Islam from later deviations and corruptions. While the Qur'an does not express interest in an earthly future (apart from the conclusion of earthly time), the hadith corpus warns of dystopian scenarios before the final battle and provides an abundance of hints and signs as alerts for the coming of the end times. In a famous hadith, the Prophet warns of a future in which Islam is divided into seventy-three sects, with only one capable of representing true Islam.[2] Bida' leads to difference, and difference destroys Islam.

For a Deleuzian analysis, such verses and hadiths raise immediate red flags: the Salafi binary opposition of sunna vs. bida' subordinates human imagination and the unstable flows and vibrations of life to judgments under a nonnegotiable divine order. This anti-innovation weaponry, however, has been picked up by just about everyone, including those who would wield it against the Salafiyya. The "religion vs. culture" discourse has proliferated with such success in Muslim communities that intellectuals and activists argue for feminism-compatible Islam not as a radical transformation or the creation of something new, but as a retrieval of the pure and unchanging Real from centuries of historical contamination and misreadings. Feminist and antifeminist Islamic revivals often work within the same logic, in which "true Islam" is defined by its timelessness, privileged as transcendent above culture, and contrasted with Islam as reproduced in human subjectivity, necessarily an inferior copy of the Real.

For the sacred sources to undergo change would mean that they became immanent in the world and history rather than transcendent above it, no longer floating above our reach. Tradition-making forces seal off those potential openings: the Qur'an offers a perfect reproduction of God's timeless uncreated speech, and Muhammad's Sunna cannot be stained by innovation. Even Muhammad's body remains unchanging: though early narrations of Muhammad's death depicted Companions as confirming his death by observing typical signs of human decomposition, later sources would affirm that prophets remained alive in their graves and that the earth was prohibited from consuming their bodies. The concept of Muhammad's bodily integrity and sentience in his grave soothed anxieties that if Muhammad could not bear witness to the prayers and deeds of his community, they would go undocumented.[3] For the prophetic body to do what prophetic bodies do, it must remain intact.

The problem with the Qur'an and hadith literature conceptualizing innovation as deviance, as in the case with Deleuze's scapegoat cutting out from the center to the edge, is that without bida', the regime could not exist. This was Abu Bakr's caution in Sunni accounts when, after a number of Qur'an memorizers were killed in battle, "Umar suggested that they compile the Qur'an's verses into a book. Abu Bakr asks, 'How can I do a thing that I did not see the Messenger of God do?' 'Umar answers, "By God, it is good.""[4] Likewise, the hadith corpus would not have been possible without a creation of new machines: the isnad, the chain of transmission by which an oral tradition could be tracked and vetted; the practice of compiling hadiths in written collections, which was initially resisted by hadith masters who saw the writing of hadiths as a caliphal takeover of their territory (and who made their point by circulating hadiths in which Muhammad or his Companions condemned the writing of hadiths); the introduction of paper technology through Chinese prisoners of war in the eighth century CE, which made hadith books easier to produce; and an evolving doctrine that held the Companions—eventually defined as anyone who met Muhammad, accepted Islam while Muhammad was still alive, and her/himself died as a Muslim—to have been universally trustworthy as a class of reporters, despite a history of ruptures in which the Companions themselves accused each other of lying and even killed each other on the battlefield. The intensification of these conflicts into long-lasting partisan divides apparently contributed to the development of hadith science. In Muslim's *Sahih*, Ibn Sirin narrates that it was not until after the Fitna that anyone asked about chains of transmission for hadiths: from then on, "They would look to the People of Sunna and take their hadiths, and look to the People of Bida' but not take their hadiths."[5]

This moment exposes a fissure in the construction of bida'. The Prophet did not transfer his experiences of revelation into a book between two covers, present his followers with a methodology for vetting statements attributed to him, or develop a legal system with its own logic through which a jurist could answer new questions in the Prophet's absence. Muhammad did not leave behind a formal "school" of theological or legal thought that could give stability and coherence to what had been an unpredictable twenty-three-year run of intense bodily possessions. A community that had lost its prophet needed the spirit to become structure. Without the possibility of more Qur'an coming, the smooth space of "Islam" on which these forces traveled had to become striated, mapped and gridded into a predictable system with limited pathways. The Sunna, the truthmaking precedent of Muhammad as reliably transmitted by his Companions and the generation after them, the Successors, is supposed to preserve the sacred past, but cannot do so without breaking from it. The Qur'an never uses the word sunna in reference to Muhammad's habit as *the* Sunna, instead describing the sunnas of past nations that were wiped out for their wickedness.[6] The development of the Sunna as a concept, along with its associated technologies—hadiths, sophisticated methods of assessing hadiths for their reliability, the preservation of hadiths in massive collections and the supplementary literatures of transmitter catalogs—responds to a crisis that would not have existed at the origins. The Prophet warns that bida' is always error, but without bida', the Sunna is gone.

When everything becomes bida', the tag of ahl al-bida' loses its polemical thrust. Deleuze's scapegoat runs across the concentric circles from the center into the desert, reviled and cast away as everything that the despot-god must condemn and destroy, but Deleuze's scapegoat is also that on which the despot-god's existence depends. Here I want to write some Deleuzian scapegoat fan fiction, following the scapegoat's wanderings across the smooth desert, where the new combinations that it forms with other bodies makes it more powerful—but this in turn enhances the power from the center despot-god that exiled the scapegoat. Everything to which the scapegoat connects also becomes connected to the center: the line of flight is not only an escape but a tunnel for smuggling things *in*. The bida' expelled from the center can find its way back, and the atheism secreted from within Islam's unresolved internal heterogeneity remains an *Islamic* atheism, made and defined by Islam machines.

Islam secretes atheism when the ideal of a pure and unchanged tradition, transcendent to history, falls apart and we are left only with the flimsy efforts of human beings and communities to make sense of these materials on the plane of immanence. The brilliant work of Qur'an interpreters to reread and produce new understandings of the text does not go "deeper" into the words but remains on the surface. This is the prerequisite for Deleuzo-Islamic theology, rather than taking Islamic theology for granted and trying to do Deleuzian work inside it: asking not how Deleuze might read alongside "what Islamic theology says" but instead asking how this assemblage of Islamic theology was made, what conditions enabled the meeting of forces that brought it into being, and what kinds of life powers are harnessed or regulated in the process. Deleuzo-Islamic theology is atheist because it frees the texts from interpretation, surrenders purity, and finds dirty historical monisms on the ground in which the inside and outside are already connected. Islam's real power would be its power of immanence, its capacity for creative movement and change and meaning-making at this level of being, the only level.

Some well-worn tropes, coming from both Muslim and non-Muslim sources (either calling for adherence to the timeless tradition against pressures from outside or demonizing Islam as the "antimodern"), name Islam's essence as nonnegotiable resistance to change. Both pious neo-traditionalists and anti-Muslim racists depend on a very narrow and selective image of what counts as "Islam" to make their case. To varying degrees based on the particular neo-traditionalism that they espouse, neo-traditional revivalists would see Islamic multiplicity as the problem: if Muslims erase intellectual and cultural differences and return to the unity of a transcendently pure origin, they would theoretically replicate the golden age. But Muslims' past unity is transcendent because it has never existed in this world; it has no precedent in earthly time. And what gets called "Islamic fundamentalism" is itself ironically a rhizome, not the tree of its own self-imagination: it was made outside, in exchange with the outside. It's no accident that "Islamic fundamentalism" flourished alongside other religious revivalist projects and divine nationalisms, pseudo-secular ethno-state revivalisms, and modern border-policing chauvinisms. The charge that Islamic feminism achieves some unprecedented break from the Real fails to recognize that it's *all* breaks, the entire endlessly fragmented tradition, forever rhizomatically open to its outside. It's not a question of whether a project "mixes" an otherwise consistent and self-contained Islam with outside resources, because we have no access to an Islam that precedes such "mixture." A better question: what can *you* mix? What promiscuous new connections can you achieve with your powers, and why do you open portals to some connections but block others? Like Allah (the former Clarence 13X) said when he held up a plate, "Whoever made this plate is the god of this plate."[7] Allah was not a Muslim by his own self-identification, but he was Allah, life-god, lord and judge over his own creative energies against the orders of a lord-judge-creator outside. Five Percenter theology can find expression in a completely materialist rejection of supernaturalist theology as Deleuze's "science of nonexisting entities,"[8] favoring life itself as a god, or filter through Sufism and become pantheism; you're the god of your plate.

> I do not say that God is in Herself constrained by us. However, our conceptions of God are at best what the Hindu yogi recognizes as the sixth *chakrah*, the place of our "notions of God." We cannot linger everlastingly at the seventh *chakrah*, or the crown, the place of "God beyond all names and forms," except for the twinkling of an eye. Or else we be gods ourselves, and though ultimately there is truth in that, our corporeal forms will only allow us intoxicated glimpses of this Reality.
>
> —AMINA WADUD, *Inside the Gender Jihad*[9]

My theology, "already several," is an assemblage—remembering that the assemblage is not only a hodge-podge of random accidental forces thrown together, but deliberately collected and sorted. In Deleuzian terms, my theology assemblage went from neurotic organization (the pursuit and maintenance of controlled unity) to a more schizophrenic mode of connections. My collection of resources includes the Sunni and Shi'i masjids available to me, but also Ibn al-'Arabi, South Asian Sufi poets, the

Nimatullahi Sufi order, Five Percenters, and dr. wadud, who manifests in the quoted excerpt as an assemblage, too, an intersection of lines that produce this Qur'an scholar referring to God with feminine pronouns, making references to chakrahs, and allowing for degrees of both immanence ("Or else we be gods ourselves") and transcendence ("Our corporeal forms will only allow us intoxicated glimpses"). Much of my archive represents Muslim Pseudo, the scapegoat and pro-bida' and anti-caliph rhizome tradition, Islam with a life-affirming openness to its margins and multiplicity and secretions of Islamic atheism as a gift from historical incoherence. Muslim Pseudo has gathered all the materials but cannot organize them to restore a perfect and pure original form.

Deleuze does not want to destroy the world beyond any chance of reassembly and coherence—again, at least not the Deleuze writing *A Thousand Plateaus* with Guattari, compared to the revolutionary energies of their *Anti-Oedipus*—but seeks a freedom of experimentation and connections to the outside. Muslim Pseudo is not reducible to a "postmodern" Islam deconstructed beyond any ability to hold meanings or make demands, but a pre-Islamic milieu, a stage on which multiple Islams form. Referring to plural "Islams" isn't critically satisfying, since it forces the question of where one would draw the line that separates one Islam from the others, but Islam has always been multiple. Muslim Pseudo lives on the Islamic plane of immanence, "the formless, unlimited absolute, neither surface nor volume but always fractal . . . like a desert that concepts populate without dividing up."[10] "Seal" in this case does not have to mean "conclusion." The Arabic *kh-t-m* root expresses meanings of closure and finality, but also fulfillment and confirmation, like the seal that signs or endorses a document. The Qur'an names Muhammad as "Seal of the Prophets" but does not define the term; the Qur'an only tells us, "Muhammad is not the father of any of your men, but he is the Messenger of God and Seal of the Prophets" (33:40). With the reference appearing within a sequence of verses that cancels Muhammad's paternity of his adopted son Zayd and read alongside hadiths in which Muhammad says that his son Ibrahim would have been a prophet if he lived to adulthood, the finality of prophethood becomes bound to Muhammad's lack of a son.[11]

Every prophet is a "sealing" of prophethood, at least in the Deleuzian sense of repetition as inevitably creation of the new. Every repetition of prophethood is unique, even if typical apologetic claims hold that all prophets followed the same religion; no repetition of the Sunna can perfectly match any repetition that precedes it, because relations to a specific repetition's unique external environment will change the repetition. If Islam was not completed at some originary moment from which every future Islam must be a doomed copy of a copy of a copy, it's *all* simulacra, it's all bida'. A significant challenge for Deleuzian engagements of Islam, rather than a reconciliation of immanence and transcendence, would be the question of Islamic relations to change: how, and under what circumstances, does Islam undergo change through its encounters with outside forces? Or rather, since a historian would recognize "tradition" as an ongoing fluid construction and change as the natural condition, what resources do we find in the tradition for seeing creatively energized transformations, experimentations, ruptures, breaks, and fragmentations as positive things? As in Deleuze's Nietzschean project of inverting Platonism, Deleuzo-Islamic theology—again, necessarily a heresiology—would affirm bida' and zandaqa, change and impurity. Pursue those lines of flight over the molar lines, prioritize creativity over consistency, and manifest an unpredictable Islam of infinite possibilities that passionately self-destructs but can reassemble itself the next day.

The Seal often appears in hadith traditions not only as a rank but also as a material artifact, an observable sign of Muhammad's status on his back between his shoulders, though hadith sources vary in the details. Numerous accounts give eyewitness testimony that the Seal was an organic birthmark, sometimes describing the Seal as resembling a cyst. In other reports, the Seal appears as a literal stamp upon Muhammad's body, closing the incision after angels cut him open, extract and clean his heart, cut away "Satan's share," and return the heart along with a pouring of wisdom into Muhammad's torso. Traditions also differ as to when this event occurred, locating the angelic surgery either in Muhammad's childhood (preparing his body for the physical trauma of the Qur'an's revelation?) or just prior to his heavenly ascension (enabling his body to transcend the world). My favorite version of the Seal origin story, found in al-Tayalisi's *Musnad*, combines the Seal with the story of the very first revelation that Muhammad experiences at the start of his prophethood. The cutting open of Muhammad's chest and washing of his heart precedes the descent of the Qur'an's first revealed verse, the famous "Recite" (96:1). While canonically privileged reports of the first revelation depict Muhammad running down the mountain in a panic to tell his wife Khadija what had happened, this version has her in the cave with him: given the tight confines of the cave, she would have been holding him through the surgery.[12]

The account is attributed to A'isha, but weakened by a broken chain: the student who reports from her goes unnamed, appearing simply as "a man."[13] Hadiths with transmission problems can flow through Muslim networks and become public canon, as in the popular but weakly evidenced traditions of Muhammad saying, "Seek knowledge even in China" and "Paradise rests at the feet of the mother," which have proliferated in extracanonical pamphlet culture. While there is an argument to be made that flawed chains ironically reflect *older* versions of hadiths, because their origins precede the era in which increasingly professionalized and sectarian hadith scholars grew obsessed over citation and sometimes forged perfect chains,[14] a Deleuzian relation to the Prophet could favor effects over authenticity. The power of the hadith lies not in the chain of transmission that authenticates its pure origin, but rather what it *does*—as the Prophet himself reportedly promised that if a hadith soothes your hair and skin, you know that it's truly from him.[15] The human-bacteria assemblage of my personal rhizosphere reacts to the text of the hadith and the varied affect-transformers that come with it—the air or "vibe" in the room, the aesthetics of the book or the voice and energy of the speaker, the Islam-coded scents of an oiled book or body—and processes all of that to restore Muhammad here, in this universe, the Muhammad of hair and skin. So my body makes Muhammad, but not because I'm a transcendent I-Self-Lord-Allah-Master over these worlds; Muhammad's activations of my hair and skin also make *me*, the fluid multiplicity pursuing these Muhammad-Deleuze connections.

The Muhammad produced in reactions of my hair and skin meets my Deleuze, the two of them quite a crowd already, and they sit facing each other, knees touching, Deleuze's hands on Muhammad's thighs. My Muhammad complains that the revelation has ceased because his Companions don't cut their fingernails.[16] My Deleuze recites melodically in the original Arabic, "We will show them our signs in the horizons and within themselves" (41:53). The throne trembles and new monsters are born. Their contact zone secretes me into being, belonging to both. On the plane of immanence, hair and skin become agents and meaning-makers, doing things in themselves rather than only boosting signals from unseen masters. Trusting the waves of energy between our bodies to answer theological problems might result in a doctrinal incoherence or Islamic "atheism," or it could produce an Islamic plane of immanence and make its own god, not a higher god that we *manifest* or *express* in this low sublunar world or one that descends at special times for closer proximity to us, but a future god always local to life, a god closer to us than our jugular veins (50:16).

Acknowledgments

This book is an assemblage of more people than I can name. First, Sadaf makes the world in which this book is possible. My work and thoughts became a book-in-process during my time at the 2020 Deleuze and Guattari World Congress camp and conference at Jamia Millia Islamia, where I was honored to present a paper that would later flow into this book's fourth chapter, and additionally had the chance to engage leading Deleuze scholars as well as Delhi's rich Sufi histories. That experience and its various encounters became this book.

My deepest gratitude to Richard Morrison's patience and encouragement, as well as the thoughtful feedback from three anonymous peer reviewers. This book is stronger for both the support and the critiques.

Finally, I'm grateful for the generosity of readers who have decided to share their time with me. I look forward to the future connections that this book might have enabled, whatever they might be.

Notes

Introduction: Secrets and Secretions

1. Gilles Deleuze and Felix Guattari, *A Thousand Plateaus: Capitalism and Schizophrenia*, trans. Brian Massumi (London and New York: Continuum, 1987), 158–59.
2. Dominique Sila-Khan, *Crossing the Threshold: Understanding Religious Identities in South Asia* (London: I. B. Tauris, 2004), 6.
3. Anand Vivek Taneja, "Jinnealogy: Everyday Life and Islamic Theology in Post-Partition Delhi," *HAU: Journal of Ethnographic Theory* 3 (2013): 139–65.
4. Ibid.
5. Peer Syed Mohd. Ahmad Chisti et al., *Life History of Hazrat Sufi Shaheed Sarmad*, trans. Badar Makhmoor (Delhi: Kutub Khana Sarmadi, n.d.), 41.
6. Nathan Katz, "The Identity of a Mystic: The Case of Sa'id Sarmad, a Jewish-Yogi-Sufi Courtier of the Mughals," *Numen* 47, no. 2 (2000): 142–60.
7. A. Azfar Moin, *The Millennial Sovereign: Sacred Kingship & Sainthood in Islam* (New York: Columbia University Press, 2014).
8. Chisti et al., *Life History of Hazrat Sufi Shaheed Sarmad*, 47.
9. Ibid., 44–45.
10. Judith Butler, *Gender Trouble: Feminism and the Subversion of Identity* (New York: Routledge, 1990), xvi.
11. John S. Strong, *Buddhisms: An Introduction* (Oxford: Oneworld, 2015), 287.
12. Sadaf Jaffer, "Trivializing Consent and Minimizing Slavery within American Academia," *AltMuslimah* (February 27, 2017), http://www.altmuslimah.com/2017/02/trivializing-consent-minimizing-slavery-withinamerican-academia/; accessed August 10, 2020.
13. Daniel W. Smith, *Essays on Deleuze* (Edinburgh: Edinburgh University Press, 2012), 286.
14. Daniel Colucciello Barber, *Deleuze and the Naming of God: Post-Secularism and the Future of Immanence* (Edinburgh: Edinburgh University Press, 2013), 13.
15. Ibid., 77.

16. Ibid., 12.

17. Ibid., 106.

18. Ibid., 13–14.

19. Daniel Tutt, "Deleuzian Theology and the Immanence of the Act of Being," *SCTIW Review* (December 1, 2015), http://sctiw.org/sctiwreviewarchives/archives/870.

20. Jon Roffe, *Badiou's Deleuze* (Montreal: McGill-Queen's University Press, 2012), 20.

21. Laura U. Marks, "A Deleuzian Ijtihad," in *Deleuze and Race*, ed. Arun Saldanha and Jason Michael Adams (Edinburgh: Edinburgh University Press, 2012), 51–72.

22. Cyrus Zargar, *Polished Mirror: Storytelling and the Pursuit of Virtue in Islamic Philosophy and Sufism* (Oxford: OneWorld, 2017).

23. Stephen F. Brown, "Avicenna and the Unity of the Concept of Being: The Interpretations of Henry of Ghent, Duns Scotus, Gerard of Bologna, and Peter Aureoli," *Franciscan Studies* 25 (1965): 117–50.

24. Alexander Kynsh, *Ibn 'Arabi in the Later Islamic Tradition: The Making of a Polemical Image in Medieval Islam* (Albany: State University of New York Press, 1999), 13–14.

25. Smith, *Essays on Deleuze*, 19–25.

26. Ian Almond, *Sufism and Deconstruction: A Comparative Study of Derrida and Ibn 'Arabi* (London and New York: Routledge, 2004).

27. Petra Carlsson Redell, *Mysticism as Revolt: Foucault, Deleuze and Theology Beyond Representation* (Aurora: Davies Group, 2014), 159.

28. Ibid., 165–66.

29. Deleuze describes his vision of philosophy as "a sort of buggery. . . . I saw myself as taking an author from behind and giving him a child that would be his own offspring, yet monstrous"; Gilles Deleuze, *Negotiations: 1972–1990*, trans. Martin Joughin (New York: Columbia University Press, 1995), 6.

30. Gilles Deleuze and Claire Parnet, *Dialogues*, trans. Hugh Tomlinson and Barbara Habberjam (New York: Athlone Press, 1987), 46–47.

31. Kecia Ali, *The Lives of Muhammad* (Cambridge, Mass.: Harvard University Press, 2015).

32. Gilles Deleuze and Felix Guattari, *What Is Philosophy?*, trans. Hugh Tomlinson and Graham Burchell (New York: Columbia University Press, 1994), 92.

33. Ibid.

34. Ibid.

35. Deleuze and Guattari, *A Thousand Plateaus*, 3.

36. Maria Isabel Fierro Bello, "Accusations of 'Zandaqa' in Al-Andalus," *Quaderni di Studi Arabi* 5/6 (1987–88): 251–58.

37. Deleuze and Guattari, *A Thousand Plateaus*, 15.

38. Alexander G. Weheliye, *Habeas Viscus: Racializing Assemblages, Biopolitics, and Black Feminist Theories of the Human* (Durham, N.C.: Duke University Press, 2014), 47.

39. Ian Buchanan, *Assemblage Theory and Method* (London and New York: Bloomsbury Academic, 2021).

40. Weheliye, *Habeas Viscus*, 47.

41. Christopher L. Miller, "The Postidentitarian Predicament in the Footnotes of *A Thousand Plateaus*: Nomadology, Anthropology, and Authority," *Diacritics* 23, no. 3 (Autumn 1993): 6–35.

42. For more on the genealogy of Deleuze's nomadology, see El Mokhtar Ghambou, *Nomadism and Its Frontiers* (New York: New York University, Graduate School of Arts and Science, 2001).

43. Nick Land, *The Dark Enlightenment*, http://www.thedarkenlightenment.com/the-dark-enlightenment-by-nick-land/; Justin Murphy, *Based Deleuze* (Other Life, 2019).

44. Gilles Deleuze, *Two Regimes of Madness: Texts and Interviews 1975–1995*, ed. David Lapoujade, trans. Ames Hodges and Mike Taormina (Cambridge, Mass.: MIT Press, 2007), 363–64.

45. Deleuze and Guattari, *A Thousand Plateaus*, 11.

46. Ibid., 10.

47. Michael Muhammad Knight, *Magic in Islam* (New York: TarcherPerigee, 2016), 107–36.

48. Deleuze and Guattari, *A Thousand Plateaus*, 161.

49. Ibid., 159–60.

50. Ibid., 160.

51. Ahmad ibn Hanbal, *Al-Musnad* (Beirut: 'Alam al-Kutub, 1998), no. 8266.

1. Deleuze and Tafsir: The Rhizomatic Qur'an

1. Gilles Deleuze and Felix Guattari, *A Thousand Plateaus: Capitalism and Schizophrenia*, trans. Brian Massumi (London: Continuum, 1987), 4.

2. Gilles Deleuze and Claire Parnet, *Dialogues*, trans. Hugh Tomlinson and Barbara Habberjam (New York: Athlone, 1987), 6.

3. Deleuze and Guattari, *A Thousand Plateaus*, 127.

4. Ibid., 126.

5. Tomoko Masuzawa, *The Invention of World Religions: Or, How European Universalism Was Preserved in the Language of Pluralism* (Chicago: University of Chicago Press, 2005), 197.

6. Edward Said, *Orientalism* (1978; New York: Vintage, 1994), 151.

7. Dietrich Jung, *Orientalists, Islamists and the Global Public Sphere: A Genealogy of the Modern Essentialist Image of Islam* (Oakville, Conn.: Equinox, 2011), 131.

8. Ibid., 199.

9. Masuzawa, *Invention of World Religions*, 197.

10. Shahab Ahmed, *What Is Islam?: The Importance of Being Islamic* (Princeton, N.J., and Oxford: Princeton University Press, 2017), 99.

11. Masuzawa, *Invention of World Religions*, 200–201.

12. W. R. W. Stephens, *Christianity & Islam: The Bible and the Koran; Four Lectures by the Rev. W. R. W. Stephens* (New York: Scribner, Armstrong, 1877), 61–62.

13. Lucy M Garnett, *Turkey of the Ottomans* (London: Sir Isaac Pitman & Sons, 1911), 110.

14. Anders Gerdmar, *Roots of Theological Anti-Semitism: German Biblical Interpretation and the Jews, from Herder and Semler to Kittel and Bultmann* (Leiden: Brill, 2009), 25.

15. Gregory A. Lipton, *Rethinking Ibn 'Arabi* (Oxford: Oxford University Press, 2018), 165.

16. Stefan Arvidsson, *Aryan Idols: Indo-European Mythology as Ideology and Science* (Chicago: University of Chicago Press, 2006), 111.

17. Ian Almond, *History of Islam in German Thought* (New York: Routledge, 2009), 37.

18. J. P. Widney, *The Genesis and Evolution of Islam and Judaeo-Christianity* (Los Angeles: Pacific, 1932), 83.

19. S. W. Koelle, *Mohammed and Mohammedanisim Critically Considered* (London: Rivingtons, 1889), 23, 122, 464.

20. Garnett, *Turkey of the Ottomans*, 39, 40.

21. Duncan Black MacDonald, *Development of Muslim Theology, Jurisprudence, and Constitutional Theory* (New York: Charles Scribner's Sons, 1903), 51, 60–62.

22. Masuzawa, *Invention of World Religions*, 199.

23. H. G. Wells, *The Outline of History: Being a Plain History of Life and Mankind*, 3rd ed. (New York: Macmillan, 1921), 581.

24. James T. Bixby, "Mohammed and the Koran," *Arena* 12, no. 64 (March 1895): 17.

25. Ibid., 30.

26. Ibid., 32.

27. C. P. Tiele, *The Religion of the Iranian Peoples*, trans. G. K. Nariman (Bombay: "Parsi," 1912), 106.

28. Charles Morris, *The Aryan Race: Its Origins and Its Achievements* (Chicago: S. C. Griggs, 1888), 229.

29. H. A. R. Gibb, *Mohammedanism: An Historical Survey*, 2nd ed. (Oxford: Oxford University Press, 1962), 36, 37, 62, 113.

30. Ahmed, *What Is Islam?*, 187–88.

31. William Montgomery Watt, *Muhammad at Mecca* (Oxford: Clarendon, 1953), 51.

32. Arvidsson, *Aryan Idols*, 111.

33. Ibid., 241.

34. Gilles Deleuze, "How Do We Recognize Structuralism?," in *Desert Islands and Other Texts, 1953–1974* (New York: Semiotext(e), 2004), 180.

35. Gilles Deleuze and Felix Guattari, *What Is Philosophy?*, trans. Hugh Tomlinson and Graham Burchell (New York: Columbia University Press, 1994), 223n5.

36. Jeremy R. Carrette, *Foucault and Religion: Spiritual Corporality and Political Spirituality* (London and New York: Routledge, 2000), 139.

37. Steven M. Wasserstrom, *Religion after Religion: Gershom Scholem, Mircea Eliade, and Henry Corbin at Eranos* (Princeton, N.J.: Princeton University Press, 1999), 135.

38. Ibid., 150.

39. Hamid Algar, "The Study of Islam: The Work of Henry Corbin," *Religious Studies Review* 6, no. 2 (1980): 89.

40. Lipton, *Rethinking Ibn 'Arabi*, 125.

41. Ibid., 179–81.

42. Thomas Nesbit, *Henry Miller and Religion* (New York and London: Routledge, 2007), 9.

43. Deleuze and Guattari, *A Thousand Plateaus*, 15.

44. Gilles Deleuze and Felix Guattari, *Anti-Oedipus: Capitalism and Schizophrenia*, trans. Robert Hurley, Mark Seem, and Helen R. Lane (Minneapolis: University of Minnesota Press, 1983), 205.

45. Ibid., 206.

46. Rudolph T. Ware III, *The Walking Qur'an: Islamic Education, Embodied Knowledge, and History in West Africa* (Chapel Hill: University of North Carolina Press, 2014), 58.

47. Travis Zadeh, "Touching and Ingesting: Early Debates over the Material Qur'an," *Journal of the American Oriental Society* 129, no. 3 (2009): 443–66.

48. Ingrid Mattson, *The Story of the Qur'an: Its History and Place in Muslim Life* (Chichester: Wiley-Blackwell, 2013), 159.

49. John S. Strong, *Buddhisms: An Introduction* (Oxford: Oneworld, 2015), 90.

50. Horst Junginger, "From Buddha to Adolf Hitler: Walther Wust and the Aryan Tradition," in *The Study of Religion under the Impact of Fascism*, ed. Horst Junginger (Leiden: Brill, 2008): 107–78.
51. Deleuze and Guttari, *A Thousand Plateaus*, 2.
52. Ibid., 121.
53. Ibid., 117.
54. Ibid., 121.
55. Ibid., 122.
56. Ibid.
57. Ibid., 123.
58. Ibid.
59. Ibid., 127.
60. Ibid., 126.
61. Ibid., 127.
62. Ibid.
63. Ibid., 5.
64. Janell Watson, "The Face of Christ: Deleuze and Guattari on the Politics of Word and Image," *The Bible and Critical Theory* 1, no. 2 (2005): 04.1–04.14.
65. Deleuze and Guattari, *A Thousand Plateaus*, 140.
66. Christopher Melchert, "The Early Controversy over Whether the Prophet Saw God," *Arabica* 62 (2015): 459–76.
67. Deleuze and Guattari, *Anti-Oedipus*, 127.
68. Deleuze and Guattari, *A Thousand Plateaus*, 6.
69. Ibid., 126–27.
70. Ibid., 7–13.
71. Christopher Melchert, "The Controversy over Reciting the Qur'ān with Tones," *JIQSA* 4 (2019): 85–109.
72. Salman H. Bashier, *Ibn al-'Arabi's Barzakh: The Concept of the Limit and the Relationship between God and the World* (Albany: State University of New York Press, 2004), 3.
73. Shahzad Bashir, *Fazlallah Astarabadi and the Hurufis* (Oxford: OneWorld, 2005), 112.
74. Pierre Lory, "The Symbolism of Letters and Language in the Work of Ibn 'Arabi," *Eye of the Heart: A Journal of Traditional Wisdom* 1 (2008): 141–50.
75. Michael Muhammad Knight, *Magic in Islam* (New York: TarcherPerigee, 2016), 60.
76. Brent Adkins, *Deleuze and Guattari's "A Thousand Plateaus": A Critical Introduction and Guide* (Edinburgh: Edinburgh University Press, 2015), 24.
77. Anna Bigelow, *Sharing the Sacred: Practicing Pluralism in Muslim North India* (Oxford: Oxford University Press, 2010), 265.
78. Ware, *The Walking Qur'an*.
79. Deleuze and Guattari, *A Thousand Plateaus*, 10.
80. Ibid.
81. Stephen Hirtenstein, *The Unlimited Mercifier: The Spiritual Life and Thought of Ibn 'Arabi* (Oxford and Ashland: Anqa and White Cloud, 1999), 237.
82. Michael Muhammad Knight, *Why I Am a Five Percenter* (New York: Tarcher/Penguin, 2011), 251–52.

83. "Surah Al-Fatihah," https://noblequran.com/surah-alfatihah/; accessed August 10, 2020.
84. Adkins, *Deleuze and Guattari's "A Thousand Plateaus,"* 24.
85. Said, *Orientalism*, 152.
86. Michael Muhammad Knight, *Why I Am a Salafi* (Berkeley: Counterpoint, 2015), 57–61.
87. Kevin van Bladel, "Heavenly Cords and Prophetic Authority in the Quran and Its Late Antique Context," *Bulletin of the School of Oriental and African Studies* 70 (2007): 223–46.
88. Michael Muhammad Knight, *Metaphysical Africa: Truth and Blackness in the Ansaru Allah Community* (University Park: Pennsylvania State University Press, 2020).
89. Knight, *Magic in Islam*, 129.
90. Tamara M. Green, *The City of the Moon God: Religious Traditions of Harran* (Leiden: Brill, 2007), 137.
91. Yasir Qadhi, "Collector's Edition: An Intro to Sahih al-Bukhari," Seminar at University of Calgary, June 5–7, 2015.
92. Deleuze and Guattari, *A Thousand Plateaus*, 21.
93. Ibid., 9.
94. Ibid., 9.
95. Ibid., 12.
96. Ibid.
97. Ibid., 15.
98. Frank Griffel, "Muslim Philosophers' Rationalist Explanation of Muhammad's Prophecy," in *The Cambridge Companion to Muhammad*, ed. Jonathan E. Brockopp (Cambridge: Cambridge University Press, 2010), 158–79.
99. Ja'far al-Sadiq, *Spiritual Gems: The Mystical Qur'an Commentary Ascribed to Ja'far al-Sadqi as Contained in Sulami's Haqa'iq al-Tafsir*, trans. Farhana Mayer (Louisville: Fons Vitae, 2011), 1.
100. Kristin Zahra Sands, *Sufi Commentaries on the Qur'an in Classical Islam* (London and New York: Routledge, 2006), 44.
101. Ibid.
102. Farouk Mitha, *Al-Ghazali and the Isma'ilis: A Debate on Reason and Authority in Medieval Islam* (London and New York: I. B. Tauris, 2001), 69–70.
103. Lipton, *Rethinking Ibn 'Arabi*, 55–83.
104. Deleuze and Guattari, *A Thousand Plateaus*, 9.
105. Ibid., 122.
106. Christopher L. Miller, "The Postidentitarian Predicament in the Footnotes of *A Thousand Plateaus*: Nomadology, Anthropology, and Authority," *Diacritics* 23, no. 3 (Autumn 1993).
107. Deleuze and Guattari, *A Thousand Plateaus*, 539n11.
108. Timothy J. Gianootti, *Al-Ghazali's Unspeakable Doctrine of the Soul: Unveiling the Esoteric Psychology and Eschatology of the Ihya'* (Leiden: Brill, 2001), 169, 180.
109. Deleuze and Guattari, *A Thousand Plateaus*, 127.

2. People of the Sunna and the Assemblage: Deleuzian Hadith Theory

1. Jonathan A. C. Brown, "The Rules of Matn Criticism: There Are No Rules," *Islamic Law and Society* 19 (2012): 356–96.

2. Ibid.
3. Gilles Deleuze and Felix, Guattari, *A Thousand Plateaus: Capitalism and Schizophrenia*, trans. Brian Massumi (London and New York: Continuum, 1987), 40–41.
4. G. H. A. Juynboll, *Muslim Tradition* (Cambridge: Cambridge University Press, 1983), 51.
5. Deleuze and Guattari, *A Thousand Plateaus*, 15.
6. Michael Muhammad Knight, *Magic in Islam* (New York: TarcherPerigee, 2016), 20–24.
7. Scott Lucas, *Constructive Critics, Hadith Literature, and the Articulation of Sunni Islam: The Legacy of the Generation of Ibn Sa'd, Ibn Ma'in, and Ibn Hanbal* (Leiden: Brill, 2004), 19–20.
8. Patricia Crone and Martin Hinds, *God's Caliph: Religious Authority in the First Centuries of Islam* (Cambridge: Cambridge University Press, 1986), 54.
9. Yasin Dutton, *The Origins of Islamic Law: The Qur'an, the Muwatta' and Madinan Amal* (New York: Routledge, 1999), 15.
10. Michael Muhammad Knight, *Why I Am a Salafi* (Berkeley, Calif.: Counterpoint, 2015), 106–9.
11. Juynboll, *Muslim Tradition*, 193.
12. Ibid., 46–47.
13. Ibid., 68; Juynboll, *The Encyclopedia of Canonical Hadith* (Leiden: Brill, 2007), 433, 471.
14. Asma Sayeed, *Women and the Transmission of Religious Knowledge in Islam* (Cambridge: Cambridge University Press, 2013), 30–31.
15. Wilferd Madelung, *The Succession to Muhammad: A Study of the Early Caliphate* (Cambridge: Cambridge University Press, 1997), 100–109.
16. Herbert Berg, "The Isnad and the Production of Cultural Memory: Ibn 'Abbas as a Case Study," *Numen* 58 (2011): 259–83.
17. Badruddin Muhammad bin Bahadir al-Zarkashi, *Al-Ijaba li-Iradi Ma Istadrakatuhu A'isha 'Ala al-Sahaba* (Syria: Al-Kutub al-Islamiyya, 1939).
18. Rkia Cornell, *Early Sufi Women: Dhikr an-Niswa al-Muta'abbidat al-Sufiyyat* (Louisville: Fons Vitae, 1999), 62.
19. Michael Lecker, "Biographical Notes on Ibn Shihab al-Zuhri," *Journal of Semitic Studies* 41, no. 1 (Spring 1996): 21–63.
20. Ibid., 21.
21. Juynboll, *Muslim Tradition*, 41.
22. Fred Donner, *Narratives of Islamic Origins: The Beginnings of Islamic Historical Writing* (Princeton, N.J.: Darwin, 1998), 227.
23. Lecker, "Biographical Notes on Ibn Shihab al-Zuhri."
24. Gregor Schoeler, "Oral Torah and Hadith: Transmission, Prohibition of Writing, Redaction," in *Hadith: Origins and Developments*, ed. Harald Motzki (New York: Routledge, 2016), 86.
25. Gregor Schoeler, *The Oral and Written in Early Islam* (New York: Routledge, 2006), 124–26.
26. Feryal Salem, *The Emergence of Early Sufi Piety and Sunni Scholasticism: 'Abdallah b. al-Mubarak and the Formation of Sunni Identity in the Second Islamic Century* (Leiden: Brill, 2016), 54–55.
27. Lucas, *Constructive Critics*, 133.
28. Juynboll, *Muslim Tradition*, 20.

29. Ibid., 164.

30. R. Marston Speight, *The Musnad of al-Tayalisi: A Study of Islamic Hadith as Oral Literature* (Hartford, Conn.: Hartford Seminary Foundation, 1970), 13.

31. Juynboll, *Encyclopedia of Canonical Hadith*, 471.

32. Speight, *Musnad of al-Tayalisi*, 12.

33. Christopher Melchert, "Sectaries in the Six Books: Evidence for Their Exclusion from the Sunni Community," *Muslim World* 82 (1992): 287–95.

34. Asma Sayeed, "Women in Imami Biographical Collections," in *Law and Tradition in Classical Islamic Thought*, ed. Michael Cook, Najam Haider, Intisar Rabb, and Asma Sayeed (New York: Palgrave, 2013), 81–97.

35. Huseyin Hansu, "Debates on the Authority of Hadith in Early Islamic Intellectual History: Identifying al-Shafi'i's Opponents in Jima' al-'Ilm," *Journal of the American Oriental Society* 136, no. 3 (July–September 2016): 515–33.

36. Scott C. Lucas, "Al-Hakim al-Naysaburi and the Companions of the Prophet: An Original Sunni Voice in the Shi'i Century," in *The Heritage of Arabo-Islamic Learning: Studies Presented to Wadad Kadi*, ed. Maurice A. Pomerantz and Aram Shahin (Leiden: Brill, 2015), 236–49.

37. Ahmad ibn Hanbal, *Al-Musnad* (Beirut: 'Alam al-Kutub, 1998).

38. Nimrod Hurvitz, *Ahmad Ibn Hanbal and the Formation of Islamic Orthodoxy* (Princeton, N.J.: Princeton University Press, 1994), 48.

39. Ibid., 542.

40. Ibid., 461.

41. Ibid., 543.

42. Ibid.

43. Ibid.

44. Ibid., 481.

45. Melchert, "Sectaries in the Six Books."

46. Hurvitz, *Ahmad Ibn Hanbal and the Formation of Islamic Orthodoxy*, 536.

47. Christopher Melchert, "The Musnad of Ahmad ibn Hanbal: How It Was Composed and What Distinguishes It from the Six Books," *Der Islam* 82, no. 1 (2005): 32–51.

48. Ibid.

49. Hurvitz, *Ahmad Ibn Hanbal and the Formation of Islamic Orthodoxy*, 48.

50. Melchert, "Sectaries in the Six Books."

51. Christopher Melchert, "The Destruction of Books by Traditionists," *Al-Qantara* 35 (2014): 213–31.

52. Sayeed, *Women and the Transmission of Religious Knowledge in Islam*, 186–87.

53. Melchert, "Sectaries in the Six Books," 287–95.

54. Lyall R. Armstrong, *The Qussas of Early Islam* (Leiden: Brill, 2017), 118–20.

55. John Nawas, "The Contribution of the Mawali to the Six Sunnite Canonical Hadith Collections," in *Ideas, Images, and Methods of Portrayal: Insights into Classical Arabic Literature and Islam*, ed. Sebastian Gunther (Leiden: Brill, 2005), 141–51.

56. Arnold Pacey, *Technology in World Civilization* (Cambridge, Mass.: MIT Press, 1990), 41.

57. DeLanda, *Assemblage Theory*, 29.

58. Lucas, *Constructive Critics*, 19.

59. Deleuze and Guattari, *A Thousand Plateaus*, 40.

60. Ibid., 42.

61. Amr Osman, "'Adalat al-Sahaba: The Construction of a Religious Doctrine," *Arabica* 60 (2013): 272–305.
62. Deleuze and Guattari, *A Thousand Plateaus*, 88.
63. Ibid.
64. Deleuze and Guattari, *A Thousand Plateaus*, 11.
65. Leah Kinberg, "The Legitimization of the Mahdahib through Dreams," *Arabica* 32 (1985): 47–79.
66. Anand Vivek Taneja, "Jinnealaogy: Everyday Life and Islamic Theology in Post-Partition Delhi," *HAU: Journal of Ethnographic Theory* 3 (2013): 141.
67. Ibid.
68. Brown, "Rules of Matn Criticism."
69. Christopher Melchert, "The Early Controversy over Whether the Prophet Saw God," *Arabica* 62 (2015).
70. Deleuze and Guattari, *A Thousand Plateaus*, 9.
71. Melchert, "The Early Controversy over Whether the Prophet Saw God."
72. Michael Muhammad Knight, *Muhammad: Forty Introductions* (Berkeley, Calif.: Counterpoint, 2019), 255–64.
73. Deleuze and Guattari, *A Thousand Plateaus*, 163.
74. Ibid., 160.
75. M. J. Kister, "The Massacre of the Banu Qurayza: A Re-examination of a Tradition," *Jerusalem Studies in Arabic and Islam* 8 (1986): 61–96.
76. Deleuze and Guattari, *A Thousand Plateaus*, 161.

3. Beyond Theology: Sufism as Arrangement and Affect

1. Ibid.
2. Gilles Deleuze and Felix Guattari, *A Thousand Plateaus: Capitalism and Schizophrenia*, trans. Brian Massumi (London and New York: Continuum, 1987), 88.
3. Lloyd Ridgeon, "Mysticism in Medieval Sufism," in *The Cambridge Companion to Sufism*, ed. Lloyd Ridgeon (Cambridge: Cambridge University Press, 2014), 125–49.
4. Ibid.
5. Louis Massignon, *The Passion of al-Hallaj*, trans. H. Mason (Princeton, N.J.: Princeton University Press, 1994), 136.
6. Deleuze and Guattari, *A Thousand Plateaus*, 142.
7. M. Malamud, "Gender and Spiritual Self-Fashioning: The Master-Disciple Relationship in Classical Sufism," *Journal of the American Academy of Religion* 64, no. 1 (Spring 1996): 89–117.
8. Nathan Hofer, *The Popularisation of Sufism in Ayyubid and Mamluk Egypt, 1173–1325* (Edinburgh: Edinburgh University Press, 2015), 24, 35.
9. Ibid., 84–85.
10. Mehdi Amin Razavi Aminrazavi, *Suhrawardi and the School of Illumination* (New York: Routledge, 1997), 4.
11. Huseyin Yilmaz, *Caliphate Redefined: The Mystical Turn in Ottoman Political Thought* (Princeton, N.J.: Princeton University Press, 2018), 49, 97.
12. Ahmet T. Karamustafa, *God's Unruly Friends* (Oxford: Oneworld, 2006), 83–84.
13. Ruhollah Khomeini, *The Wine of Love: Mystical Poetry of Imam Khomeini*, trans. Ghulam-Rida A'wani and Muhammad Legenhausen (Tehran: Institute for the Compilation and Publication of Imam Khomeini's Works, 2002), 63.

14. Carl Ernst, *The Shambhala Guide to Sufism* (Boston: Shambhala, 1997), 120.
15. Michael Muhammad Knight, *Muhammad: Forty Introductions* (Berkeley, Calif.: Counterpoint, 2019), 136.
16. M. P. Connell, *The Ni'matullahi Sayyids of Taft: A Study of the Evolution of a Late Medieval Iranian Sufi Tariqah* (Cambridge, Mass.: Harvard University Press, 2004), 130.
17. Deleuze and Guattari, *A Thousand Plateaus*, 314.
18. Connell, *Ni'matullahi Sayyids of Taft*, 130.
19. J. Burton-Page, "'Abd Allah Wali, Shah Ni'mat Allah Nur al-Din b. (1330/31–)," in *Biographical Encyclopedia of Sufis: Central Asia & Middle East*, ed. N. Hanif (New Delhi: Sarup & Sons, 2002), 2–8.
20. Jeffrey Rothschild, *Bestower of Light: A Portrait of Dr. Javad Nurbakhsh, Master of the Nimatullahi Sufi Order* (London and New York: Khaniqahi Nimatullahi, 1999), 79.
21. Laury Silvers, "The Teaching Relationship in Early Sufism: A Reassessment of Fritz Meier's Definition of the *shaykh al-tarbiya* and the *shaykh al-ta'līm*," *Muslim World* 93, no. 1 (2003): 69–97.
22. Terry Graham, "Shah Ni'matullah Wali: Founder of the Ni'matullahi Sufi Order," in *The Legacy of Mediaeval Persian Sufism*, ed. Leonard Lewisohn (London and New York: Khaniqahi Nimatullahi, 1992), 173–90.
23. Ernst, *Shambhala Guide to Sufism*, 112–13, 123.
24. Ibid., 133.
25. Javad Nurbakhsh, *The Great Satan "Eblis"* (London: Khaniqahi Nimatullahi, 1986); *Dogs from a Sufi Point of View* (London: Khaniqahi Nimatullahi, 1989); *Jesus in the Eyes of the Sufis* (London: Khaniqahi Nimatullahi, 1992).
26. Javad Nurbakhsh, *Sufi Symbolism*, 16 vols. (London: Khaniqahi Nimatullahi, 1987–2004).
27. Dominique Sila-Khan, *Crossing the Threshold: Understanding Religious Identities in South Asia* (London: I. B. Tauris, 2004), 1–7, 26–27.
28. James R. Newell, "Unseen Power: Aesthetic Dimensions of Symbolic Healing in Qawwālī," *Muslim World* 97 (October 2007): 640–56.
29. Brian Massumi, *Parables for the Virtual: Movement, Affect, Sensation* (Durham, N.C.: Duke University Press, 2002), 15.
30. Rosi Braidotti, "Nomadic Ethics," in *The Cambridge Companion to Deleuze*, ed. Daniel W. Smith and Henry Somers-Hall (Cambridge: Cambridge University Press, 2012), 170–97.
31. Nasrollah Pourjavady, "Stories of Ahmad al-Ghazali Playing the Witness," in *Reason and Inspiration in Islam*, ed. T. Lawson (London: I. B. Tauris, 2005), 200–220.
32. Jenna Supp-Montgomerie, "Affect and the Study of Religion," *Religion Compass* 9/10 (2015): 335–45.
33. Gilles Deleuze, *The Logic of Sense*, trans. Mark Lester with Charles Stivale, ed. Constantin V. Boundas (London: Athlone, 1990), 281.
34. Alexander Treiger, "Monism and Monotheism in al-Ghazali's Mishkat al-Anwar," *Journal of Qur'anic Studies* 9, no. 1 (2007): 1–27.

4. The Immanence of Baraka: Bodies and Territory

1. Al-Tabari, *The History of al-Tabari*, vol. 15, *The Crisis of the Early Caliphate*, trans. R. Stephen Humphreys (Albany: State University of New York Press, 1990), 248–49.

2. Leor Halevi, *Muhammad's Grave: Death Rites and the Making of Islamic Society* (New York: Columbia University Press, 2007), 37.

3. Daniella Talmon-Heller, "Historiography in the Service of the Mufti: Ibn Taymiyya on the Origins and Fallacies of Ziyarat," *Islamic Law and Society* 26 (2019): 227–51.

4. Ibid.

5. Donna L. Zamiska, "The Ikhwan of Saudi Arabia Past and Present" (Ph.D. diss., McGill University, 1993), 13–14.

6. Johann Lewis Burckhardt, *Travels in Arabia: Comprehending an Account of Those Territories in Hedjaz Which the Mohammedans Regard as Sacred* (London: Henry Colburn, 1829), 222–23.

7. Ibid.

8. Irfan Ahmed, "The Destruction of the Holy Sites in Mecca and Medina," *Islamica* 15 (2006): 71–74.

9. Afshin Shahi, *The Politics of Truth Management in Saudi Arabia* (New York: Routledge, 2013), 51.

10. Ahmed, "Destruction of the Holy Sites in Mecca and Medina."

11. Shahab Ahmed, *What Is Islam?: The Importance of Being Islamic* (Princeton, N.J., and Oxford: Princeton University Press, 2017), 532–37.

12. Ibid.

13. Ian Buchanan, "Assemblage Theory and Its Discontents," *Deleuze Studies* 9, no. 3 (2015): 382–92.

14. Gilles Deleuze and Felix Guattari, *A Thousand Plateaus: Capitalism and Schizophrenia*, trans. Brian Massumi (London and New York: Continuum, 1987), 88.

15. Nasa'i, *Sunan, kitab al-jana'za: Bab al-amri bi-l-steghfari lil-muminin*, Sunnah .com, https://sunnah.com/nasai/21; accessed August 10, 2020.

16. Tirmidhi, *Jami', kitab al-munaqib 'an rasl Allah*, Sunnah.com, https://sunnah .com/tirmidhi/49; accessed August 10, 2020.

17. Gilles Deleuze, *Foucault*, trans. and ed. Sean Hand (Minneapolis: University of Minnesota Press, 1988), 47.

18. Ahmed, *What Is Islam?*, 362.

19. Ibid.

20. Deleuze and Guattari, *A Thousand Plateaus*, 20.

21. Samer Akkach, "The Eye of Reflection: Al-Nabulusi's Spatial Interpretation of Ibn 'Arabi's Tomb," *Muqarnas* 32 (2015): 79–95.

22. Ahmed, *What Is Islam?*, 93.

23. Huseyin Yilmaz, *Caliphate Redefined: The Mystical Turn in Ottoman Political Thought* (Princeton, N.J.: Princeton University Press, 2018).

24. Stefan Winter, *Shiites of Lebanon under Ottoman Rule, 1516–1788* (Cambridge: Cambridge University Press, 2010), 26.

25. Ahmed, *What Is Islam?*, 460.

26. Ibid., 406.

27. Deleuze and Guattari, *A Thousand Plateaus*, 143.

28. Ahmed, *What Is Islam?*, 532–37.

29. Ibid., 534.

30. Ibid., 82–84.
31. Umar Bin Ibad, *Sufi Shrines and the Pakistani State: The End of Religious* Pluralism (London and New York: I. B. Tauris, 2019), 4–7.
32. Katherine Ewing, "The Politics of Sufism: Redefining the Saints of Pakistan," *Journal of Asian Studies* 42, no. 2 (February 1983): 251–68.
33. Kristien Justaert, *Theology After Deleuze* (New York: Continuum, 2012); Daniel Colucciello Barber, *Deleuze and the Naming of God: Post-Secularism and the Future of Immanence* (Edinburgh: Edinburgh University Press, 2015).
34. G. S. Colin, "Baraka," in *Encyclopedia of Islam*, 2nd ed., ed. P. Bearman et al. (Brill Online, 2016), http://dx.doi.org/10.1163/1573-3912_islam_SIM_1216.
35. Josef Meri, "Aspects of Baraka (Blessings) and Ritual Devotion among Medieval Muslims and Jews," *Medieval Encounters* 5, no. 1 (1999): 46–49.
36. Ahmed, *What Is Islam?*, 92.
37. Omid Safi, "Bargaining with Baraka: Persian Sufism, 'Mysticism,' and Premodern Politics," *Muslim World* 90, no. 3/4 (2000): 259–88.
38. Deleuze and Guattari, *A Thousand Plateaus*, 20.
39. Gregory Lipton, *Rethinking Ibn 'Arabi* (Oxford: Oxford University Press, 2018), 17.

5. Arm Leg Leg Arm Head: Five Percenter Theologies of Immanence

1. Gilles Deleuze and Felix Guattari, *What Is Philosophy?*, trans. Hugh Tomlinson and Graham Burchell (New York: Columbia University Press, 1994), 92.
2. F. LeRon Shults, *Iconoclastic Theology: Gilles Deleuze and the Secretion of Atheism* (Edinburgh: Edinburgh University Press, 2014), 61.
3. Ibid., 21.
4. Ibid., 214.
5. Gilles Deleuze, *Logic of Sense*, trans. Mark Lester with Charles Stivale, ed. Constantin V. Boundas (London: Athlone, 1990), 281.
6. Gilles Deleuze and Felix Guattari, *A Thousand Plateaus: Capitalism and Schizophrenia*, trans. Brian Massumi (London and New York: Continuum, 1987), 161.
7. Shahab Ahmed, *What Is Islam? The Importance of Being Islamic* (Cambridge, Mass.: Harvard University Press, 2015).
8. Shults, *Iconoclastic Theology*, 191–92.
9. Christopher Melchert, "The Early Controversy over Whether the Prophet Saw God," *Arabica* 62, no. 4 (2015): 459–76.
10. Ibid.
11. Huseyin Yilmaz, *Caliphate Redefined: The Mystical Turn in Ottoman Political Thought* (Princeton, N.J.: Princeton University Press, 2018).
12. Sherman Jackson, "Ibn Taymiyya on trial in Damascus," *Journal of Semitic Studies*, no. 39 (1994): 41–85.
13. Deleuze, *Expressionism in Philosophy*, 46.
14. Christopher Melchert, "God Created Adam in His Image," *Journal of Qur'anic Studies* 13, no. 1 (2011): 113–24.
15. Joseph Lumbard, *Ahmad al-Ghazali, Remembrance, and the Metaphysics of Love* (Albany: State University of New York Press, 2016).
16. Binyamin Abrahamov, *Ibn al-'Arabi's Fusus al-hikam: An Annotated Translation of "The Bezels of Wisdom"* (New York: Routledge, 2015), 3.

17. Alexander Knysh, *Ibn Arabi in the Later Islamic Tradition: The Making of a Polemical Image in Medieval Islam* (Albany: State University of New York Press, 1999), 106, 124.
18. Abrahamov, *Ibn al-'Arabi's Fusus al-hikam*, 38.
19. Ibid., 38.
20. Ibid., 40.
21. Ibid.
22. Ibid., 42.
23. Abrahamov, *Ibn al-'Arabi's Fusus al-hikam*, 36.
24. Josef Van Ess, "The Youthful God: Anthropomorphism in Early Islam," University Lecture in Religion at Arizona State University, 1988.
25. Ian Almond, *Sufism and Deconstruction: A Comparative Study of Derrida and Ibn 'Arabi* (London and New York: Routledge, 2004).
26. Carl W. Ernst, *Hallaj: Poems of a Sufi Martyr* (Evanston, Ill.: Northwestern University Press, 2018).
27. Patricia Crone, *The Nativist Prophets of Early Islamic Iran: Rural Revolt and Local Zoroastrianism* (Cambridge: Cambridge University Press, 2012), 221–25.
28. Ibid., 212, 223.
29. Ahmet T. Karamustafa, *God's Unruly Friends* (Oxford: Oneworld, 2006), 48.
30. Ibid., 22.
31. Deleuze and Guattari, *A Thousand Plateaus*, 40.
32. Ibid., 158–59.
33. Knysh, *Ibn Arabi in the Later Islamic Tradition*, 217–18.
34. Erdmann Doane Beynon, "The Voodoo Cult among Negro Migrants in Detroit," *American Journal of Sociology* 43, no. 6 (1938): 906.
35. Righteousdisorder, "Louis Farrakhan in Egypt answering question about W. D. Fard —World Friendship Tour," https://www.youtube.com/watch?v=RU7AolKdE50&t =174s; accessed August 10, 2020.
36. Nasrollah Pourjavady and Peter Lamborn Wilson, *Kings of Love: The History & Poetry of the Ni'matullahi Sufi Order of Iran* (Tehran: Imperial Iranian Academy of Philosophy, 1978), 43. Translation modified by author.
37. Louis Farrakhan, *Put on the New Man* (Final Call, 2010), DVD.
38. Erykah Badu, "On and On," *Baduizm* (Kedar/Universal Labels, 1997), CD.
39. Michael Muhammad Knight, *The Five Percenters: Islam, Hip-Hop, and the Gods of New York* (Oxford: Oneworld, 2007).
40. Rakim, "The Mystery (Who Is God)." *The 18th Letter* (Universal Records, 1997).
41. Deleuze and Guattari, *A Thousand Plateaus*, 161.
42. Claude Andrew Clegg III, *An Original Man: The Life and Times of Elijah Muhammad* (New York: St. Martin's, 1997), 317.
43. The Supreme Wisdom Lessons, 10:40.
44. L. E. Goodman, *Avicenna* (London and New York: Routledge, 1992), 164.

Conclusion: The Seal of Muslim Pseudo

1. Muslim ibn al-Hajjaj, *Sahih Muslim (kitab al-hajj)*, Sunnah.com, https://sunnah.com/muslim/15/534; accessed August 10, 2020.
2. Ibn Majah, *Sunan Ibn Majah (kitab al-fitan)*, Sunnah.com, https://sunnah.com/ibnmajah/36/67; accessed August 10, 2020.

3. Michael Muhammad Knight, *Muhammad's Body: Baraka Networks and the Prophetic Assemblage* (Chapel Hill: The University of North Carolina Press, 2020), 141.

4. Muhammad ibn Isma'il al-Bukhari, *Sahih (kitab al-akham)*, Sunnah.com, https://sunnah.com/bukhari/93; accessed August 10, 2020.

5. Muslim ibn al-Hajjaj, *Sahih Muslim (al-muqaddima)*, Sunnah.com, https://sunnah.com/muslim/introduction/26; accessed August 10, 2020.

6. Michael Muhammad Knight, *Why I Am a Salafi* (Berkeley, Calif.: Soft Skull, 2015), 100.

7. Michael Muhammad Knight, *William S. Burroughs vs. the Qur'an* (Berkeley, Calif.: Soft Skull, 2012), 184.

8. Gilles Deleuze, *The Logic of Sense*, trans. Mark Lester with Charles Stivale, ed. Constantin V. Boundas (London: Athlone, 1990), 281.

9. amina wadud, *Inside the Gender Jihad* (Oxford: Oneworld, 2006), 198.

10. Gilles Deleuze and Felix Guattari, *What Is Philosophy?*, trans. Hugh Tomlinson and Graham Burchell (New York: Columbia University Press, 1994), 36.

11. Knight, *Muhammad's Body*, 122.

12. Ibid., 56–57.

13. Ibid.

14. Shahab Ahmed, *Before Orthodoxy: The Satanic Verses in Early Islam* (Cambridge, Mass.: Harvard University Press, 2017), 32–33.

15. Michael Muhammad Knight, *Muhammad: Forty Introductions* (Berkeley, Calif.: Counterpoint, 2019), 291–300.

16. Knight, *Muhammad's Body*, 52.

Bibliography

Abrahamov, Binyamin. *Ibn al-'Arabi's Fusus al-hikam: An Annotated Translation of "The Bezels of Wisdom."* New York: Routledge, 2015.
Adkins, Brent. *Deleuze and Guattari's "A Thousand Plateaus": A Critical Introduction and Guide.* Edinburgh: Edinburgh University Press, 2015.
Ahmed, Irfan. "The Destruction of the Holy Sites in Mecca and Medina." *Islamica* 15 (2006): 71–74.
Ahmed, Shahab. *Before Orthodoxy: The Satanic Verses in Early Islam.* Cambridge, Mass.: Harvard University Press, 2017.
———. *What Is Islam?: The Importance of Being Islamic.* Princeton, N.J., and Oxford: Princeton University Press, 2017.
Akkach, Samer. "The Eye of Reflection: Al-Nabulusi's Spatial Interpretation of Ibn 'Arabi's Tomb." *Muqarnas* 32 (2015): 79–95.
Algar, Hamid. "The Study of Islam: The Work of Henry Corbin." *Religious Studies Review* 6, no. 2 (1980): 89.
Ali, Kecia. *The Lives of Muhammad.* Cambridge, Mass.: Harvard University Press, 2015.
Almond, Ian. *History of Islam in German Thought.* New York: Routledge, 2009.
———. *Sufism and Deconstruction: A Comparative Study of Derrida and Ibn 'Arabi.* London and New York: Routledge, 2004.
Aminrazavi, Mehdi Amin Razavi. *Suhrawardi and the School of Illumination.* New York: Routledge, 1997.
Armstrong, Lyall R. *The Qussas of Early Islam.* Leiden: Brill, 2017.
Arvidsson, Stefan. *Aryan Idols: Indo-European Mythology as Ideology and Science.* Chicago: University of Chicago Press, 2006.
Barber, Daniel Colucciello. *Deleuze and the Naming of God: Post-Secularism and the Future of Immanence.* Edinburgh: Edinburgh University Press, 2013.

Bashier, Salman H. *Ibn al-'Arabi's Barzakh: The Concept of the Limit and the Relationship between God and the World*. Albany: State University of New York Press, 2004.

Bashir, Shahzad. *Fazlallah Astarabadi and the Hurufis*. Oxford: OneWorld, 2005.

Bello, Maria Isabel Fierro. "Accusations of 'Zandaqa' in Al-Andalus." *Quaderni di Studi Arabi* 5/6 (1987–88): 251–58.

Berg, Herbert. "The Isnad and the Production of Cultural Memory: Ibn 'Abbas as a Case Study." *Numen* 58 (2011): 259–83.

Beynon, Erdmann Doane. "The Voodoo Cult among Negro Migrants in Detroit." *American Journal of Sociology* 43, no. 6 (1938): 894–907.

Bigelow, Anna. *Sharing the Sacred: Practicing Pluralism in Muslim North India*. Oxford: Oxford University Press, 2010.

Bin Ibad, Umar. *Sufi Shrines and the Pakistani State: The End of Religious Pluralism*. London and New York: I. B. Tauris, 2019.

Bixby, James T. "Mohammed and the Koran." *Arena* 12, no. 64 (March 1895): 17.

Braidotti, Rosi. "Nomadic Ethics." In *The Cambridge Companion to Deleuze*, edited by Daniel W. Smith and Henry Somers-Hall, 170–97. Cambridge: Cambridge University Press, 2012.

Brown, Jonathan A. C. "The Rules of Matn Criticism: There Are No Rules." *Islamic Law and Society* 19 (2012): 356–96.

Brown, Stephen F. "Avicenna and the Unity of the Concept of Being: The Interpretations of Henry of Ghent, Duns Scotus, Gerard of Bologna, and Peter Aureoli." *Franciscan Studies* 25 (1965): 117–50.

Buchanan, Ian. "Assemblage Theory and Its Discontents." *Deleuze Studies* 9, no. 3 (2015): 382–92.

———. *Assemblage Theory and Method*. London and New York: Bloomsbury Academic, 2021.

Al-Bukhari, Muhammad ibn Isma'il. *Sahih*. Sunnah.com. Accessed August 10, 2020.

Burckhardt, Johann Lewis. *Travels in Arabia: Comprehending an Account of Those Territories in Hedjaz Which the Mohammedans Regard as Sacred*. London: Henry Colburn, 1829.

Burton-Page, J. "'Abd Allah Wali, Shah Ni'mat Allah Nur al-Din b. (1330/31–)." In *Biographical Encyclopdia of Sufis: Central Asia & Middle East*, edited by N. Hanif, 2–8. New Delhi: Sarup & Sons, 2002.

Butler, Judith. *Gender Trouble: Feminism and the Subversion of Identity*. New York: Routledge, 1990.

Carrette, Jeremy R. *Foucault and Religion: Spiritual Corporality and Political Spirituality*. London and New York: Routledge, 2000.

Chisti, Peer Syed Mohd. Ahmad, et. al. *Life History of Hazrat Sufi Shaheed Sarmad*. Translated by Badar Makhmoor. Delhi: Kutub Khana Sarmadi, n.d.

Chittick, William C. *In Search of the Lost Heart: Explorations in Islamic Thought*, edited by Mohammed Rustom, Atif Khalil, and Kazuyo Murata. Albany: State University of New York, 2012.

Clegg, Claude Andrew III. *An Original Man: The Life and Times of Elijah Muhammad.* New York: St. Martin's, 1997.
Colin, G. S. "Baraka." In *Encyclopedia of Islam.* 2nd ed. Edited by P. Bearman et al. Brill Online, 2016.
Connell, M. P. *The Ni'matullahi Sayyids of Taft: A Study of the Evolution of a Late Medieval Iranian Sufi Tariqah.* Cambridge, Mass.: Harvard University, 2004.
Cornell, Rkia. *Early Sufi Women: Dhikr an-Niswa al-Muta'abbidat al-Sufiyyat.* Louisville: Fons Vitae, 1999.
Crone, Patricia. *The Nativist Prophets of Early Islamic Iran: Rural Revolt and Local Zoroastrianism.* Cambridge: Cambridge University Press, 2012.
Crone, Patricia, and Martin Hinds. *God's Caliph: Religious Authority in the First Centuries of Islam.* Cambridge: Cambridge University Press, 1986.
DeLanda, Manuel. *Assemblage Theory.* Edinburgh: Edinburgh University Press, 2016.
Deleuze, Gilles. *Expressionism in Philosophy: Spinoza.* Translated by M. Joughin. New York: Zone, 1992.
———. *Foucault.* Translated and edited by Sean Hand. Minneapolis: University of Minnesota Press, 1988.
———. "How Do We Recognize Structuralism?" In *Desert Islands and Other Texts, 1953-1974,* edited by David Lapoujade, translated by Michael Taormina, 170–92. New York: Semiotext(e), 2004.
———. *The Logic of Sense.* Translated by Mark Lester with Charles Stivale. Edited by Constantin V. Boundas. London: Athlone, 1990.
———. *Negotiations: 1972–1990.* Translated by Martin Joughin. New York: Columbia University Press, 1995.
———. *Two Regimes of Madness: Texts and Interviews 1975–1995.* Edited by David Lapoujade. Translated by Ames Hodges and Mike Taormina. Cambridge, Mass.: MIT Press, 2007.
Deleuze, Gilles, and Felix Guattari. *Anti-Oedipus: Capitalism and Schizophrenia.* Translated by Robert Hurley, Mark Seem, and Helen R. Lane. Minneapolis: University of Minnesota Press, 1983.
———. *A Thousand Plateaus: Capitalism and Schizophrenia.* Translated by Brian Massumi. London and New York: Continuum, 1987.
———. *What Is Philosophy?* Translated by Hugh Tomlinson and Graham Burchell. New York: Columbia University Press, 1994.
Deleuze, Gilles, and Claire Parnet. *Dialogues.* Translated by Hugh Tomlinson and Barbara Habberjam. New York: Athlone, 1987.
Donner, Fred. *Narratives of Islamic Origins: The Beginnings of Islamic Historical Writing.* Princeton, N.J.: Darwin, 1998.
Dutton, Yasin. *The Origins of Islamic Law: The Qur'an, the Muwatta' and Madinan Amal.* New York: Routledge, 1999.
Ernst, Carl W. *Hallaj: Poems of a Sufi Martyr.* Evanston, Ill.: Northwestern University Press, 2018.

———. *The Shambhala Guide to Sufism*. Boston: Shambhala, 1997.
Ewing, Katherine. "The Politics of Sufism: Redefining the Saints of Pakistan." *Journal of Asian Studies* 42, no. 2 (February 1983): 251–68.
Farrakhan, Louis. *Put on the New Man*. Final Call, 2010, DVD.
Garnett, Lucy M. *Turkey of the Ottomans*. London: Sir Isaac Pitman & Sons, 1911.
Gerdmar, Anders. *Roots of Theological Anti-Semitism: German Biblical Interpretation and the Jews, from Herder and Semler to Kittel and Bultmann*. Leiden: Brill, 2009.
Ghambou, El Mokhtar. *Nomadism and Its Frontiers*. New York: New York University, Graduate School of Arts and Science, 2001.
Gianootti, Timothy J. *Al-Ghazali's Unspeakable Doctrine of the Soul: Unveiling the Esoteric Psychology and Eschatology of the Ihya'*. Leiden: Brill, 2001.
Gibb, H. A. R. *Mohammedanism: An Historical Survey*. 2nd ed. Oxford: Oxford University Press, 1962.
Goodman, L. E. *Avicenna*. London and New York: Routledge, 1992.
Graham, Terry. "Shah Ni'matullah Wali: Founder of the Ni'matullahi Sufi Order." In *The Legacy of Mediaeval Persian Sufism*, edited by Leonard Lewisohn, 173–90. London and New York: Khaniqahi Nimatullahi, 1992.
Green, Tamara M. *The City of the Moon God: Religious Traditions of Harran*. Leiden: Brill, 2007.
Griffel, Frank. "Muslim Philosophers' Rationalist Explanation of Muhammad's Prophecy." In *The Cambridge Companion to Muhammad*, edited by Jonathan E. Brockopp, 158–79. Cambridge: Cambridge University Press, 2010.
Halevi, Leor. *Muhammad's Grave: Death Rites and the Making of Islamic Society*. New York: Columbia University Press, 2007.
Hansu, Huseyin. "Debates on the Authority of Hadith in Early Islamic Intellectual History: Identifying al-Shafi'i's Opponents in Jima' al-'Ilm." *Journal of the American Oriental Society* 136, no. 3 (July–September 2016): 515–33.
Hirtenstein, Stephen. *The Unlimited Mercifier: The Spiritual Life and Thought of Ibn 'Arabi*. Oxford and Ashland: Anqa and White Cloud, 1999.
Hofer, Nathan. *The Popularisation of Sufism in Ayyubid and Mamluk Egypt, 1173–1325*. Edinburgh: Edinburgh University Press, 2015.
Hurvitz, Nimrod. *Ahmad Ibn Hanbal and the Formation of Islamic Orthodoxy*. Princeton, N.J.: Princeton University Press, 1994.
Ibn Hanbal, Ahmed. *Al-Musnad*. Beirut: 'Alam al-Kutub, 1998.
Ibn Majah. *Sunan Ibn Majah*. Sunnah.com. https://sunnah.com/ibnmajah. Accessed August 10, 2020.
Ibn Sa'd, Muhammad. *Tabaqat al-Kubra*. Edited by Muhammed Abd al-Qader 'Ata. Beirut: Dar al-Kutub al-Ilmiyah, 2012.
Jackson, Sherman. "Ibn Taymiyya on trial in Damascus." *Journal of Semitic Studies*, no. 39 (1994): 41–85.
Jaffer, Sadaf. "Trivializing Consent and Minimizing Slavery within American Academia." *AltMuslimah* (February 27, 2017). http://www.altmuslimah

.com/2017/02/trivializing-consent-minimizing-slavery-withinamerican-academia/. Accessed August 10, 2020.

Jung, Dietrich. *Orientalists, Islamists and the Global Public Sphere: A Genealogy of the Modern Essentialist Image of Islam*. Oakville, Conn.: Equinox, 2011.

Junginger, Horst. "From Buddha to Adolf Hitler: Walther Wust and the Aryan Tradition." In *The Study of Religion under the Impact of Fascism*, edited by Horst Junginger, 107–78. Leiden: Brill, 2008.

Justaert, Kristien. *Theology After Deleuze*. New York: Continuum, 2012.

Juynboll, G. H. A. *The Encyclopedia of Canonical Hadith*. Leiden: Brill, 2007.

———. *Muslim Tradition*. Cambridge: Cambridge University Press, 1983.

Karamustafa, Ahmet T. *God's Unruly Friends*. Oxford: Oneworld, 2006.

Katz, Nathan. "The Identity of a Mystic: The Case of Sa'id Sarmad, a Jewish-Yogi-Sufi Courtier of the Mughals." *Numen* 47, no. 2 (2000): 142–60.

Khomeini, Ruhollah. *The Wine of Love: Mystical Poetry of Imam Khomeini*. Translated by Ghulam-Rida A'wani and Muhammad Legenhausen. Tehran: Institute for the Compilation and Publication of Imam Khomeini's Works, 2002.

Kinberg, Leah. "The Legitimization of the Mahdahib through Dreams." *Arabica* 32 (1985): 47–79.

Kister, M. J. "The Massacre of the Banu Qurayza: A Re-examination of a Tradition." *Jerusalem Studies in Arabic and Islam* 8 (1986): 61–96.

Knight, Michael Muhammad. *The Five Percenters: Islam, Hip-Hop, and the Gods of New York*. Oxford: Oneworld, 2007.

———. *Magic in Islam*. New York: TarcherPerigee, 2016.

———. *Metaphysical Africa: Truth and Blackness in the Ansaru Allah Community*. University Park: Pennsylvania State University Press, 2020.

———. *Muhammad's Body: Baraka Networks and the Prophetic Assemblage*. Chapel Hill: The University of North Carolina Press, 2020.

———. *Muhammad: Forty Introductions*. Berkeley, Calif.: Counterpoint, 2019.

———. *Why I Am a Five Percenter*. New York: Tarcher/Penguin, 2011.

———. *Why I Am a Salafi*. Berkeley, Calif.: Counterpoint, 2015.

———. *William S. Burroughs vs. the Qur'an*. Berkeley, Calif.: Soft Skull Press, 2012.

Koelle, S. W. *Mohammed and Mohammedanisim Critically Considered*. London: Rivingtons, 1889.

Knysh, Alexander. *Ibn 'Arabi in the Later Islamic Tradition: The Making of a Polemical Image in Medieval Islam*. Albany: State University of New York Press, 1999.

Lecker, Michael. "Biographical Notes on Ibn Shihab al-Zuhri." *Journal of Semitic Studies* 41, no. 1 (Spring 1996): 21–63.

Lory, Pierre. "The Symbolism of Letters and Language in the Work of Ibn 'Arabi." *Eye of the Heart: A Journal of Traditional Wisdom* 1 (2008): 141–50.

Lucas, Scott C. "Al-Hakim al-Naysaburi and the Companions of the Prophet: An Original Sunni Voice in the Shi'i Century." In *The Heritage of*

Arabo-Islamic Learning: Studies Presented to Wadad Kadi, edited by Maurice A. Pomerantz and Aram Shahin, 236–49. Leiden: Brill, 2015.

———. *Constructive Critics, Hadith Literature, and the Articulation of Sunni Islam: The Legacy of the Generation of Ibn Sa'd, Ibn Ma'in, and Ibn Hanbal.* Leiden: Brill, 2004.

Lipton, Gregory A. *Rethinking Ibn 'Arabi.* Oxford: Oxford University Press, 2018.

Lumbard, Joseph. *Ahmad al-Ghazali, Remembrance, and the Metaphysics of Love.* Albany: State University of New York Press, 2016.

MacDonald, Duncan Black. *Development of Muslim Theology, Jurisprudence, and Constitutional Theory.* New York: Charles Scribner's Sons, 1903.

Madelung, Wilferd. *The Succession to Muhammad: A Study of the Early Caliphate.* Cambridge: Cambridge University Press, 1997.

Malamud, M. "Gender and Spiritual Self-Fashioning: The Master-Disciple Relationship in Classical Sufism." *Journal of the American Academy of Religion* 64, no. 1 (Spring 1996): 89–117.

Marks, Laura U. "A Deleuzian Ijtihad." In *Deleuze and Race*, edited by Arun Saldanha and Jason Michael Adams, 51–72. Edinburgh: Edinburgh University Press, 2012.

Massignon, Louis. *The Passion of al-Hallaj.* Translated by H. Mason. Princeton, N.J.: Princeton University Press, 1994.

Massumi, Brian. *Parables for the Virtual: Movement, Affect, Sensation.* Durham, N.C.: Duke University Press, 2002.

Masuzawa, Tomoko. *The Invention of World Religions: Or, How European Universalism Was Preserved in the Language of Pluralism.* Chicago: University of Chicago Press, 2005.

Mattson, Ingrid. *The Story of the Qur'an: Its History and Place in Muslim Life.* Chichester: Wiley-Blackwell, 2013.

Melchert, Christopher. "The Controversy over Reciting the Qur'ān with Tones." *JIQSA* 4 (2019): 85–109.

———. "The Destruction of Books by Traditionists." *Al-Qantara* 35 (2014): 213–31.

———. "The Early Controversy over Whether the Prophet Saw God." *Arabica* 62 (2015): 459–76.

———. "God Created Adam in His Image." *Journal of Qur'anic Studies* 13, no. 1 (2011): 113–24.

———. "The Musnad of Ahmad ibn Hanbal: How It Was Composed and What Distinguishes It from the Six Books." *Der Islam* 82, no. 1 (2005): 32–51.

———. "Sectaries in the Six Books: Evidence for Their Exclusion from the Sunni Community." *Muslim World* 82 (1992): 287–95.

Meri, Josef. "Aspects of Baraka (Blessings) and Ritual Devotion among Medieval Muslims and Jews." *Medieval Encounters* 5, no. 1 (1999): 46–49.

Miller, Christopher L. "The Postidentitarian Predicament in the Footnotes of *A Thousand Plateaus*: Nomadology, Anthropology, and Authority." *Diacritics* 23, no. 3 (Autumn 1993): 6–35.

Mitha, Farouk. *Al-Ghazali and the Isma'ilis: A Debate on Reason and Authority in Medieval Islam*. London and New York: I. B. Tauris, 2001.
Moin, A. Azfar. *The Millennial Sovereign: Sacred Kingship & Sainthood in Islam*. New York: Columbia University Press, 2014.
Morris, Charles. *The Aryan Race: Its Origins and Its Achievements*. Chicago: S. C. Griggs, 1888.
Murphy, Justin. *Based Deleuze*. Other Life, 2019.
Muslim ibn al-Hajjaj. *Sahih Muslim*. Sunnah.com/muslim. Accessed August 10, 2020.
Al-Nasa'i. *Sunan*. Sunnah.com. https://sunnah.com/nasai. Accessed August 10, 2020.
Nawas, John. "The Contribution of the Mawali to the Six Sunnite Canonical Hadith Collections." In *Ideas, Images, and Methods of Portrayal: Insights into Classical Arabic Literature and Islam*, edited by Sebastian Gunther, 141–51. Leiden: Brill, 2005.
Nesbit, Thomas. *Henry Miller and Religion*. New York and London: Routledge, 2007.
Newell, James R. "Unseen Power: Aesthetic Dimensions of Symbolic Healing in Qawwālī." *Muslim World* 97 (October 2007): 640–56.
Nurbakhsh, Javad. *Dogs from a Sufi Point of View*. London: Khaniqahi Nimatullahi, 1989.
———. *The Great Satan "Eblis."* London: Khaniqahi Nimatullahi, 1986.
———. *Jesus in the Eyes of the Sufis*. London: Khaniqahi Nimatullahi, 1992.
———. *Sufi Symbolism*. 16 vols. London: Khaniqahi Nimatullahi, 1987–2004.
Osman, Amr. "'Adalat al-Sahaba: The Construction of a Religious Doctrine." *Arabica* 60 (2013): 272–305.
Pacey, Arnold. *Technology in World Civilization*. Cambridge, Mass.: MIT Press, 1990.
Pourjavady, Nasrollah. "Stories of Ahmad al-Ghazali Playing the Witness." In *Reason and Inspiration in Islam*, edited by T. Lawson, 200–220. London: I. B. Tauris, 2005.
Pourjavady, Nasrollah, and Peter Lamborn Wilson. *Kings of Love: The History & Poetry of the Ni'matullahi Sufi Order of Iran*. Tehran: Imperial Iranian Academy of Philosophy, 1978.
Puri, Rakshat, and Kuldip Akhtar. "Sarmad, the Naked Faqir." *India International Centre Quarterly*, MONSOON 1993, vol. 20, no. 3 (1993): 65–78.
Qadhi, Yasir. "Collector's Edition: An Intro to Sahih al-Bukhari." Seminar at University of Calgary, June 5–7, 2015.
Redell, Petra Carlsson. *Mysticism as Revolt: Foucault, Deleuze and Theology Beyond Representation*. Aurora: Davies Group, 2014.
Ridgeon, Lloyd. "Mysticism in Medieval Sufism." In *The Cambridge Companion to Sufism*, edited by Lloyd Ridgeon, 125–49. Cambridge: Cambridge University Press, 2014.
Roffe, Jon. *Badiou's Deleuze*. Montreal: McGill-Queen's University Press, 2012.

Rothschild, Jeffrey. *Bestower of Light: A Portrait of Dr. Javad Nurbakhsh, Master of the Nimatullahi Sufi Order*. London and New York: Khaniqahi Nimatullahi, 1999.
al-Sadiq, Ja'far. *Spiritual Gems: The Mystical Qur'an Commentary Ascribed to Ja'far al-Sadqi as Contained in Sulami's Haqa'iq al-Tafsir*. Translated by Farhana Mayer. Louisville: Fons Vitae, 2011.
Safi, Omid. "Bargaining with Baraka: Persian Sufism, 'Mysticism,' and Premodern Politics." *Muslim World* 90, no. 3/4 (2000): 259–88.
Said, Edward. *Orientalism*. New York: Vintage, 1994. Originally published in 1978.
Salem, Feryal. *The Emergence of Early Sufi Piety and Sunni Scholasticism: 'Abdallah b. al-Mubarak and the Formation of Sunni Identity in the Seecond Islamic Century*. Leiden: Brill, 2016.
Sands, Kristin Zahra. *Sufi Commentaries on the Qur'an in Classical Islam*. London and New York: Routledge, 2006.
Sayeed, Asma. *Women and the Transmission of Religious Knowledge in Islam*. Cambridge: Cambridge University Press, 2013.
———. "Women in Imami Biographical Collections." In *Law and Tradition in Classical Islamic Thought*, edited by Michael Cook, Najam Haider, Intisar Rabb, and Asma Sayeed, 81–97. New York: Palgrave, 2013.
Schoeler, Gregor. *The Oral and Written in Early Islam*. New York: Routledge, 2006.
———. "Oral Torah and Hadith: Transmission, Prohibition of Writing, Redaction." In *Hadith: Origins and Developments*, edited by Harald Motzki, 67–108. New York: Routledge, 2016.
Shahi, Afshin. *The Politics of Truth Management in Saudi Arabia*. New York: Routledge, 2013.
Shults, F. LeRon. *Iconoclastic Theology: Gilles Deleuze and the Secretion of Atheism*. Edinburgh: Edinburgh University Press, 2014.
Sila-Khan, Dominique. *Crossing the Threshold: Understanding Religious Identities in South Asia*. London: I. B. Tauris, 2004.
Silvers, Laury. "The Teaching Relationship in Early Sufism: A Reassessment of Fritz Meier's Definition of the *shaykh al-tarbiya* and the *shaykh al-ta'līm*." *Muslim World* 93, no. 1 (2003): 69–97.
Smith, Daniel W. *Essays on Deleuze*. Edinburgh: Edinburgh University Press, 2012.
Speight, R. Marston. *The Musnad of al-Tayalisi: A Study of Islamic Hadith as Oral Literature*. Hartford, Conn.: Hartford Seminary Foundation, 1970.
Stephens, W. R. W. *Christianity & Islam: The Bible and the Koran; Four Lectures by the Rev. W.R.W. Stephens*. New York: Scribner, Armstrong, 1877.
Strong, John S. *Buddhisms: An Introduction*. Oxford: Oneworld, 2015.
Supp-Montgomerie, Jenna. "Affect and the Study of Religion." *Religion Compass* 9/10 (2015): 335–45.

Al-Tabari. *The History of al-Tabari*. Vol. 15, *The Crisis of the Early Caliphate*. Translated by R. Stephen Humphreys. Albany: State University of New York Press, 1990.

Talmon-Heller, Daniella. "Historiography in the Service of the Mufti: Ibn Taymiyya on the Origins and Fallacies of Ziyarat." *Islamic Law and Society* 26 (2019): 227–51.

Taneja, Anand Vivek. "Jinnealogy: Everyday Life and Islamic Theology in Post-Partition Delhi." *HAU: Journal of Ethnographic Theory* 3 (2013): 139–65.

Tiele, C. P. *The Religion of the Iranian Peoples*. Translated by G. K. Nariman. Bombay: "Parsi" Publishing, 1912.

Tirmidhi. *Jami'*. Sunnah.com/tirmidhi. Accessed August 2020.

Treiger, Alexander. "Monism and Monotheism in al-Ghazali's Mishkat al-Anwar." *Journal of Qur'anic Studies* 9, no. 1 (2007): 1–27.

Tutt, Daniel. "Deleuzian Theology and the Immanence of the Act of Being." *SCTIW Review* (December 1, 2015). http://sctiw.org/sctiwreviewarchives/archives/870.

van Bladel, Kevin. "Heavenly Cords and Prophetic Authority in the Quran and Its Late Antique Context." *Bulletin of the School of Oriental and African Studies* 70 (2007): 223–46.

Van Ess, Josef. "The Youthful God: Anthropomorphism in Early Islam." University Lecture in Religion at Arizona State University, 1988.

wadud, amina. *Inside the Gender Jihad*. Oxford: Oneworld, 2006.

Ware, Rudolph T. III. *The Walking Qur'an: Islamic Education, Embodied Knowledge, and History in West Africa*. Chapel Hill: University of North Carolina Press, 2014.

Wasserstrom, Steven M. *Religion after Religion: Gershom Scholem, Mircea Eliade, and Henry Corbin at Eranos*. Princeton, N.J.: Princeton University Press, 1999.

Watson, Janell. "The Face of Christ: Deleuze and Guattari on the Politics of Word and Image." *The Bible and Critical Theory* 1, no. 2 (2005): 04.1–04.14.

Watt, William Montgomery. *Muhammad at Mecca*. Oxford: Clarendon Press, 1953.

Weheliye, Alexander G. *Habeas Viscus: Racializing Assemblages, Biopolitics, and Black Feminist Theories of the Human*. Durham, N.C.: Duke University Press, 2014.

Wells, H. G. *The Outline of History: Being a Plain History of Life and Mankind*. 3rd ed. New York: Macmillan, 1921.

Widney, J. P. *The Genesis and Evolution of Islam and Judaeo-Christianity*. Los Angeles: Pacific Publishing, 1932.

Winter, Stefan. *Shiites of Lebanon under Ottoman Rule, 1516–1788*. Cambridge: Cambridge University Press, 2010.

Yilmaz, Huseyin. *Caliphate Redefined: The Mystical Turn in Ottoman Political Thought*. Princeton, N.J.: Princeton University Press, 2018.

Zadeh, Travis. "Touching and Ingesting: Early Debates over the Material Qur'an." *Journal of the American Oriental Society* 129, no. 3 (2009): 443–66.

Zamiska, Donna L. "The Ikhwan of Saudi Arabia Past and Present." Ph.D. diss., McGill University, 1993, 13–14.

Zargar, Cyrus. *Polished Mirror: Storytelling and the Pursuit of Virtue in Islamic Philosophy and Sufism*. Oxford: OneWorld, 2017.

al-Zarkashi, Badruddin Muhammad bin Bahadir. *Al-Ijaba li-Iradi Ma Istadrakatuhu A'isha 'Ala al-Sahaba*. Syria: Al-Kutub al-Islamiyya, 1939.

Index

'Abbasid dynasty, 67, 76, 146
'Abd Allah ibn Mu'awiya, 132
'Abd Allah Intizam, 93
Abu Bakr, 66, 105, 106, 109, 148
Abu Dharr, 124
Abu Hurayra, 111, 140
Abu Mu'awiyya (d. 185-95/801-11), 75
'adalat al-sahaba, Companions of Muhammad and, 78
Adkins, Brent, 43, 48
affect theory, 101, 102
al-Ahad (al-Ikhlas) sura, 53
Ahmed, Shahab, 109, 110, 112, 113, 114-15, 116-17, 122
A'isha (wife of Muhammad), (d. 58/678), 65-70, 73, 75, 105, 111, 124, 153
Akbar (Emperor), 96
Akhtar, Kuldip, 1
Algar, Hamid, 31
Ali, Asghar, *87*
Ali, Yusuf, 140, 143
'Ali (4th Caliph), 62, 64, 66-68, 91, 106
Allah, 104; Buddha and, 47; Fard Muhammad as, 135, 136; God, 10, 13, 23, 24, 28, 31, 62, 95, 119, 123-25, 128-43, 147, 151-52; Ibn al-'Arabi as, 134; as surname, 139
Allah (the former Clarence 13X), 22-23, 119, 120, 137-39, 141, *142*, 143
Allah, Universal Shamgaudd, 139-40
Allah Born God (Bilal), 138
allegories (*ishara*), 55

Alphabets, Supreme, 143
al-A'mash (d. 148-56 / 745-52), 71, 72
Amina (mother of Muhammad), 108
Andjuman-i Ukhuwwat (Society of Brotherhood), 93
angels, 46, 47, 82, 104, 123-24, 133, 139
Anis, Mir Babar Ali (1803-74), 5
anthropomorphism, 124-29, 136
anti-jinn talisman, 43, 44
Anti-Oedipus (Deleuze and Guattari), 19, 32, 34, 58, 152
anti-Semitism, 28, 86
Arabic letters, 41, 42-43, 54, 55, 147, 152
Aristotle, 12
Armstrong, Lyall R., 76
art, 30, 37, 42, 53, 54, 122
Aryanism, 31-32, 33
Aryanist ideology, 28-29
Aryans (Persians), 28-29
Aryan spirituality, 86
The Aryan Race (Morris), 30
Ash-Shu'ara ("The Poets"), 46
asignifying rupture, rhizome, 40, 53-54
Assemblage Theory (Delanda), 61
astrology, 51
atheism, 14, 119-20, 121, 123, 136-37. *See also* Islamic atheism
Aurangzeb (Mughal crown prince), 6-8
authority, from genealogy, 92
Avicenna (Ibn Sina), 11-12, 14, 19, 110, 117
ayahuasca, 100, 102

182 / INDEX

Ayat al-Kursi, 53–54
Azreal (John Kennedy), 139

Baba, Tajuddin (1861–1925), 97, 98
Badiou, Alan, 11
Badu, Erykah, 137
"Balkans-to-Bengal complex," 114–15
Baqi' al-Gharqad. *See* Jannat al-Baqi cemetery
baraka (energy flow, force), 3–4, 7, 78, 92, 98, 102, 104; with immanence and transcendence, 116, 118; Jannat al-Baqi cemetery and, 22, 105–9; as territory, 117
baraka nails, 5, 5–6
Barber, Daniel Coluciello, 10–11
al-Basri, Hasan (d. 110/728), 62, 72, 92
Battle of the Camel, 66, 67
al-Bayhaqi, 82
b-d-'a root, 147
"becoming a Sufi" (tasawwuf), 84, 85, 99
Bektashis, 90
Berg, Herbert, 67
Bey, Hakim, 2
Bezels of Wisdom (*Fusus al-Hikam*) (Ibn al-'Arabi), 52, 128–29
the Bible, 30, 34, 36, 47, 50–51, 59
bida', 16, 146–50, 152–53
Bigelow, Anna, 43
Bilal (Allah Born God), 138
al-Bistami, Abu Yazid, 92, 96
Bixby, James T., 29–30
Black godhood, 23, 24, 119, 136, 141–42
Black Stone, 19, 141
bodies, 8, 20, 76, 78, 90, 141; corporeal anthropomorphism, 124, 136; of God, 130; God in, 132; isnads and, 80–81; of Muhammad (Prophet), 124, 148, 153–54; Qur'an and, 45–46, 60; representation and divine, 123–27; Sufism, 21–22, 85, 92, 97–103. *See also* hadith corpus; Jannat al-Baqi cemetery
body system, religion as, 2
Body without Organs. *See* BwO
book culture, 77, 80, 149
Braidotti, Rosi, 101
"Brothers of Purity" (Ikhwan as-Safa'), 51
Brown, Jonathan A. C., 9
Buddha, 33–34, 47, 140
Buddhism, 9, 33, 86
Al-Bukhari, Muhammad ibn Isma'il, 76, 77, 82
Bullhe Shah, 23, 140

Burckhardt, Johann Lewis, 107–8
burial shrouds, 91
al-Bushanji, Abu Hasan, 84–85, 91
Butler, Judith, 8
BwO (Body without Organs), 16, 36, 78, 82, 133, 141; Deleuze and Guattari on, 20; deterritorialization of, 125; Islam as, 19; Sarmad and, 6

calligraphy, 41, 42–43, 54, 55
Capitalism and Schizophrenia (Deleuze and Guattari), 26, 32, 36, 58. *See also Anti-Oedipus*; *A Thousand Plateaus*
Carlyle, Thomas (1795–1881), 48
cartography, rhizome, 40, 54–55
cemetery. *See* Jannat al-Baqi cemetery
chakrahs, 151, 152
Chand, Abhay, 6
Chan Pir shrine, 88
Chaudhry, Ayesha, 40
China, 47, 77, 149, 153
Christianity, 10, 11, 15, 30, 36, 86, 140; atheism of, 14, 119–20, 123; Judaism and, 28, 37
Clarence 13X (Clarence Edward Smith, Allah). *See* Allah (the former Clarence 13X)
The Clear Fountain on the Forty Paths (al-Sanusi), 94
clerical scholars ('ulama), 4, 21, 55, 82, 90, 115, 122, 146
cloth, white, 91
coins, 91, 122
Colin, G. S., 116
Companions (al-Sahaba) of Muhammad, 114, 124, 130, 149; hadith corpus and, 62–72, 74, 77, 78; isnads and, 63, 81; with musnad genre, 64–68; *tabi'in* and *tabi' al-tabi'in*, 68–72, 78–79; women, 66, 67–69
connection, rhizome, 40–50
consistent adherence to a legal school (taqlid), 144, 145
Con-Text, 110, 112–14, 117, 122, 139
Corbin, Henri, 31
corporeal anthropomorphism, 124, 136
"creeping shari'a," 18
Crone, Patricia, 132
cultures: books, 77, 80, 149; hadiths, 70; religion vs., 148; shrine, 22, 96–98

Dara Shikoh (Mughal crown prince), 6–8, 46, 50

INDEX / 183

dargahs, 1–5, 14, 19
al-Dastawa'i, Hisham, 79
Day of Sorrow (Yaum-e-Gham), 108
decalcomania, rhizome, 40, 54–55
Delanda, Manuel, 61, 77
Deleuze, Gilles, 4, 10, 15; *Anti-Oedipus*, 19, 32, 34, 58, 152; on BwO, 20; *Capitalism and Schizophrenia*, 26, 32, 36, 58; *Expressionism in Philosophy*, 119, 127; on philosophy, 158n29; *What Is Philosophy?*, 1, 13, 119. See also *A Thousand Plateaus*; specific topics
Deleuze and Guattari camp/conference, 1, 2–3
Deleuze and the Naming of God (Barber), 10
Deleuzian theology, 8–20, 102, 132–33
Deleuzo-Islamic theology, 11, 13–16, 133, 144, 146, 150, 153
Delhi, 4, 5, 7, 15
Della Vida, Giorgio Levi, 27
Derrida, Jacques, 12
dervish groups, Sufism, 90, 91–92, 94, 95
despotic machine, 32–36
deterritorialization, 19, 41, 81, 113; of BwO, 125; reterritorialization and, 45, 54, 57, 77, 93, 111, 114; Sufism and, 85, 94, 95, 96; tashbih and, 125–26
dice, geomancy, 51
dimethyltryptamine (DMT), 60, 100
The Divinity of the Human Soul (Khan), 3
DNA, 80
Dogs from a Sufi Point of View (Nurbakhsh), 95–96
domes, 105, 107, 109, 110, 113, 114, 116
"Dot-ists" (Nuqtaviyya), 43
drinking or ingesting, Qur'an, 33, 34, 43
drugs (medicine), 60, 96–97, 100, 102
Dumezil, Georges (1898–1986), 31
Duns Scotus, John, 12, 21, 87

Egypt, 33, 89, 90
energy flow. See baraka
Enlightenment, 28
Enoch (Idris, Hermes), 51
Ernst, Carl, 94
Expressionism in Philosophy (Deleuze), 119, 127

fada'il al-sahaba ("virtues of the Companions"), 77
family trees, 23, 27
Farrakhan, Louis, 136, 139
fascicular root-book, 20, 35–40, 57

fascism, 31, 54
al-Fatiha sura, 52–53, 55
Fatima az-Zahra (daughter of Muhammad), 60, 100, 106, 108
Fatima bt. Asad, 105
FBI, 138
Female Singers' Prohibition Act (1943), 115
feminists, 17, 38, 57, 148, 151
Firoz Shah Kotla palace complex, 5
Five Percenters: Allah (the former Clarence 13X) and, 22–23, 119, 120, 137–39, 141, 142, 143; Black godhood and, 23, 24, 119, 136, 141–42; hip hop and, 23, 138, 140; Muslim Gods and, 131–43; Nation of Islam and, 23, 119, 134–37, 139–41; theology, 23–24, 151
"five pillars" model, Islam and, 13
force. See baraka
Foucault, Michel, 110
Fusus al-Hikam (*Bezels of Wisdom*) (Ibn al-'Arabi), 52, 128–29

Gabriel (angel), 82, 104, 123–24
Garnett, Lucy M., 28
gender, 8, 66, 69, 73, 151, 152
Gender Trouble (Butler), 8
genealogy: authority from, 92; Qur'an and colonial, 26–36. See also isnads
geomancy dice, 51
al-Ghazali, Abu Hamid, 11, 14, 56, 85, 92, 101, 144
al-Ghazali, Ahmad, 92, 101, 127
Ghoray Shah (d. 1594), 18, 19
Gibb, H. A. R., 30
Gobineau, Arthur de, 31
God, 10, 13, 28, 31, 62, 95, 151–52; Allah Born God, 138; Black godhood, 23, 24, 119, 136, 141–42; Five Percenters and, 23; Muslim, 131–43; in Qur'an, 123–25, 128–30, 147. See also Allah
graves, pilgrimage to, 106–7, 111, 114. See also Jannat al-Baqi cemetery
Great Collection of Fabrications (*al-Mawdu'at al-Kubra*) (Ibn al-Jawzi), 82
The Great Satan "Eblis" (Nurbakhsh), 96
Guattari, Felix, 15, 20; *Anti-Oedipus*, 19, 32, 34, 58, 152; *Capitalism and Schizophrenia*, 26, 32, 36, 58; Deleuze and Guattari camp/conference, 1, 2–3; *What Is Philosophy?*, 1, 13, 119. See also *A Thousand Plateaus*; specific topics
Gunabadi lineage, 93

184 / INDEX

Habeas Viscus (Weheliye), 17
haddathani ("he narrated to me"), 76
hadith corpus: baraka and, 3; Companions of Muhammad and, 62–72, 74, 77, 78; formation of, 61–62; from Ibn al-Hajjaj to musnads, 72–83; isnads and, 21, 148; matn and, 62; *Musnad* of al-Tayalisi and, 63–70, 72–74, 82, 153; *Musnad* of Ibn Hanbal, 74, 75, 76, 82; oral traditions and, 62, 67; Qur'an and, 48, 123–24, 147; Six Books canon, 76–77, 82, 147; Sunna based on, 65, 73; with *tabi'in* and *tabi' al-tabi'in*, 68–72, 78–79
"Hadith of Cringing," 80–81
"Hadith of the Slave Girl," 129
hadiths, 70, 73–74, 154; horse-sweat, 62, 82, 130–31; isnads and, 62–64, 69, 71, 72, 80, 93
Hafsa bt. Sirin, 69
Halevi, Leor, 106
al-Hallaj, Mansur, 88, 89, 102, 131–32, 134
Hallajian Abstract Machine, 88–89
Hallajiyya, 94
Hanbali Abstract Machine, 89
Hanbali school, 48, 50, 113
haramayn (Islamic holy cities), 105. *See also* Mecca; Medina
Hartmann, Martin, 27
Hatimiyya, 94
Haydar, Amir, 87
Haydaris, 90
"he narrated to me" (*haddathani*), 76
Hermes (Idris, Enoch), 51
heterogeneity, rhizome, 40, 50–52
al-Hilali, Muhammad Taqi-ud-Din, 48
Hilali-Khan translation of Qur'an, 47–48, 52
Hinduism, 37, 86, 96
hip hop, 23, 138, 140
Hitler, Adolf, 33
"holy fool" (*majdhub* saint), 97
horse-sweat hadith, 62, 82, 130–31
al-Hujwiri, 94
hulul (incarnationism), 126, 132, 133, 135
Hurufiyya ("Lettrists"), 42–43, 132
Hurvitz, Nimrod, 74, 75
Husayn (Prophet's grandson), 5

Ibn 'Abbas, 'Abd Allah (d. 68/687–88), 65–69, 73–74, 80
Ibn 'Abd al-Malik, Hisham (r. 105–25 / 724–43), 71

Ibn 'Abd al-Muttalib, 'Abbas (uncle of Muhammad), 105
Ibn 'Abd al-Wahhab, Muhammad (1703–92), 113
Ibn Abi Mulayka (d. 117/735), 69
Ibn al-'Arabi (1165–1240), 7, 17, 21, 42, 43, 46, 52, 56–57, 81, 131; as Allah, 134; Five Percenters and, 23, 140; influence of, 85, 101; on Noah, 128–29; shrine of, 112; Sufism and, 90, 99
Ibn al-Hajjaj, Shu'ba (d. 160/776), 72–83
Ibn al-Hakam, Hisham, 130
Ibn 'Ali, Hasan (grandson of Muhammad), 105
Ibn al-Jarrah, Waki' (d. 814/198), 75
Ibn al-Jawzi, 82
Ibn al-Zubayr, 'Urwa, 68
Ibn Anas, Malik (711–795), 65, 74, 82, 83, 106
Ibn Bashir, Hushaym (d. 799/183), 74
Ibn Da'ima, Qatada, 71, 72
Ibn Habib al-Isbahani, Yunus (d. 267/881), 74
Ibn Hanbal, Ahmad (d. 241/855), 74–77, 79, 82–83, 88–89, 127
Ibn Harn, Yazid, 75
Ibn Ishaq (704–68), 83
Ibn Ja'far, Isma'il, 92
Ibn Mahdi, 'Abd al-Rahman (d. 198/814), 74, 75
Ibn Malik, Anas (d. 91–93/710–12), 65–70, 72–73, 82
Ibn Mas'ud, 'Abd Allah (d. 32/652), 65–69, 73
Ibn Sina (Avicenna), 11–12, 14, 19, 110, 117
Ibn Sirin, Muhammad, 68, 149
Ibn Taymiyya (1263–1328), 106–7, 108, 116, 126
Ibn 'Ulayya (d. 809/193), 74
Ibn 'Uyayna, Sufyan (d. 198/814), 75
Ibrahim (son of Muhammad), 105
idolatry, shrines and, 107
Idris (Enoch, Hermes), 51
al-Ijaba li-Iradi Ma Istadrakatuhu A'isha 'Ala al-Sahaba, 68
ijtihad (independent reasoning), 144, 145
al-Ikhlas (al-Ahad) sura, 53
Ikhwan as-Safa' ("Brothers of Purity"), 51
'Ikrima, 68
immanence: baraka and, 116, 118; Islamic theology and, 22, 120, 133; pure, 8, 12, 22, 142; transcendence and, 10
Inayat Khan, Hazrat (1882–1927), 2

INDEX / 185

incarnationism (hulul), 126, 132, 133, 135
independent reasoning (ijtihad), 144, 145
India, 33, 88, 93
Indonesia, 33
Inside the Gender Jihad (Wadud), 151
interpretation, of Qur'an, 48–49, 57
interpretosis, 13, 25, 57–58, 143
The Invention of World Religions (Masuzawa), 27
Iran, 28, 31, 33, 86, 90, 92–95, 132
ishara (allegories), 55
ISIS, 22, 115
Islam, 4, 13, 27, 41, 66, 85, 96, 105; as BwO, 19; of Islamic atheism, 121–23, 127, 131, 150, 152; monotheism, 28, 29, 30, 32; Nation of Islam, 23, 119, 134–37, 139–41; Qur'an as Bible of, 34, 36, 47, 59; Qur'an as center of, 30, 39; Sufism and, 86, 88; Sunni, 7, 79, 88–89, 91, 111–13, 145–46; "true," 15, 104, 126; *What Is Islam?*, 109, 110, 122
Islamic atheism, 13–14, 61, 103; BwO and, 82; Five Percenters, 141; Islam of, 121–23, 127, 131, 150, 152; Nation of Islam and, 119; Qur'an and, 58
Islamic Center of Los Angeles, 100
"Islamic fundamentalism," 151
Islamic holy cities (haramayn), 105. See also Mecca; Medina
Islamic theology: anthropomorphism, 129; Deleuzo-, 11, 13–16, 133, 144, 146, 150, 153; horse-sweat hadith and, 130–31; immanence and, 22, 120, 133; Muslim Gods and, 131; Platonism and, 113; Qur'an and, 145–46
Isma'il I (d. 1524), 90
Isma'ilis, 56
isnads: Companions of Muhammad and, 63, 81; hadith corpus and, 21, 148; hadiths and, 62–64, 69, 71, 72, 80, 93; women disappearing from, 76
Ithna Ash'ari Shi'i imamate, 110–11

Jabal al-Nur (Mountain of Light), 104–5
Jama Masjid, Delhi, 5, 7, 15
Jamia Millia Islamia, 1
Jannat al-Baqi (Baqi' al-Gharqad) cemetery, Medina: baraka and, 22, 105–9; as territory, 109–18
al-Jawaliqi, Hisham, 130
al-Jawaribi, Dawud, 130
Jehangir (emperor), 122
Jesus, 28, 95, 136–37, 147

Jesus in the Eyes of the Sufis (Nurbakhsh), 95
jinns, 5, 43, 44, 80
Judaism, 28–30, 34, 37
Juynboll, G. H., 66, 72

Ka'ba, 19, 44, 131
Kant, Immanuel (1724–1804), 28, 29
Karamustafa, Ahmet T., 132
Khadija (wife of Muhammad), 153
Khan, Dominique-Sila, 4, 96
Khan, Muhsin, 47–48, 52
khanaqah (Sufi lodge), 21, 85, 89, 91–92, 95, 98–100, 102
Khomeini (Ayatollah), 37, 90, 93
kh-t-m root, 152
Khusrow, Amir (1253–1325), 1
King, Martin Luther, Jr., 138
kitab ("writing"/"book"), 41
Kuryluk, Eva, 37

lata'if (subtleties), 55
legislator gods, 31
"Lettrists" (Hurufiyya), 42–43, 132
Lindsay, John, 138
Lipton, Gregory A., 32
lobster god, 13, 62

MacCulloch, John Arnott, 27
machines: despotic, 32–36; DMT, 60; Hallajian Abstract, 88–89; Hanbali Abstract, 89; Qur'an, 36–58
magical technologies, texts, 33
magician gods, 31
majdhub saint ("holy fool"), 97
Malamatiyya, 95
Mamluks, 89, 90
Manichaeism, 86
Marks, Laura, 11
Marwan I, 106
masjids, 5, 7, 15, 105, 108
Massumi, Brian, 101
Masuzawa, Tomoko, 27
Mathematics, Supreme, 143
matn, hadith corpus and, 62
mausolea, 22, 105, 108, 110, 114, 115, 116. See also Jannat al-Baqi cemetery
al-Mawdu'at al-Kubra (*Great Collection of Fabrications*) (Ibn al-Jawzi), 82
Mecca, 67, 75, 104, 134; Medina and, 105; pilgrimage to, 107–9, 114, 141; as sole authentic "holy place," 4, 114; "Wahhabism" and, 38

medicine (drugs), 60, 96–97, 100, 102
Medina, 65, 66, 68, 70, 71, 72, 74, 83; Jannat al-Baqi cemetery, 22, 105–18; Mecca and, 105; "Wahhabism" and, 38
Melchert, Christopher, 41–42, 73, 75, 76
mental illness, 97
Meri, Joseph, 116
Mirza (Munis) 'Ali Shah, 93, 94
Mohammedanism (Gibb), 30
monotheism: Islam, 28, 29, 30, 32; Qur'an, 30
Morris, Charles, 30
Moses (biblical figure), 36, 37, 47, 95
Mosque No. 7, Harlem, 119, 137–38
Mothership, Noah and, 127–31
Mountain of Light (Jabal al-Nur), 104–5
Mu'awiyya (caliph), 106
Mughals, 6–8, 122
Muhaiyaddeen, Bawa, 96
Muhammad (Prophet), 6–7, 20, 37, 52, 62, 66; ascension of, 133–34; baraka and, 3, 92, 98; body of, 124, 148, 153–54; God and, 123–24; "Hadith of Cringing" and, 80–81; as Moses, 36; Qur'an and, 104, 123, 152; shrine to, 107; transcendence and, 11. *See also* Companions of Muhammad
Muhammad, Burnsteen Sharrieff, 136
Muhammad, Elijah, 19, 23, 135, 136, 137–38, 141, 142–43
Muhammad, Master Fard, 134–36, 138, 143
Muhammadiyya path, 95
Muir, William (1819–1905), 27
Mukhammisa, 132
Mulla Sadra, 6, 12
multiplicity, rhizome, 40, 52–53
Munawwar Ali Shah, 93
Munis 'Ali Shah. *See* Mirza 'Ali Shah
al-Muqanna, 132
music, 1, 96–97, 115, 122
Music in Muslim Shrines Act (1942), 115
"Muslim Christ," Qur'an as, 37
Muslim Gods, 131–43
Muslim Pseudo, 24, 152
Muslims, 23, 54, 101, 115
Musnad (al-Tayalisi), 63–70, 72–74, 82, 153
Musnad (Ibn Hanbal), 74, 75, 76, 82
musnads: Companions of Muhammad with, 64–68; Ibn al-Hajjaj to, 72–83
Mu'tazila, 76, 126, 145–46
Muwahidun ("Wahhabism"), 38, 52, 107, 110, 113
mystics, 5, 7, 88, 97, 102, 127, 132

Nabi without Organs (NwO), 82
nails, baraka, 5, 5–6
namaz, 1, 8, 99
Nation of Islam, 23, 119, 134–37, 139–41
Nawas, John, 76
negation (ta'til), 124, 125–26
Nimatullahi order, 90–95, 99–100, 136, 139, 143, 152
Nimatullah Wali, Sayyid Nur al-Din Shah, 92–94, 136
Nizamuddin Awliya (1238–1325), 1, 2
Noah, Mothership and, 127–31
Nubian Islamic Hebrews, 50–51
Nuqtaviyya ("Dot-ists"), 43
Nurbakhsh, Javad, 93–94, 95–96, 100
nutmeg, 91
NwO (Nabi without Organs), 82

"On and On," 137
oral traditions, 21, 62, 67, 70, 71, 77, 148
orchid, wasp and, 45
Orientalism, 26, 27, 34, 58
Orientalism (Said), 58
orthodoxy, 16, 132–33
Otman Baba, 132
Ottoman Empire, 7, 37, 90, 108, 111–13

paganism, 28, 31
Pahlavi regime, 31
Pakistan, 4, 33, 88, 115
paper technology, 77, 149
Persians (Aryans), 28–29
Pfleiderer, Otto, 29
philosophy: Deleuze on, 158n29; *Expressionism in Philosophy*, 119, 127; "Sufi-philosophical amalgam," 112; Sufism and, 87, 98; *What Is Philosophy?*, 1, 13, 119
pilgrimage (ziyarat), 106–9, 111, 114, 116–17, 141
pir (title for Sufi spiritual guide), 87, 87
Plato, 12, 113, 153
"The Poets" (*Ash-Shu'ara*), 46
prisoners, Chinese, 77, 149
prison system, Five Percenters and, 23
pure immanence, 8, 12, 22, 142
Puri, Rakshat, 1

Qadhi, Yasir, 145
Qadiriyya, 93, 94, 96, 98
al-Qaeda, 115
Qalandars, 90, 95
al-Qarani, Uways, 95
qawwali musical tradition, 1

Qur'an, 121; as "Bible" of Islam, 34, 36, 47, 59; body and, 45–46, 60; as center of Islam, 30, 39; colonial genealogy of one half-sentence, 26–36; despotic machine, 32–36; drinking or ingesting, 33, 34, 43; Five Percenters and, 142–43; God in, 123–25, 128–30, 147; hadith corpus and, 48, 123–24, 147; interpretation of, 48–49, 57; Islamic atheism and, 58; Islamic theology and, 145–46; levels of meaning, 55–56; machines, 36–58; Muhammad (Prophet) and, 104, 123, 152; reading, 48–49, 52–53; Revelation and, 50–51; as rhizome, 36, 40; Sufism and, 99, 140; tajwid, 41–42; in *A Thousand Plateaus*, 25, 26; translations of, 47–48, 52, 55
"Qur'anists," 53

ar-Rahman sura, 53
Rahmat 'Ali Shah, 93
Rakim, 138
reading, Qur'an, 48–49, 52–53
reciting the Qur'an with tones (tajwid), 41–42
Redell, Petra Carlsson, 12
religion, 2, 27, 85, 86, 89, 148
Religion, Its Origin and Forms (MacCulloch), 27
Renan, Ernest (1823–92), 28–29
representation: with atheism of Christianity, 119–20; divine body and, 123–27
reterritorialization: deterritorialization and, 45, 54, 57, 77, 93, 111, 114; Sufism and, 84, 93; tanzih, 125
Revelation, Qur'an and, 50–51
rhizome-book, 20, 35, 37, 40, 48, 59
rhizomes: asignifying rupture, 40, 53–54; cartography, 40, 54–55; connection, 40–50; decalcomania, 40, 54–55; defined, 40; heterogeneity, 40, 50–52; multiplicity, 40, 52–53; principles, 40–41, 50–55; as Qur'an, 36, 40; trees and, 34, 63, 94
ring, 91
rock candy, 91
root-book, 20, 27, 35–37, 39–41, 46, 59, 61

as-Sadiq, Ja'far, 55
Safi 'Ali-Shahiyya lineage, 93
Safiya (aunt of Muhammad), 105
al-Sahaba. See Companions of Muhammad
Said, Edward, 58
Sain, Pappu, 96
saints, 4, 5, 97

Saladin, 89–90
the Salaf, 33, 107, 113
salat, 1, 142
al-Sanusi al-Idrisi, Muhammad (1787–1859), 94–95
Sarmad, Muhammad Sa'id (d. 1659), 1, 5–8
"Sarmad, the Naked Faqir" (Puri and Akhtar), 1
Satan, 92, 96, 153
Saudi Arabia, 48, 115
Saudi state, 22, 37–38, 80, 88, 112–13, 116, 125; with Mecca, 4; Mountain of Light and, 104–5; with sacred sites demolished, 108; self-legitimation of, 105, 115
Sayeed, Asma, 69, 76
Schuon, Frithjof (1907–98), 31–32
"Seal of the Prophets," Muhammad as, 152
the Seal, origin story, 153
sedimentary rock, creation of, 61
Selim (Sultan), 112
sex, 43, 58
sexualities, illicit, 127
al-Shafi'i (d. 204/820), 73
shahadah, 6, 8, 13, 127
shahidbazi ("witness play"), 127
Shah Jamal (1588–1671), 96–97
shajaras, Sufism, 92–93, 95
Shambhala Guide to Sufism (Ernst), 94
Al-Shibli, 43
Shi'ism, 23, 73, 90, 93–95, 112–14
Shikoh, Dara, 46, 50
shrines, 88, 112, 113, 115; bulldozing of, 4, 7, 22; culture, 22, 96–98; domed, 107, 108
Shults, F. LeRon, 119–20, 123
Silvers, Laury, 94
sira projects, 83
Sirin family, 68–69
Six Books canon, 76–77, 82, 147
slavery, 9–10, 69, 91, 129
Smith, Clarence Edward. See Allah (the former Clarence 13X)
Smith, Daniel W., 10
Smith, Robertson, 27
smooth space, 4, 50, 70, 79, 133–34, 140, 149
Society of Brotherhood (Andjuman-i Ukhuwwat), 93
sola scriptura arguments, 38
South Asian shrine culture, 96
Speight, R. Marston, 73
Sphinx, 90
Spinoza, Baruch, 12, 14, 21, 87, 98, 119
spirituality: Aryan, 86; shrine culture and, 97; Sufism and, 85–87, 92

"strata" (tabaqat), 77–78
subtleties (*lata'if*), 55
Successors (*tabi'in*), 68–72, 78–79, 149
Successors of the Successors (*tabi' al-tabi'in*), 68–72, 78–79
Sufi lodge (khanaqah), 21, 85, 89, 91–92, 95, 98–100, 102
Sufi orders (tariqas), 89–96, 99–100, 136, 139, 143, 152
"Sufi-philosophical amalgam," 112
Sufism, 32, 112, 113, 115; affects, 97–101; Aryanist ideology and, 28–29; bodies, 21–22, 85, 92, 97–103; deterritorialization and, 85, 94, 95, 96; *Dogs from a Sufi Point of View*, 95–96; *The Great Satan "Eblis"*, 96; *Jesus in the Eyes of the Sufis*, 95; order and assemblage, 88–97; philosophy and, 87, 98; Qur'an and, 99, 140; reterritorialization and, 84, 93; shajaras, 92–93, 95; *Shambhala Guide to Sufism*, 94; spirituality and, 85–87, 92; "theoretical" orders, 94–95
Sufi Symbolism (Nurbakhsh), 100
Suhrawardi, 12, 19, 87, 90, 96
Sunna, 148; as concept, 149; hadith-based, 65, 73; Ibn Hanbal and, 76
Sunni Islam, 7, 79, 88–89, 91, 111–13, 145–46
Supp-Montgomerie, Jenna, 102
sura, 39, 43, 45–46, 52–55
surname, Allah as, 139
Syed Abdullah Shah, 97–98

tabaqat ("strata"), 77–78
al-Tabarani, 82
al-Tabari, 88
tabi' al-tabi'in (Successors of the Successors), 68–72, 78–79
tabi'in (Successors), 68–72, 78–79, 149
tajwid (reciting the Qur'an with tones), 41–42
talisman, anti-jinn, 43, 44
Taneja, Anand Vivek, 80
tanzih (transcendence), 124–25, 128, 133
taqlid (consistent adherence to a legal school), 144, 145
tariqas (Sufi orders), 89–96, 99–100, 136, 139, 143, 152
tasawwuf ("becoming a Sufi"), 84, 85, 99
tashbih (anthropomorphism), 124–26, 128–29
ta'til (negation), 124, 125–26
tawhid, 13, 124, 126, 128

al-Tayalisi, Sulayman Abu Dawud (133–204 / 751–820), 63–70, 72–76, 78–79, 82, 153
technologies: modern media, 80; paper, 77, 149; texts and magical, 33
telepathy, 95
"10 percent," Nation of Islam and, 137
territory: baraka as, 117; Jannat al-Baqi cemetery as, 109–18
texts: magical technologies, 33; oral traditions as, 77
al-Thawri, Sufyan (d. 778/161), 75
theologies: Christian, 11; defined, 120; Deleuzian, 8–20, 102, 132–33; Five Percenters, 23–24, 151; negative, 12, 120, 125; Noah and Mothership, 127–31; radical liberation, 135; with representation and divine body, 123–27. *See also* Islamic theology
"theoretical" orders, Sufism, 94–95
A Thousand Plateaus (Deleuze and Guattari), 15, 19, 81, 144, 152; colonial genealogy of one half-sentence in, 26–36; "587 B.C.–A.D. 70," 34; Qur'an in, 25, 26; rhizome defined in, 40; "7000 B.C.," 31; "1227," 31
threshold concept, 4
Timurid monarchs, 7
title for Sufi spiritual guide (pir), 87, *87*
tourism, shrine culture, 96–97
transcendence: baraka and, 116, 118; immanence and, 10; Muhammad (Prophet) and, 11; tanzih, 124–25, 128, 133
translations, of Qur'an, 47–48, 52, 55
trees: of Buddha, 34; family, 23, 27; model, 23, 63, 131; rhizomes and, 34, 63, 94; shajara charts and, 93
Turkey, 33, 90

'ulama (clerical scholars), 4, 21, 55, 82, 90, 115, 122, 146
'Umar (caliph), 105, 109
'Umar II (r. 98–102 / 717–20), 71
'Umayyad caliphate, 67, 70–71, 76, 77
Umm Sulaym, 66, 104
Um Salama (Prophet's widow), 92
the unity of being (wahdat al-wujud), 132
Upanishads, 46, 50
'Urwa, 70
'Uthman b. Maz'un (d. 624), 106, 108
'Uthman ibn 'Affan (third rashidun caliph), 67, 71, 106, 109, 111
Uwaysiyya, 95

Vast Aire "Vishnu Allah," 140
Vedas, 6, 38
"virtues of the Companions" (*fada'il al-sahaba*), 77
Vishnu, 6, 19

Wadud, Amina, 151, 152
wahdat al-wujud (the unity of being), 132
Wahhabi movement, 22, 37
"Wahhabism" (Muwahidun), 38, 52, 107, 110, 113
Waliullah, Shah (1703–62), 80
Ware, Rudolph, 33
wasp, orchid and, 45
Wasserstrom, Steven M., 31
Watson, Janell, 37
Watt, M. Montgomery, 30–31
"way of life," Islam as, 30
Weheliye, Alexander G., 17
Wells, H. G., 29
What Is Islam? (Ahmed), 109, 110, 122
What Is Philosophy? (Deleuze and Guattari), 1, 13, 119
white supremacy, 31, 32, 86, 135
wine cup, 122

"witness play" (*shahidbazi*), 127
women, 145; Companions of Muhammad, 66, 67–69; "Hadith of the Slave Girl," 129; hadiths and, 74; isnads and disappearance of, 76; Jannat al-Baqi cemetery and, 108
"writing"/"book" (*kitab*), 41
Wu Tang Clan, 138

X, Joseph, 138
X, Malcolm, 10, 20, 22, 137

Al-Yafi'i, 'Abd Allah, 92, 94
Ya Sin sura, 53
Yaum-e-Gham (Day of Sorrow), 108
Yemen, 33, 134

Zafar Jinn, 5
zandaqa, 16, 153
Zempleni, Andras, 33, 34
ziyarat (pilgrimage), 106–9, 111, 114, 116–17, 141
Zodiac plate, brass, 51, *51*
Zoroastrianism, 19, 86
al-Zuhri, Shihab (d. 124/742), 69–71, 72

Michael Muhammad Knight is assistant professor of religion and cultural studies at the University of Central Florida. He is the author of numerous books including, most recently, *Muhammad's Body: Baraka Networks and the Prophetic Assemblage.*

www.ingramcontent.com/pod-product-compliance
Lightning Source LLC
Chambersburg PA
CBHW020411080526
44584CB00014B/1274